Legal Notice

This book is copyright 2017 with all rights reserved. It is illegal to copy, distribute, or create derivative works from this book in whole or in part or to contribute to the copying, distribution, or creating of derivative works of this book.

BOOKS FROM THE GET 800 COLLECTION

28 New SAT Math Lessons to Improve Your Score in One Month
    Beginner Course
    Intermediate Course
    Advanced Course
New SAT Math Problems arranged by Topic and Difficulty Level
320 SAT Math Problems arranged by Topic and Difficulty Level
SAT Verbal Prep Book for Reading and Writing Mastery
320 SAT Math Subject Test Problems
    Level 1 Test
    Level 2 Test
Vocabulary Builder
28 ACT Math Lessons to Improve Your Score in One Month
    Intermediate Course
    Advanced Course
320 ACT Math Problems arranged by Topic and Difficulty Level
320 GRE Math Problems arranged by Topic and Difficulty Level
320 AP Calculus AB Problems
320 AP Calculus BC Problems
Physics Mastery for Advanced High School Students
400 SAT Physics Subject Test and AP Physics Problems
SHSAT Verbal Prep Book to Improve Your Score in Two Months
555 Math IQ Questions for Middle School Students
555 Advanced Math Problems for Middle School Students
555 Geometry Problems for High School Students
Algebra Handbook for Gifted Middle School Students
1000 Logic and Reasoning Questions for Gifted and Talented
    Elementary School Students

CONNECT WITH DR. STEVE WARNER

www.facebook.com/SATPrepGet800

www.youtube.com/TheSATMathPrep

www.twitter.com/SATPrepGet800

www.linkedin.com/in/DrSteveWarner

www.pinterest.com/SATPrepGet800

plus.google.com/+SteveWarnerPhD

28 ACT Math Lessons to Improve Your Score in One Month

Intermediate Course

For Students Currently Scoring Between 20 and 25 in ACT Math

Dr. Steve Warner

© 2017, All Rights Reserved

Table of Contents

Actions to Complete Before You Read This Book   vi

Introduction: Studying for Success   7
     1. Using this book effectively   7
     2. Calculator use   8
     3. Tips for taking the ACT   10
         Check your answers properly   10
         Take a guess whenever you cannot
             solve a problem   11
         Pace yourself   11
         Attempt the right number of questions   11

28 SAT Math Lessons
     Lesson 1: Number Theory   13
         Optional Material   22
     Lesson 2: Algebra   23
         Optional Material   33
     Lesson 3: Geometry   35
         Optional Material   44
     Lesson 4: Statistics   45
         Optional Material   52
     Lesson 5: Number Theory   54
         Optional Material   66
     Lesson 6: Algebra   68
     Lesson 7: Geometry   77
         Optional Material   89
     Lesson 8: Counting   90
         Optional Material   98
     Lesson 9: Number Theory   100
     Lesson 10: Algebra   106
         Optional Material   113
     Lesson 11: Geometry   114
         Optional Material   126
     Lesson 12: Probability   128
     Lesson 13: Number Theory   136
     Lesson 14: Algebra   144
         Optional Material   156

Lesson 15: Geometry	158
Optional Material	168
Lesson 16: Logic and Sets	169
Lesson 17: Number Theory	180
Optional Material	190
Lesson 18: Algebra	191
Optional Material	202
Lesson 19: Trigonometry	203
Optional Material	212
Lesson 20: Statistics	213
Optional Material	216
Lesson 21: Number Theory	217
Optional Material	225
Lesson 22: Functions	227
Optional Material	236
Lesson 23: Geometry	239
Optional Material	247
Lesson 24: Counting and Probability	248
Lesson 25: Number Theory	252
Lesson 26: Algebra and Functions	259
Lesson 27: Geometry and Trigonometry	266
Lesson 28: Probability and Statistics	274
Afterword: Your Road to Success	**283**
Actions to Complete After You Have Read This Book	**284**
About the Author	*285*
Books by Dr. Steve Warner	**286**

ACTIONS TO COMPLETE BEFORE YOU READ THIS BOOK

1. **Purchase a TI-84 or equivalent calculator**

   It is recommended that you use a TI-84 or comparable calculator for the ACT. Answer explanations in this book will always assume you are using such a calculator.

2. **Take a practice ACT from the Real ACT Prep Guide to get your preliminary ACT math score**

   Your score should be at least a 20. If it is lower, you should use *320 ACT Math Problems* until your score on practice tests increases to 20 or higher.

3. **Claim your FREE bonus**

   Visit the following webpage and enter your email address to receive solutions to all the supplemental problems in this book.

   ## www.satprepget800.com/28LesInt

4. **Like my Facebook page**

   This page is updated regularly with ACT prep advice, tips, tricks, strategies, and practice problems.

   ## www.facebook.com/ACTPrepGet800

INTRODUCTION
STUDYING FOR SUCCESS

This book was written specifically for the student currently scoring between a 20 and 25 in ACT math. Results will vary, but if you are such a student and you work through the lessons in this book, then you will see a substantial improvement in your score.

The book you are now reading is self-contained. Each lesson was carefully created to ensure that you are making the most effective use of your time while preparing for the ACT. The initial lessons are quite focused, ensuring that the reader learns and practices one strategy and one topic at a time. In the beginning the focus is on Level 1, 2 and 3 problems, and little by little Level 4 problems will be added into the mix. It should be noted that a score of 30 can usually be attained without ever attempting a Level 5 problem. That said, some Level 5 problems will appear late in the book for those students that show accelerated improvement. The reader of this book should not feel obligated to work on these harder problems the first time they go through this book.

1. Using this book effectively

- Begin studying at least three months before the ACT.
- Practice ACT math problems ten to twenty minutes each day.
- Choose a consistent study time and location.

You will retain much more of what you study if you study in short bursts rather than if you try to tackle everything at once. So, try to choose about a twenty-minute block of time that you will dedicate to ACT math each day. Make it a habit. The results are well worth this small time commitment. Some students will be able to complete each lesson within this ten- to twenty-minute block of time. Others may take a bit longer. If it takes you longer than twenty minutes to complete a lesson, you have two options. You can stop when twenty minutes are up and then complete the lesson the following day, or you can finish the lesson and then take a day off from ACT math prep that week.

- Every time you get a question wrong, **mark it off, no matter what your mistake**.
- Begin each lesson by first redoing the problems from previous lessons on the same topic that you have marked off.
- If you get a problem wrong again, **keep it marked off**.

As an example, before you begin the third number theory lesson (Lesson 9), you should redo all the problems you have marked off from the first two number theory lessons (Lessons 1 and 5). Any question that you get right you can "unmark" while leaving questions that you get wrong marked off for the next time. If this takes you the full twenty minutes, that is okay. Just begin the new lesson the next day.

Note that this book often emphasizes solving each problem in more than one way. Please listen to this advice. The same question is never repeated on any ACT, and so the important thing is learning as many techniques as possible. Being able to solve any specific problem is of minimal importance. The more ways you have to solve a single problem, the more prepared you will be to tackle a problem you have never seen before, and the quicker you will be able to solve that problem. Also, if you have multiple methods for solving a single problem, then on the actual ACT when you "check over" your work you will be able to redo each problem in a different way. This will eliminate all "careless" errors on the actual exam. In this book the quickest solution to any problem will always be marked with an asterisk (*).

2. Calculator use.

- Use a TI-84 or comparable calculator if possible when practicing and during the ACT.
- Make sure that your calculator has fresh batteries on test day.
- You may have to switch between DEGREE and RADIAN modes during the test. If you are using a TI-84 (or equivalent) calculator press the MODE button and scroll down to the third line when necessary to switch between modes.

Below are the most important things you should practice on your graphing calculator.

- Practice entering complicated computations in a single step.
- Know when to insert parentheses:
  - Around numerators of fractions
  - Around denominators of fractions
  - Around exponents
  - Whenever you actually see parentheses in the expression

Examples:

We will substitute a 5 in for x in each of the following examples.

Expression	Calculator computation
$\dfrac{7x+3}{2x-11}$	$(7*5+3)/(2*5-11)$
$(3x-8)^{2x-9}$	$(3*5-8)\wedge(2*5-9)$

- Clear the screen before using it in a new problem. The big screen allows you to check over your computations easily.
- Press the **ANS** button (**2nd (-)**) to use your last answer in the next computation.
- Press **2nd ENTER** to bring up your last computation for editing. This is especially useful when you are plugging in answer choices, or guessing and checking.
- You can press **2nd ENTER** over and over again to cycle backwards through all the computations you have ever done.
- Know where the $\sqrt{}$, π , and ^ buttons are so you can reach them quickly.
- Change a decimal to a fraction by pressing **MATH ENTER ENTER**.
- Press the **MATH** button – in the first menu that appears you can take cube roots and nth roots for any n. Scroll right to **NUM** and you have **lcm(** and **gcd(**. Scroll right to **PRB** and you have **nPr, nCr,** and **!** to compute permutations, combinations and factorials very quickly.
- Know how to use the **SIN, COS** and **TAN** buttons as well as **SIN^{-1}, COS^{-1}** and **TAN^{-1}**.

The following items are less important but can be useful.

- Press the **Y=** button to enter a function, and then hit **ZOOM 6** to graph it in a standard window.
- Practice using the **WINDOW** button to adjust the viewing window of your graph.
- Practice using the **TRACE** button to move along the graph and look at some of the points plotted.
- Pressing **2nd TRACE** (which is really **CALC**) will bring up a menu of useful items. For example, selecting **ZERO** will tell you where the graph hits the x-axis, or equivalently where the function is zero. Selecting **MINIMUM** or **MAXIMUM** can find the vertex of a parabola. Selecting **INTERSECT** will find the point of intersection of 2 graphs.

3. Tips for taking the ACT

Each of the following tips should be used whenever you take a practice ACT, as well as on the actual exam.

Check your answers properly: When you go back to check your earlier answers for careless errors *do not* simply look over your work to try to catch a mistake. This is usually a waste of time.

- When "checking over" problems you have already done, **always redo the problem from the beginning** without looking at your earlier work.
- If possible, use a different method than you used the first time.

For example, if you solved the problem by picking numbers the first time, try to solve it algebraically the second time, or at the very least pick different numbers. If you do not know, or are not comfortable with a different method, then use the same method, but do the problem from the beginning and do not look at your original solution. If your two answers do not match up, then you know that this is a problem you need to spend a little more time on to figure out where your error is.

This may seem time consuming, but that is okay. It is better to spend more time checking over a few problems, then to rush through a lot of problems and repeat the same mistakes.

Take a guess whenever you cannot solve a problem: There is no guessing penalty on the ACT. Whenever you do not know how to solve a problem take a guess. Ideally you should eliminate as many answer choices as possible before taking your guess, but if you have no idea whatsoever do not waste time overthinking. Simply put down an answer and move on. You should certainly mark it off and come back to it later if you have time.

Pace yourself: Do not waste your time on a question that is too hard or will take too long. After you have been working on a question for about 1 minute you need to make a decision. If you understand the question and think that you can get the answer in another 30 seconds or so, continue to work on the problem. If you still do not know how to do the problem or you are using a technique that is going to take a long time, mark it off and come back to it later if you have time.

If you cannot get the answer, feel free to take a guess. But you still want to leave open the possibility of coming back to it later. Remember that every problem is worth the same amount. Do not sacrifice problems that you may be able to do by getting hung up on a problem that is too hard for you.

Attempt the right number of questions: Many students make the mistake of thinking that they must attempt every single ACT math question when they are taking the test. There is no such rule. In fact, many students will increase their ACT score by *reducing* the number of questions they attempt. The following chart gives a general guideline for how many questions you should be attempting.

Score	Questions
< 13	15/60
13 – 14	20/60
15 – 17	28/60
18 – 20	36/60
21 – 23	40/60
24 – 27	52/60
28 – 36	60/60

For example, a student with a current score of 22 should be attempting about 40 of the 60 questions on the test.

Since the math questions on the ACT tend to start out easier in the beginning of the section and get harder as you go, then attempting the first 40 questions is not a bad idea. However, it is okay to skip several questions and try a few that appear later.

Note that although the questions tend to get harder as you go, it is not true that each question is harder than the previous question. For example, it is possible for question 25 to be easier than question 24, and in fact, question 25 can even be easier than question 20. But it is unlikely that question 50 would be easier than question 20.

If you are particularly strong in a certain subject area, then you may want to "seek out" questions from that topic even though they may be more difficult. For example, if you are very strong at number theory problems, but very weak at probability problems, then you may want to try every number theory problem no matter where it appears, and you may want to reduce the number of probability problems you attempt.

Remember that there is no guessing penalty on the ACT, so you should *not* leave any questions blank. This *does not* mean you should attempt every question. It means that if you are running out of time make sure you fill in answers for all the questions you did not have time to attempt.

For example, if you are currently scoring a 22, then it is possible you will only be attempting the first 40 questions or so. Therefore, when you are running out of time you should fill in answers for the last 20 problems. If you happen to get a chance to attempt some of them, you can always change your answer. But make sure those answers are filled in before the test ends!

Lesson 1
Number Theory

Start with the Middle Answer Choice

In many ACT math problems, you can get the answer simply by trying each of the answer choices until you find the one that works. Unless you have some intuition as to what the correct answer might be, then you should always start with the middle answer choice (C or H) as your first guess (an exception will be detailed in the next strategy below). The reason for this is simple. Answers are very often (but not always) given in increasing or decreasing order. So, if the middle choice fails you can sometimes eliminate two of the other choices as well.

Try to answer the following question using this strategy. **Do not** check the solution until you have attempted this question yourself.

Level 1: Number Theory

1. Three consecutive integers are listed in increasing order. If their sum is 138, what is the second integer in the list?

   A. 45
   B. 46
   C. 47
   D. 48
   E. 49

Solution

Begin by looking at choice C. If the second integer is 47, then the first integer is 46 and the third integer is 48. Therefore, we get a sum of $46 + 47 + 48 = 141$. This is a little too big. So, we can eliminate choices C, D, and E.

We next try choice B. If the second integer is 46, then the first integer is 45 and the third integer is 47. So, the sum is $45 + 46 + 47 = 138$. Thus, the answer is choice **B**.

Remark: You should use your calculator to compute these sums. This will be quicker and you are less likely to make a careless error.

Before we go on, try to solve this problem in two other ways.

(1) Algebraically (the way you would do it in school).
(2) With a single computation.

Here is a hint for method (2):

Hint: In a set of consecutive integers, the average (arithmetic mean) and median are equal (see Lesson 4 for definitions of average and median).

Important Note: If you have trouble understanding the following solutions, it is okay. Just do your best to follow the given explanations.

Solutions

(1) An algebraic solution: If we name the least integer x, then the second and third integers are $x + 1$ and $x + 2$, respectively. So, we have

$$x + (x + 1) + (x + 2) = 138$$
$$3x + 3 = 138$$
$$3x = 135$$
$$x = 45$$

The second integer is $x + 1 = 46$, choice **B**.

Important: Always remember to check what the question is asking for before choosing your answer. Many students would accidently choose choice A here as soon as they discovered that $x = 45$.

Note: The following is a bit more efficient.

$$x + (x + 1) + (x + 2) = 138$$
$$3x + 3 = 138$$
$$3(x + 1) = 138$$
$$x + 1 = 46$$

* **(2) A quick, clever solution:** Simply divide 138 by 3 to get 46, choice **B**.

When NOT to Start with the Middle Answer Choice

If the word **least** appears in the problem, then start with the smallest number as your first guess. Similarly, if the word **greatest** appears in the problem, then start with the largest number as your first guess.

Try to answer the following question using this strategy. **Do not** check the solution until you have attempted this question yourself.

LEVEL 2: NUMBER THEORY

2. What is the least positive integer divisible by the integers 3, 7 and 14?

   F. 168
   G. 126
   H. 84
   J. 42
   K. 28

Solution

Begin by looking at choice K since it is the smallest. 28/3 comes to approximately 9.33 in our calculator. Since this is not an integer, 28 is **not** divisible by 3. We can therefore eliminate choice K. We next try choice J.

$$42/3 = 14 \quad 42/7 = 6 \quad 42/14 = 3$$

Since these are all integers, the answer is choice **J**.

Before we go on, try to solve this problem directly (without using the answer choices).

Solutions

(1) The question is asking for the **least common multiple** of 3, 7 and 14. Here is one way to find it.

Step 1: Find the prime factorization of each integer in the set.

$$3 = 3$$
$$7 = 7$$
$$14 = 2 \cdot 7$$

Step 2: Choose the highest power of each prime that appears in any of the factorizations.

2, 3 and 7 (in this example the highest power of each prime is 1)

Step 3: Multiply these numbers together to get the least common multiple.

$$2 \cdot 3 \cdot 7 = 42, \text{ choice } \mathbf{J}.$$

***(2) Getting the answer quickly:** Starting from 3, write down the prime factors of each number, skipping any that do not contribute to the least common multiple. So, we would write 3, then 7. We would then think of 14 as $2 \cdot 7$, and so we would write down 2 (we do not write 7 again because we have already written it). So, we have 3 7 2. We then multiply these numbers together to get $3 \cdot 7 \cdot 2 = 42$, choice **J**.

(3) Calculator solution: We use the **lcm** feature on our graphing calculator (found under NUM after pressing the MATH button). Our calculator can only handle two numbers at a time. So, compute $\text{lcm}(3,7) = 21$, and then $\text{lcm}(21,14) = 42$ choice **J**.

You're doing great! Let's just practice a bit more. Try to solve each of the following problems by using one of the two strategies you just learned. Then, if possible, solve each problem another way. The answers to these problems, followed by full solutions are at the end of this lesson. **Do not look at the answers until you have attempted these problems yourself.** Please remember to mark off any problems you get wrong.

LEVEL 1: NUMBER THEORY

3. Which of the following numbers is less than 0.416?

    A. 0.4106
    B. 0.4161
    C. 0.4166
    D. 0.42
    E. 0.421

4. Which of the following numbers disproves the statement "A number that is divisible by 4 and 8 is also divisible by 12"?

    F. 24
    G. 48
    H. 56
    J. 72
    K. 96

5. The absolute value of which of the following numbers is the greatest?

   A. −0.7
   B. −0.073
   C. −0.0079
   D. 0.07
   E. 0.078

6. Which of the following numbers is NOT a factor of 252 ?

   F. 6
   G. 14
   H. 27
   J. 42
   K. 63

7. What is the least integer greater than $\sqrt{67}$?

   A. 7
   B. 8
   C. 9
   D. 10
   E. 11

LEVEL 2: NUMBER THEORY

8. What is the greatest positive integer that is a divisor of 14, 49, and 63?

   F. 1
   G. 3
   H. 5
   J. 7
   K. 14

9. Among the following rational numbers, which has the greatest value?

   A. 0.25
   B. 0.2$\overline{5}$
   C. 0.$\overline{25}$
   D. 0.252
   E. 0.2507

Level 3: Number Theory

10. What is the largest positive integer value of k for which 3^k divides 18^4?

    F. 2
    G. 4
    H. 6
    J. 7
    K. 8

Definitions Used in This Lesson

The **integers** are the counting numbers together with their negatives.

$$\{\ldots, -4, -3, -2, -1, 0, 1, 2, 3, 4, \ldots\}$$

The **positive integers** consist of the positive numbers from that set.

$$\{1, 2, 3, 4, \ldots\}$$

Consecutive integers are integers that follow each other in order. The difference between consecutive integers is 1. Here are two examples.

$1, 2, 3$ these are three consecutive integers

$-3, -2, -1, 0, 1$ these are five consecutive integers

In general, if x is an integer, then $x, x+1, x+2, x+3, \ldots$ are consecutive integers.

An integer n is **divisible** by an integer d if there is another integer k such that $n = dk$. For example, 42 is divisible by 7 because $42 = 7 \cdot 6$. In practice, we can check if n is divisible by d simply by dividing n by d in our calculator. If the answer is an integer, then n is divisible by d. If the answer is not an integer (it contains digits after the decimal point), then n is not divisible by d. If n is divisible by d, we say that d is a **divisor** (or **factor**) of n. We also say that n is a **multiple** of d.

The **least common multiple (lcm)** of a set of positive integers is the smallest positive integer that is divisible by each integer in the set.

The **greatest common divisor (gcd)** of a set of positive integers is the largest positive integer that each integer in the set is divisible by.

Answers

1. B   6. H
2. J   7. C
3. A   8. J
4. H   9. B
5. A   10. K

Full Solutions

3.
We can compare two decimals by looking at the first position where they disagree. For example, 0.415 is less than 0.416 because 5 is less than 6. If a digit is missing, there is a hidden 0 there. Thus, 0.4 is also less than 0.416 because 0.4 is the same as 0.400 and 0 is less than 1 (remember that we look at the **first** position where the decimals disagree). Since 0 is less than 6, the answer is choice **A**.

* **Quick Solution:** Answers are often given in increasing or decreasing order on the ACT (in this problem they are given in increasing order). Therefore, choice **A** is the only reasonable answer.

Remark: The words "less than" would seem to indicate we should start by looking at the smallest answer choice. In this case that is choice A. Note that we have essentially used the second strategy from this lesson here (we started with the smallest answer choice).

4.
* **Solution by starting with choice H:** We want a number that is divisible by 4 and 8, but **not** by 12. Use your calculator and begin with choice H. When we divide 56 by 4, 8 and 12 we get 14, 7 and approximately 4.67. Since 14 and 7 are integers we see that 56 is divisible by 4 and 8. Since 4.67 is **not** an integer, 56 is not divisible by 12. Therefore, the answer is choice **H**.

5.
* A quick glance at the answer choices shows that they are listed in increasing order. Since we are looking for the absolute value of the choices, the answer must be either choice A or E. The absolute value of −0.7 is 0.7, and the absolute value of 0.078 is 0.078. Since 0.7 is greater than 0.078, the answer is choice **A**.

19

Notes: (1) When we take the absolute value of a real number, we simply remove the minus sign if there is one (otherwise we do nothing). So, the absolute values of the choices, beginning with choice A, are 0.7, 0.073, 0.0079, 0.07, and 0.078.

(2) Although it is not necessary to understand this problem, the standard notation for taking the absolute value of a number is to put the number between two vertical lines. So, for example, the absolute value of -0.7 can be written as $|-0.7|$, and we have $|-0.7| = 0.7$.

6.

* Solution by starting with choice H: We divide 252 by 27 in our calculator to get approximately 9.333. Since this is not an integer, 27 is not a factor of 252, and the answer is choice **H**.

Notes: (1) The prime factorization of 252 is $2^2 \cdot 3^2 \cdot 7$. So, a factor of 252 has at most two factors of 2 and 3, and at most one factor of 7 (and no other prime factors).

(2) The factors of 252 are 1, 2, $2^2 = 4$, 3, $2 \cdot 3 = 6$, $2^2 \cdot 3 = 12$, $3^2 = 9$, $2 \cdot 3^2 = 18$, $2^2 \cdot 3^2 = 36$, 7, $2 \cdot 7 = 14$, $2^2 \cdot 7 = 28$, $3 \cdot 7 = 21$, $2 \cdot 3 \cdot 7 = 42$, $2^2 \cdot 3 \cdot 7 = 84$, $3^2 \cdot 7 = 63$, $2 \cdot 3^2 \cdot 7 = 126$, and $2^2 \cdot 3^2 \cdot 7 = 252$.

7.

Solution by starting with choice A: Since the word "least" appears in the problem, let's start with the smallest answer choice, choice A. We have $7^2 = 49$. This is too small. Let's try choice B. We have $8^2 = 64$, still a bit too small. So, the answer is most likely choice C.

Let's check: $9^2 = 81$. Since $8^2 < 67$, and $9^2 > 67$, the answer is **C**.

* Quick solution: If we take the square root of 67 in our calculator we get approximately 8.185. The least integer greater than this is 9, which is choice **C**.

8.

* Solution by starting with choice K: Pull out your calculator. Since the question has the word **"greatest"** in it, we will start with the greatest answer choice, which is choice K, and we will divide each of the three numbers by 14. Since 49 divided by 14 is 3.5 (not an integer), choice K is not the answer. We next try choice J. The divisions give us 2, 7 and 9, respectively. Since these are all integers, the answer is choice **J**.

Note that the three given integers are all divisible by 1, but choice A is not the answer because 7 is greater.

Direct solution: We are being asked to find the **greatest common divisor** of 14, 49 and 63, which is 7, choice **J**.

Finding the greatest common divisor:

Here are two ways to find the greatest common divisor of the given integers.

    (1) List all divisors of each integer and look for the biggest one they have in common.

Divisors of 14: $\{1, 2, 7, 14\}$
Divisors of 49: $\{1, 7, 49\}$
Divisors of 63: $\{1, 3, 7, 9, 21, 63\}$
Common Divisors: $\{1, 7\}$

Thus, the greatest common divisor is 7.

    (2) Here is a more sophisticated method (this method is much quicker if the given integers are large).

<u>Step 1</u>: Find the prime factorization of each number in the set.

$$14 = 2 \cdot 7$$
$$49 = 7^2$$
$$63 = 3^2 \cdot 7$$

<u>Step 2</u>: Choose the lowest power of each prime that appears in **all** the factorizations. In this case, this is just 7.

<u>Step 3</u>: Multiply these numbers together to get the greatest common divisor. (In this case there is nothing to multiply since there is only one prime factor that the three integers have in common.)

Remark: We can also write the above prime factorizations as follows:

$$14 = 2^1 \, 3^0 \, 7^1$$
$$49 = 2^0 \, 3^0 \, 7^2$$
$$63 = 2^0 \, 3^2 \, 7^1$$

It is easy to see in this form that the lowest power of 2 is $2^0 = 1$, and similarly the lowest power of 3 is $3^0 = 1$.

9.
* $0.2\overline{5} = 0.255555...$ and $0.\overline{25} = 0.252525...$ We see that the greatest value is choice **B**.

10.
* **Solution by starting with choice K:** Pull out your calculator. Since the question has the word **"largest"** in it, we will start with the largest answer choice which is choice **K**, and we will divide 18^4 by 3^8. We type 18^4 / 3^8 into our calculator and the output is 16. Since 16 is an integer, the answer is choice **K**.

Note that all five answer choices give an integer, but 8 is the largest positive integer that works.

Direct solution: The prime factorization of 18 is $18 = 2 \cdot 3^2$. Therefore,
$$18^4 = (2 \cdot 3^2)^4 = 2^4(3^2)^4 = 2^4 \cdot 3^8.$$
From this prime factorization, it should be clear that 3^8 divides 18^4, but 3^9 does not, choice **K**.

For a review of the basic laws of exponents used here see Lesson 10.

OPTIONAL MATERIAL

The following questions will test your understanding of definitions used in this lesson. These are **not** in the format of ACT questions.

1. Which of the following numbers are integers? Choose all that apply.

   $\frac{1}{2}$ -3 $.67$ $\sqrt{2}$ 0 1800 1.1 $\sqrt{4}$ $\frac{18}{3}$ $\frac{\sqrt{18}}{\sqrt{2}}$ π

2. List 10 consecutive integers beginning with -6. Which of these are positive integers?

Answers

1. $-3, 0, 1800, \sqrt{4} = 2, \frac{18}{3} = 6, \frac{\sqrt{18}}{\sqrt{2}} = \sqrt{\frac{18}{2}} = \sqrt{9} = 3$
2. $-6, -5, -4, -3, -2, -1, 0, 1, 2, 3$ positive integers: 1, 2, 3

LESSON 2
ALGEBRA

Turn to Lesson 1 and review the strategy **Start with the Middle Answer Choice**. Then try to answer the following question using this strategy. **Do not** check the solution until you have attempted this question yourself.

LEVEL 1: ALGEBRA

1. If $\frac{7}{x} = 0.7$, then $x = ?$

    A. 0.07
    B. 0.1
    C. 0.7
    D. 7
    (E.) 10

Solution

Begin by looking at choice C, and let $x = 0.7$. Using our calculator, we have $\frac{7}{x} = \frac{7}{0.7} = 10$. This is too big. It follows that we need to divide by a *larger* number, and so we can eliminate choices A, B, and C.

We can eliminate choice D quite easily because $\frac{7}{7} = 1$, and so the answer is choice **E**.

Note: For completeness, let's just check choice E. Using our calculator, we have $\frac{7}{x} = \frac{7}{10} = 0.7$.

Before we go on, try to solve this problem algebraically.

Solution

Algebraic solution:

$$\frac{7}{x} = \frac{0.7}{1}$$
$$0.7x = 7 \cdot 1$$
$$0.7x = 7$$
$$x = \frac{7}{0.7} = 10, \text{ choice } \mathbf{E}.$$

Notes: (1) We chose to rewrite 0.7 as $\frac{0.7}{1}$ so that it is easy to see how to cross multiply. However, it was not necessary to do this. We could have simply multiplied each side of the equation $\frac{7}{x} = 0.7$ by x to get $7 = 0.7x$ (this is equivalent to the third equation above).

(2) We got from the third equation above to the fourth equation by dividing each side by 0.7. We can simply perform the division 7 / 0.7 in our calculator to get 10.

(3) We can also divide 7 by 0.7 by hand easily by first multiplying the numerator and denominator of $\frac{7}{0.7}$ by 10. Note that multiplying a number by 10 is equivalent to moving the decimal point one place to the right, or placing a zero on the right if there is no decimal point. So $\frac{7}{0.7} = \frac{70}{7} = 10$.

(4) We can solve the equation $\frac{7}{x} = 0.7$ *informally* by simply answering the question "7 divided by what equals 0.7?" Well moving the decimal point one place to the left is equivalent to dividing by 10. So, the answer is 10, choice E.

(5) See the Optional Material at the end of this lesson for a review of both informal and formal algebra.

Turn to Lesson 1 and review the strategy **When NOT to Start with the Middle Answer Choice.** Then try to answer the following question using this strategy. **Do not** check the solution until you have attempted this question yourself.

LEVEL 2: ALGEBRA

2. What is the greatest integer x that satisfies the inequality $3 + \frac{x}{5} < 8$?

    F. 20
    G. 22
    H. 24
    J. 25
    K. 26

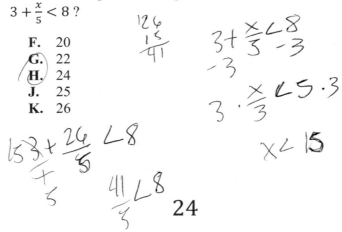

Solution

Since the word "greatest" appears in the problem, let's start with the largest answer choice, choice K. Now $3 + \frac{26}{5} = 8.2$ (use your calculator). This is too big, so we can eliminate choice K.

Let's try choice J next. We have $3 + \frac{25}{5} = 8$. This is just barely too big, and so the answer is choice **H**.

Before we go on, try to solve this problem algebraically.

Solution

* **Algebraic solution:** Let's solve the inequality. We start by subtracting 3 from each side of the given inequality to get $\frac{x}{5} < 5$. We then multiply each side of this inequality by 5 to get $x < 25$. The greatest integer less than 25 is 24, choice **H**.

You're doing great! Let's just practice a bit more. Try to solve each of the following problems by using one of the two strategies you just reviewed. Then, if possible, solve each problem another way. The answers to these problems, followed by full solutions are at the end of this lesson. **Do not** look at the answers until you have attempted these problems yourself. Please remember to mark off any problems you get wrong.

LEVEL 1: ALGEBRA

3. For what value of x is $7x - 6 = 5x + 4$

   A. 10
   B. 5
   C. 1
   D. $\frac{1}{2}$
   E. $\frac{3}{4}$

25

4. If $3c + 2 < 11$, which of the following CANNOT be the value of c?

    F. -1
    G. 0
    H. 1
    J. 2
    K. 3

5. If $\sqrt{h} = k$ and $k = 25$, then $h = ?$

    A. 5
    B. 12.5
    C. 50
    D. 250
    E. 625

LEVEL 2: ALGEBRA

6. Given that $\sqrt{3x} - 6 = 3$, $x = ?$

    F. -27
    G. -9
    H. 3
    J. 27
    K. 54

7. Jessica bakes treats for 7 hours every Sunday. It takes her 40 minutes to bake each oatmeal treat and 50 minutes to bake each chocolate treat. This Sunday, Jessica will bake twice as many chocolate treats as oatmeal treats. How many of the chocolate treats will she bake this Sunday?

    A. 3
    B. 4
    C. 5
    D. 6
    E. 8

8. If $6^{x+1} = 7776$, what is the value of x?

   F. 6
   G. 5
   H. 4
   J. 3
   K. 2

9. For which nonnegative value of b is the expression $\frac{1}{36-b^2}$ undefined?

   A. 0
   B. 6
   C. 18
   D. 36
   E. 72

LEVEL 3: ALGEBRA

10. For what two values of x is the equation $x^2 + 3x - 10 = 0$ true?

    F. -2 and -5
    G. 2 and -5
    H. 2 and 5
    J. -2 and 5
    K. -2 and 2

Definitions Used in This Lesson

$x < y$ means "x is less than y."

For example, $2 < 3$ and $-4 < 0$ are TRUE, whereas $6 < 5$ is FALSE.

$x > y$ means "x is greater than y."

For example, $3 > 2$ and $0 > -4$ are TRUE, whereas $5 > 6$ is FALSE.

It sometimes helps to remember that for $<$ and $>$, the symbol always points to the smaller number.

Answers

1. E   6. J
2. H   7. D
3. B   8. H
4. K   9. B
5. E   10. G

Full Solutions

3.

Solution by starting with choice C: We start with choice C, and substitute 1 in for x in the given equation.

$$7x - 6 = 5x + 4$$
$$7 \cdot 1 - 6 = 5 \cdot 1 + 4$$
$$7 - 6 = 5 + 4$$
$$1 = 9$$

Since the last equation is false, we can eliminate choice C.

Let's try choice B next, and substitute 5 for x.

$$7x - 6 = 5x + 4$$
$$7 \cdot 5 - 6 = 5 \cdot 5 + 4$$
$$35 - 6 = 25 + 4$$
$$29 = 29$$

This is correct, and so the answer is choice **B**.

* Algebraic solution:

$$7x - 6 = 5x + 4$$
$$2x = 10$$
$$x = 5$$

So, the answer is choice **B**.

Notes: (1) We got from the first to the second equation by subtracting $5x$ from each side, and then adding 6 to each side.

(2) We got from the second to the third equation by dividing by 2.

4.

Solution by starting with choice K: We start with choice K, and substitute 3 in for c in the given inequality.

$$3c + 2 < 11$$
$$3 \cdot 3 + 2 < 11$$
$$9 + 2 < 11$$
$$11 < 11$$

Since this is FALSE, the answer is choice **K**.

* Remark: This is a slight variation of the second strategy reviewed in this lesson. A moment's thought should tell you that we are looking for a number that is too big. So, the largest number given must be the answer.

Algebraic solution:
$$3c + 2 < 11$$
$$3c < 9$$
$$c < 3$$

Thus, the answer is choice **K**.

5.

Solution by starting with choice C: We start with choice C, substitute 50 in for h, and use our calculator to get $\sqrt{h} = \sqrt{50} \approx 7.07$. Since this is less than 25, we can eliminate choices A, B, and C.

Let's try choice E next, and substitute 625 in for h. Using our calculator, we get $\sqrt{h} = \sqrt{625} = 25$. This is correct, and so the answer is choice **E**.

* Algebraic solution: We are given $\sqrt{h} = 25$. We square both sides of this equation to get $h = 25^2 = 625$, choice **E**.

6.

Solution by starting with choice H: Let's start with choice H, and substitute 3 for x in the equation.

$$\sqrt{3x} - 6 = 3$$
$$\sqrt{3 \cdot 3} - 6 = 3$$
$$\sqrt{9} - 6 = 3$$
$$3 - 6 = 3$$
$$-3 = 3$$

The last equation is false, and so we can eliminate choice H.

Let's try choice J next, and substitute 27 for x.

$$\sqrt{3x} - 6 = 3$$
$$\sqrt{3 \cdot 27} - 6 = 3$$
$$81 - 6 = 3$$
$$9 - 6 = 3$$
$$3 = 3$$

This is correct, and so the answer is choice **J**.

* **Algebraic solution:**

$$\sqrt{3x} - 6 = 3$$
$$\sqrt{3x} = 9$$
$$3x = 81$$
$$x = 27$$

This is choice **J**.

7.

* **Solution by starting with choice C:** Let's start with choice C, and guess that Jessica will bake 5 chocolate treats this Sunday. Since she bakes twice as many chocolate treats as oatmeal treats, it follows that she bakes 2.5 oatmeal treats. Baking fractional parts of treats is unlikely, and so we can probably eliminate choice C (and choice A for the same reason).

Let's try choice D next, and guess that Jessica bakes 6 chocolate treats. She therefore bakes 3 oatmeal treats. The total number of minutes it takes her to bake all these treats is then $3 \cdot 40 + 6 \cdot 50 = 420$. Since 7 hours is equal to $7 \cdot 60 = 420$ minutes, the answer is choice **D**.

Algebraic solution: First note that 7 hours is $7 \cdot 60 = 420$ minutes. Let x be the number of oatmeal treats, and y the number of chocolate treats that Jessica will bake this Sunday. We have the following system of equations.

$$40x + 50y = 420$$
$$y = 2x$$

We substitute $2x$ for y into the first equation to get

$$40x + 50 \cdot 2x = 420$$
$$40x + 100x = 420$$
$$140x = 420$$
$$x = \frac{420}{140} = 3$$

The number of chocolate treats Jessica will make this Sunday is $y = 2x = 2 \cdot 3 = 6$, choice **D**.

Note: The algebraic solution for this problem involves solving a system of linear equations. This solution is much more difficult than plugging in. See Lesson 14 for more on solving systems of linear equations.

8.
Solution by starting with choice H: Let's start with choice H, and substitute 4 in for x in the given equation. We type in our calculator $6\wedge(4 + 1) = 7776$. Thus, the answer is choice **H**.

Calculator notes: (1) If you find yourself getting the wrong answer when you use your calculator, please review the second example under Calculator Use on page 9.

(2) Instead of typing $6\wedge(4 + 1)$ in our calculator, we can add 4 and 1 in our head (to get 5), and type $6\wedge5$ instead.

* **Algebraic solution:** We rewrite the equation so that each side has the same base (in this case the common base is 6). $6^{x+1} = 6^5$. Now that the bases are the same, so are the exponents. Thus, $x + 1 = 5$, and therefore $x = 4$, choice **H**.

9.
* **Solution by plugging in answer choices:** We want to find a nonnegative value for b that makes the denominator of the fraction zero. Normally we would start with choice C, but in this case, it's easy to see that choice B will work. Indeed, $36 - 6^2 = 36 - 36 = 0$. So, the answer is choice **B**.

Algebraic solution: The expression is undefined when the denominator is zero. So, we need to solve the equation $36 - b^2 = 0$. Factoring the left-hand side gives the equation $(6 - b)(6 + b) = 0$. So, $6 - b = 0$ or $6 + b = 0$. Therefore, we have $b = 6$ or $b = -6$. Since the question is asking for the nonnegative value of b, we choose $b = 6$, choice **B**.

Notes: (1) The given expression is a **rational function**. A rational function is a quotient of polynomials (one polynomial divided by another polynomial). A rational function is undefined when the denominator is zero (see Lesson 6 for the definition of a polynomial).

(2) The expression $36 - b^2$ is the **difference of two squares**. In general, the difference of two squares $x^2 - y^2$ factors as $(x - y)(x + y)$.

See Lesson 18 for more details on the difference of two squares.

(3) We can also solve the equation $36 - b^2 = 0$ by adding b^2 to each side of the equation to get $36 = b^2$, and then using the **square root property** to get $\pm 6 = b$.

Note that the **square root property** says that if $x^2 = k^2$, then $x = \pm k$. This is different from taking a square root since it leads to two solutions.

See Lesson 18 for more on the square root property.

10.
* Solution by starting with choice H: Let's start with choice H. We first try $x = 2$. We have $2^2 + 3 \cdot 2 - 10 = 4 + 6 - 10 = 0$. So $x = 2$ works. Now let's try $x = 5$. We have $5^2 + 3 \cdot 5 - 10 = 25 + 15 - 10 = 30$. So, 5 does not work. We can therefore eliminate choices C and D.

Let's try choice G next. We already know that $x = 2$ works. So let's just try $x = -5$. We have $(-5)^2 + 3(-5) - 10 = 25 - 15 - 10 = 0$. So, $x = -5$ works, and the answer is choice **G**.

Solution by factoring:
$$x^2 + 3x - 10 = 0$$
$$(x - 2)(x + 5) = 0$$
$$x - 2 = 0 \text{ or } x + 5 = 0$$
$$x = 2 \text{ or } x = -5$$

This is choice **G**.

Note: There are several more ways to solve a quadratic equation like this, including completing the square, using the quadratic formula, and using our graphing calculator. See Lesson 18 for more details.

OPTIONAL MATERIAL

Informal and Formal Algebra

Suppose we are asked to solve for x in the following equation:
$$x + 3 = 8$$
In other words, we are being asked for a number such that when we add 3 to that number we get 8. It is not too hard to see that $5 + 3 = 8$, so that $x = 5$.

I call the technique above solving this equation **informally**. In other words, when we solve algebraic equations informally we are solving for the variable very quickly in our heads. I sometimes call this performing **"mental math."**

We can also solve for x **formally** by subtracting 3 from each side of the equation:

$$\begin{array}{r} x + 3 = 8 \\ -3 -3 \\ \hline x = 5 \end{array}$$

In other words, when we solve an algebraic equation formally we are writing out all the steps – just as we would do it on a test in school.

To save time on the ACT you should practice solving equations informally as much as possible. And you should also practice solving equations formally – this will increase your mathematical skill level.

Let's try another:
$$5x = 30$$
Informally, 5 times 6 is 30, so we see that $x = 6$.

Formally, we can divide each side of the equation by 5:

$$\begin{array}{c} \dfrac{5x}{5} = \dfrac{30}{5} \\ x = 6 \end{array}$$

Now let's get a little harder:

$$5x + 3 = 48$$

We can still do this informally. First let's figure out what number plus 3 is 48. Well, 45 plus 3 is 48. So $5x$ is 45. So x must be 9.

Here is the formal solution:

$$
\begin{aligned}
5x + 3 &= 48 \\
-3 & -3 \\
\underline{\tfrac{5x}{5}} &= \underline{\tfrac{45}{5}} \\
x &= 9
\end{aligned}
$$

Try to solve each of the following equations for x both informally, and formally. The answers are below:

1. $x + 17 = 20$
2. $6x = 24$
3. $\frac{x}{12} = 2$
4. $7x - 4 = 24$
5. $\frac{2x-3}{5} = 2$
6. $5(x - 7) = 40$
7. $2^x = 8$
8. $\frac{5+x}{2} = 8\frac{1}{2}$
9. $5^{x+1} = 125$
10. $3^x + 4 = 31$

Answers

1. 3
2. 4
3. 24
4. 4
5. 13/2 or 6.5

6. 15
7. 3
8. 12
9. 2
10. 3

Lesson 3
Geometry

Turn to Lesson 1 and review the strategy **Start with the Middle Answer Choice**. Then try to answer the following question using this strategy. **Do not** check the solution until you have attempted this question yourself.

Level 2: Geometry

1. If the perimeter of the rectangle below is 78 inches, what is the value of x, in inches?

    A. 20
    B. 19
    C. 18
    D. 17
    E. 16

Solution

* Recall that we get the **perimeter** of a rectangle by adding up the lengths of all four sides. Let's start with choice C as our first guess, so that $x = 18$. Then $x - 5 = 18 - 5 = 13$ and $x + 8 = 18 + 8 = 26$. It follows that the perimeter of the rectangle is $13 + 13 + 26 + 26 = 78$. This is correct, and so the answer is choice **C**.

Now try to solve this problem algebraically.

Solution

$$P = 2l + 2w$$
$$78 = 2(x+8) + 2(x-5)$$
$$78 = 2x + 16 + 2x - 10$$
$$78 = 4x + 6$$
$$72 = 4x$$
$$\frac{72}{4} = x$$
$$18 = x, \text{ choice } \mathbf{C}.$$

Turn to Lesson 1 and review the strategy **When NOT to Start with the Middle Answer Choice**. Then try to answer the following question using this strategy. **Do not** check the solution until you have attempted this question yourself.

LEVEL 3: GEOMETRY

2. The sum of the areas of two squares is 85. If the sides of both squares have integer lengths, what is the least possible value for the length of a side of the smaller square?

   F. 1
   G. 2
   H. 6
   J. 7
   K. 9

Solution

* Begin by looking at choice F since it is the smallest. If the side length of the smaller square is 1, then the area of the smaller square is $1 \cdot 1 = 1$. So, the area of the larger square is $85 - 1 = 84$. Since 84 is not a perfect square, we can eliminate choice F.

Let's try choice G next. If the side length of the smaller square is 2, then the area of the smaller square is 4, and the area of the larger square is $85 - 4 = 81$. Since 81 is a perfect square, the answer is choice **G**.

Remark: If it is not clear to you that 84 is not a perfect square, take the square root of 84 in your calculator. You will get approximately 9.16515. Since this is not an integer, 84 is not a perfect square.

81 is a perfect square however because $81 = 9^2$. Again, if this is not clear to you, simply take the square root of 81 in your calculator.

You're doing great! Let's just practice a bit more. Try to solve each of the following problems by using one of the two strategies you just reviewed. Then, if possible, solve each problem another way. The answers to these problems, followed by full solutions are at the end of this lesson. **Do not** look at the answers until you have attempted these problems yourself. Please remember to mark off any problems you get wrong.

LEVEL 1: GEOMETRY

3. If the degree measures of an isosceles triangle are 100°, $z°$, and $z°$, what is the value of z ?

   A. 80
   B. 70
   C. 60
   D. 40
   E. 30

4. In the triangle below, $x=$

   F. 62
   G. 64
   H. 66
   J. 68
   K. 70

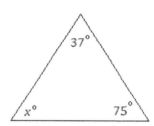

5. In the right triangle below, what is the value of y ?

   A. 15
   B. 18
   C. 21
   D. 30
   E. 60

6. In isosceles triangle ΔCAT, $\angle C$ and $\angle A$ are congruent and the measure of $\angle T$ is 52°. What is the measure of $\angle C$?

   F. 148°
   G. 128°
   H. 102°
   J. 86°
   K. 64°

LEVEL 2: GEOMETRY

7. The circumference of a circle is 40 cm. What is the length, in centimeters, of the *radius* of the circle?

   A. 2π
   B. $\frac{20}{\pi}$
   C. $\frac{40}{\pi}$
   D. 40
   E. 40π

8. If the area of a square is 49 cm², then the perimeter of the square, in centimeters, is

   F. 28
   G. 30
   H. 32
   J. 34
   K. 36

9. A rectangle has a perimeter of 16 meters and an area of 15 square meters. What is the longest of the side lengths, in meters, of the rectangle?

   A. 3
   B. 5
   C. 10
   D. 15
   E. 16

LEVEL 3: GEOMETRY

10. If the perimeter of a rectangle is 100 cm then the area of the rectangle, in centimeters, is

    F. 200
    G. 400
    H. 600
    J. 800
    K. Cannot be determined from the given information

Definitions Used in This Lesson

A **perfect square** is an integer that is equal to the square of another integer. For example, 9 is a perfect square because $9 = 3^2$.

A **triangle** is a two-dimensional geometric figure with three sides and three angles. The sum of the degree measures of all three angles of a triangle is 180.

A triangle is **isosceles** if it has two sides of equal length. Equivalently, an isosceles triangle has two angles of equal measure.

A **right triangle** has one angle that measures 90° (this angle is called a **right angle**).

A **quadrilateral** is a two-dimensional geometric figure with four sides and four angles. The sum of the degree measures of all four angles of a quadrilateral is 360.

A **rectangle** is a quadrilateral in which each angle is a right angle. That is, each angle has a measure of 90 degrees.

The **perimeter** of a rectangle is $P = 2l + 2w$, and the area of a rectangle is $A = lw$.

A **square** is a rectangle with four equal sides.

The perimeter of a square is $P = 4s$, and the area of a square is $A = s^2$.

Example:

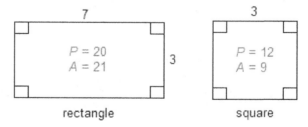

rectangle   square

A **circle** is a two-dimensional geometric figure formed of a curve surrounding a center point, every point of the curve being an equal distance from the center point. This distance is called the **radius** of the circle. The **diameter** of a circle is the distance between any two points on the circle that pass through the center of the circle.

The **circumference** of a circle is $C = 2\pi r$ and the area of a circle is $A = \pi r^2$.

Answers

1. C   6. K
2. G   7. B
3. D   8. F
4. J   9. B
5. A   10. K

Full Solutions

3.

Solution by starting with choice C: Recall that the angle measures of a triangle sum to 180 degrees. Let us start with choice C. If we guess that $z = 60$, then the angles sum to $100 + z + z = 100 + 60 + 60 = 220$ degrees. This is too large. We can therefore eliminate choices A, B, and C.

Let us try choice D next. So, we are guessing that $z = 40$. Then the angle measures sum to $100 + z + z = 100 + 40 + 40 = 180$ degrees. Since this is correct, the answer is choice **D**.

* Algebraic solution: The angle measures of a triangle sum to 180 degrees. So, we must solve the following equation.

$$100 + z + z = 180$$
$$100 + 2z = 180$$
$$2z = 80$$
$$z = 40$$

Therefore, the answer is choice D.

4.

Solution by starting with choice H: Recall that the angle measures of a triangle sum to 180 degrees, and begin by looking at choice H. If we let $x = 66$, then we have $66 + 37 + 75 = 178$. This is a bit too small, and so we can eliminate choices F, G, and H.

Let's try choice J next. If $x = 68$, we get $68 + 37 + 75 = 180$. So, the answer is choice J.

* Algebraic solution: We solve the following equation.

$$x + 37 + 75 = 180$$
$$x + 112 = 180$$
$$x = 68$$

This is answer choice **J**.

5.

Solution by starting with choice C: Recall that the angle measures of a triangle sum to 180 degrees, and begin by looking at choice C. So, we let $y = 21$. Then $5y = 5 \cdot 21 = 105$, and we have $90 + 21 + 105 = 216$. Since $216 > 180$ we can eliminate choices C, D and E.

Let's try choice A next. So, we let $y = 15$. Then $5y = 5 \cdot 15 = 75$, and we have $90 + 15 + 75 = 180$. Therefore, the answer is choice **A**.

* **Algebraic solution:** $5y + y$ must be equal to 90. So $6y = 90$, and therefore $y = \frac{90}{6} = 15$, choice **A**.

6.

Solution by starting with choice H: First note that the three angle measures in a triangle add up to 180°.

Let's start with choice H and guess that the measure of ∠C is 102°. Since ∠C and ∠A are congruent, the measure of ∠A is also 102°. But the sum $102 + 102 = 204$ is already too big. So, we can eliminate choices F, G, and H.

Let's try choice K next and guess that the measure of ∠C is 64°. Since ∠C and ∠A are congruent, the measure of ∠A is also 64°. we then have that $52 + 64 + 64 = 180$. So, the answer is choice **K**.

* **Quick solution:** $180 - 52 = 128$. So, angles C and A together measure 128°. Since ∠C and ∠A are congruent, the measure of ∠C is $\frac{128}{2} = 64°$, choice **K**.

7.

Solution by starting with choice C: The circumference of a circle is $C = 2\pi r$. Let's start with choice C as our first guess. If $r = \frac{40}{\pi}$, then we have $C = 2\pi \left(\frac{40}{\pi}\right) = 80$. Since this is too big we can eliminate choices C, D, and E.

Let's try choice B next. If $r = \frac{20}{\pi}$, then $C = 2\pi \left(\frac{20}{\pi}\right) = 40$. So, the answer is indeed choice **B**.

* **Algebraic solution:** We use the circumference formula $C = 2\pi r$, and substitute 40 in for C.

$$C = 2\pi r$$
$$40 = 2\pi r$$
$$\frac{40}{2\pi} = r$$
$$\frac{20}{\pi} = r$$

This is choice **B**.

8.

* The length of a side of the square is $s = \sqrt{49} = 7$. So, the perimeter is $P = 4(7) = 28$, choice **F**.

9.

* **Solution by starting with choice C:** Let's start with choice C and guess that the longest side of the rectangle is 10 meters long. But then the length of the two longer sides of the rectangle adds up to 20 meters which is greater than the perimeter. So, we can eliminate choices C, D, and E.

Let's try choice B next. So, we are guessing that the longest side of the rectangle is 5. Since the perimeter is 16, it follows that the shortest side must have length 3 (see Remark (1) below for more clarification). So, the area is $5 \cdot 3 = 15$. Since this is correct, the answer is choice **B**.

Remarks: (1) If one side of the rectangle has a length of 5 meters, then the opposite side also has a length of 5 meters. Since the perimeter is 16 meters, this leaves $16 - 5 - 5 = 6$ meters for the other two sides. It follows that a shorter side of the rectangle has length $\frac{6}{2} = 3$ meters.

(2) When guessing the longest side of the rectangle we can use the area instead of the perimeter to find the shortest side. For example, if we guess that the longest side is 5, then since the area is 15 it follows that the shortest side is 3. We would then check to see if we get the right perimeter. In this case, we have $P = 2(5) + 2(3) = 16$ which is correct.

Algebraic solution: We are given that $2x + 2y = 16$ and $xy = 15$. If we divide each side of the first equation by 2, we get $x + y = 8$. Subtracting each side of this equation by x, we get $y = 8 - x$.

We replace y by $8 - x$ in the second equation to get $x(8 - x) = 15$. Distributing the x on the left yields $8x - x^2 = 15$. Subtracting $8x$ and adding x^2 to each side of this equation gives us $0 = x^2 - 8x + 15$. The right-hand side can be factored to give $0 = (x - 5)(x - 3)$. So, we have $x - 5 = 0$ or $x - 3 = 0$. So, $x = 5$ or $x = 3$. Since the question asks for the longest of the side lengths, the answer is $x = 5$, choice **B**.

Here is a picture for extra clarification.

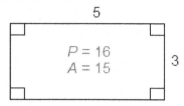

10.

Solution: If the length of the rectangle is $l = 20$, then we get

$$P = 2l + 2w$$
$$100 = 2(20) + 2w$$
$$100 = 40 + 2w$$
$$60 = 2w$$
$$30 = w$$

So, $A = lw = 20 \cdot 30 = \mathbf{600}$. This eliminates choices F, G, and J.

Now, if $l = 10$, then $w = \frac{100 - 2(10)}{2} = \frac{100 - 20}{2} = \frac{80}{2} = 40$, and therefore $A = 10 \cdot 40 = 400$. This eliminates choice H, and the answer is therefore choice **K**.

Note: Since $P = 2l + 2w$, we have $2w = P - 2l$, and it follows that $w = \frac{P - 2l}{2}$.

For example, if the perimeter of a rectangle is $P = 100$, and the length of the rectangle is $l = 20$, then the width is $w = \frac{100 - 2 \cdot 20}{2} = 30$.

So, we could have done the first computation in the solution above more quickly this way.

This is how we did the second computation.

OPTIONAL MATERIAL

The following questions will test your understanding of formulas used in this lesson. These are **not** in the format of ACT questions.

1. Find the perimeter and area of a rectangle with each of the following lengths and widths.

$\ell = 3, w = 5$ $\ell = 2.3, w = 1.7$ $\ell = x - 2, w = x + 3$ $\ell = x - 4, w = x^2 + 5$

2. Find the perimeter of a square with area 64.

3. Find the area of a square with perimeter 48.

4. Find the area of a rectangle with perimeter 60 and length 10.

5. Find the perimeter of a rectangle with area 35 and width 7.

6. Find the area of a rectangle with perimeter 60.

7. Find the circumference of a circle with each of the following radii.

$\quad\quad 3 \quad\quad \pi \quad\quad x \quad\quad x^2 + 5$

8. Find the radius of a circle with each of the following circumferences.

$\quad\quad 2\pi \quad\quad \pi \quad\quad 7\pi \quad\quad 5 \quad\quad C \quad\quad x - 2$

Answers

1. $P = 16, A = 15$; $P = 8, A = 3.91$; $P = 4x + 2, A = (x - 2)(x + 3) = x^2 + x - 6$; $P = 2x^2 + 2x + 2, A = (x - 4)(x^2 + 5) = x^3 - 4x^2 + 5x - 20$

2. $4(8) = 32$

3. $(48/4)^2 = 12^2 = 144$

4. $w = (60 - 2(10))/2 = (60 - 20)/2 = 40/2 = 20$. So $A = (10)(20) = 200$

5. $\ell = 35/7 = 5$. So $P = 2(5) + 2(7) = 10 + 14 = 24$.

6. **Cannot be determined from the given information!** For example, in question 4 we saw that A can be 200. But, for example, if $\ell = 5$, then $w = (60 - 2(5))/2 = (60 - 10)/2 = 50/2 = 25$. So $A = (5)(25) = 125$.

7. $6\pi, 2\pi^2, 2\pi x, 2\pi(x^2 + 5)$

8. $1, \frac{1}{2}, \frac{7}{2}, \frac{5}{2\pi}, \frac{C}{2\pi}, \frac{x-2}{2\pi}$

Lesson 4
Statistics

Change Averages to Sums

A problem involving averages often becomes much easier when we first convert the averages to sums. We can easily change an average to a sum using the following simple formula.

$$\textbf{Sum} = \textbf{Average} \cdot \textbf{Number}$$

Many problems with averages involve one or more conversions to sums, followed by a subtraction.

Note: The above formula comes from eliminating the denominator in the definition of average.

$$\textbf{Average} = \frac{\textbf{Sum}}{\textbf{Number}}$$

Try to answer the following question using this strategy. **Do not** check the solution until you have attempted this question yourself.

Level 1: Statistics

1. The average (arithmetic mean) of three numbers is 50. If two of the numbers are 40 and 65, what is the third number?

    A. 35
    B. 40
    C. 45
    D. 50
    E. 55

Solution

* In this case, we are averaging 3 numbers. Thus, the **Number** is 3. The **Average** is given to be 50. So, the **Sum** of the 3 numbers is $50 \cdot 3 = 150$. Since we know that two of the numbers are 40 and 65, the third number is $150 - 40 - 65 = 45$, choice **C**.

Before we go on, try to solve this problem in two other ways.

(1) By "Starting with Choice C" (see Lesson 1).
(2) Algebraically (the way you would do it in school).

Solutions

(1) Solution by starting with choice C: Let's start with choice C and guess that the third number is 45. Then the average of the three numbers is $\frac{40+65+45}{3} = \frac{150}{3} = 50$. Since this is correct, the answer is choice **C**.

(2) An algebraic solution: If we name the third number x, we have

$$\frac{40 + 65 + x}{3} = 50$$
$$105 + x = 150$$
$$x = 45.$$

So, the answer is choice **C**.

Now try to solve each of the following problems by using the strategy you just learned. The answers to these problems, followed by full solutions are at the end of this lesson. **Do not** look at the answers until you have attempted these problems yourself. Please remember to mark off any problems you get wrong.

LEVEL 1: STATISTICS

2. For which of the following lists of 5 numbers is the average (arithmetic mean) less than the median?

   F. 1, 1, 3, 4, 4
   G. 1, 2, 3, 5, 6
   H. 1, 1, 3, 5, 5
   J. 1, 2, 3, 4, 5
   K. 1, 2, 3, 4, 9

LEVEL 2: STATISTICS

3. What is the median of the list of the numbers below?

    2, 7, 4, 21, 11, 4, 6, 4, 8, 1, 5

    A. 4
    B. 5
    C. 6
    D. 7
    E. 8

4. The average (arithmetic mean) of three numbers is 114. If one of the numbers is 32, what is the sum of the other two?

    F. 82
    G. 144
    H. 214
    J. 306
    K. 310

5. Greg earned scores of 63, 72, 86, and 91 on his first 4 math tests. What is the minimum score Greg needs to earn on his 5th test so that the mean of his scores on all 5 tests is at least 3 points more than the mean of his scores on the first 4 tests?

    A. 90
    B. 91
    C. 92
    D. 93
    E. 94

6. The average (arithmetic mean) of 22, 50, and y is 50. What is the value of y?

    F. 50
    G. 72
    H. 76
    J. 78
    K. 134

Level 3: Statistics

7. Let m be the median of a set of data containing 13 items. Suppose that six data items are added to the set, three items greater than the original median, and three items less than the original median. Which of the following statements *must* be true about the median of the new data set?

   A. It is less than m.
   B. It is greater than m.
   C. It is equal to m
   D. It is the average of the 3 new lower values.
   E. It is the average of the 3 new higher values.

8. The average (arithmetic mean) of seven numbers is 20. When an eighth number is added, the average of the eight numbers is also 20. What is the eighth number?

   F. 0
   G. $\frac{8}{5}$
   H. $\frac{5}{2}$
   J. 16
   K. 20

Level 4: Statistics

9. If the average (arithmetic mean) of k and $k + 3$ is b and the average of k and $k - 3$ is c, what is the average of b and c?

   A. 1
   B. $\frac{k}{2}$
   C. k
   D. $k + \frac{1}{2}$
   E. $2k$

10. The average (arithmetic mean) of 4 numbers is m. If one of the numbers is n, what is the average of the remaining 3 numbers in terms of m and n?

   F. $\frac{m}{4}$
   G. $4m + n$
   H. $\frac{3m-n}{4}$
   J. $\frac{4m-n}{3}$
   K. $\frac{4n-m}{3}$

Definitions Used in This Lesson

The **average (arithmetic mean)** of a set of numbers is the sum of the numbers in the set divided by the quantity of the numbers in the set.

$$\text{Average} = \frac{\text{Sum}}{\text{Number}}$$

In ACT problems, we usually prefer to use the formula in the following form:

Sum = Average · Number

The **median** of a set of numbers is the middle number when the numbers are arranged in increasing order. If the total number of values in the set is even, then the median is the average of the two middle values.

Answers

1. C   6. J
2. F   7. C
3. B   8. K
4. K   9. C
5. D   10. J

Full Solutions

2.

Solution by changing averages to sums: All of these lists have a median of 3 (this is the number in the middle when the numbers are written in increasing order).

We want the **Average** to be less than 3. So, using the formula

Sum = Average · Number

we see that we want the **Sum** to be less than $3 \cdot 5 = 15$.

Let's start with choice H. The sum is $1 + 1 + 3 + 5 + 5 = 15$.

Let's try J next. $1 + 2 + 3 + 4 + 5 = 15$

Let's try G. $1 + 2 + 3 + 5 + 6 = 17$

Let's try F. $1 + 1 + 3 + 4 + 4 = 13$

Since 13 is less than 15, the answer is choice **F**.

* **Quick Solution:** With a little experience, it is not hard to see that **F** is the answer. Just look at how the numbers are "balanced" about the middle number 3. 1 is two units to the left, and 4 is only 1 unit to the right. You should still compute the sum as a check to verify that the answer is correct.

3.
* Let's rewrite the numbers in increasing order from left to right.

$$1, 2, 4, 4, 4, \mathbf{5}, 6, 7, 8, 11, 21$$

The middle number is 5, choice **B**.

4.
* **Solution by changing averages to sums:** We are averaging 3 numbers so that the **Number** is 3. The **Average** is given to be 114. Therefore, the **Sum** of the 3 numbers is $114 \cdot 3 = 342$. Since one of the numbers is 32, it follows that the sum of the other two is $342 - 32 = 310$, choice **K**.

Algebraic solution Let x, y, and 32 be the three numbers. Then we have that $\frac{x+y+32}{3} = 114$. Multiplying each side of this equation by 3 yields $x + y + 32 = 342$. Finally, subtract 32 from each side of this last equation to get $x + y = 310$, choice **K**.

Note: Notice that the steps performed in both solutions are essentially the same. The first solution is much better because it requires very little writing, and in fact the solution can be done right in your calculator without writing anything at all.

5.

* The sum of Greg's first 4 test scores is $63 + 72 + 86 + 91 = 312$, and the mean of those first 4 scores is $\frac{312}{4} = 78$. So, we want the mean of all 5 test scores to be at least $78 + 3 = 81$. Thus, the sum of the 5 scores should be at least $81 \cdot 5 = 405$. Therefore, the 5th score should be at least $405 - 312 = 93$, choice **D**.

6.

Solution by changing averages to sums: We are averaging 3 numbers so that the **Number** is 3. The **Average** is given to be 50. Thus, the **Sum** of the 3 numbers is $50 \cdot 3 = 150$. Since we know that two of the numbers are 22 and 50, the third number is $y = 150 - 22 - 50 = 78$, choice **J**.

* **Quick Method:** Since the average is 50, y must be at the same distance from 50 as 22. The distance between 22 and 50 is $50 - 22 = 28$. It follows that $y = 50 + 28 = 78$, choice **J**.

7.

* **Quick solution:** The median of a set of data is the middle number when the numbers are arranged in increasing order. If we add the same number of items greater than the median as we do that are less than the median, then the original median is still the middle number. So, the answer is choice **C**.

Note: If you don't understand the solution, try writing out 13 numbers in increasing order, and circle the middle number. Then place three numbers that are greater than the circled number, and three numbers less than the circled number. Now just observe that the circled number is still in the middle.

8.

Solution by changing averages to sums: The **Sum** of the seven numbers is $20 \cdot 7 = 140$. The sum of the eight numbers is $20 \cdot 8 = 160$. The eighth number is $160 - 140 = 20$, choice **K**

* **Quick solution:** If a list of numbers has an average of 20, then adding the number 20 does not change the average. Therefore, the answer is choice **K**.

9.

* Solution by changing averages to sums: Note that the **Sum** of k and $k+3$ is $k+(k+3) = 2k+3$, so that $2k+3 = 2b$. Similarly, the **Sum** of k and $k-3$ is $k+(k-3) = 2k-3$ so that $2k-3 = 2c$. So,

$$2b + 2c = 4k$$
$$2(b+c) = 4k$$
$$\frac{b+c}{2} = k.$$

Thus, the answer is choice **C**.

Note: This problem can also be solved by picking numbers. See Lesson 5 for more details.

10.

* Solution by changing averages to sums: The **Sum** of the 4 numbers is $4m$. The **Sum** of the remaining 3 numbers (after removing n) is $4m - n$. So, the **Average** of the remaining 3 numbers is $\frac{4m-n}{3}$, choice **J**.

Note: This problem can also be solved by picking numbers. See Lesson 5 for more details.

OPTIONAL MATERIAL

The following questions will test your understanding of the definitions used in this lesson. These are **not** in the format of ACT questions.

Compute the average (arithmetic mean) and median of the following lists of numbers.

1. $1, 2, 3, 4, 5$
2. $3, 3, 3, 3, 3$
3. $5, 3, 1, -1, -3, -5$
4. $21, 57, 32, 48, 1, 101$
5. $1, 2, 3, 4, 5, \ldots, 99$
6. x, y, z, where $x < y < z$
7. $1, 2, 5, 6, 10, 14, 15, 18, 19$

Answers

1. average = median = 3
2. average = median = 3
3. average = median = 0
4. average = $43\frac{1}{3} = \frac{130}{3} \approx 43.3$, median = 40
5. average = median = 50
6. average = $\frac{x+y+z}{3}$, median = y
7. average = median = 10

Tips for Computing These Quickly

You can (and should) compute each of these directly. But in addition, you should try to get the answers quickly using some shortcuts.

1. In a list of consecutive integers, the average (arithmetic mean) and median are equal.

2. If all the numbers in a list are the same, the average and median are equal to that number.

3. **Method 1:** Notice how all the numbers are "balanced" about 0.

Method 2: Note that the sum is 0 (a quick way to see this is by observing that for each positive number the corresponding negative number is there also).

5. In a list of consecutive integers, the average (arithmetic mean) and median are equal to the average of the first and last number:

$$\frac{1+99}{2} = \frac{100}{2} = 50.$$

7. Notice how all the numbers are "balanced" about 10 (for example, the distance from 6 to 10 is the same as the distance from 14 to 10).

Lesson 5
Number Theory

Reminder: Before beginning this lesson remember to redo the problems from Lesson 1 that you have marked off. Do not "unmark" a question unless you get it correct.

Take a Guess

Sometimes the answer choices themselves cannot be substituted in for the unknown or unknowns in the problem. But that does not mean that you cannot guess your own numbers. Try to make as reasonable a guess as possible, but do not over think it. Keep trying until you zero in on the correct value.

Try to answer the following question using this strategy. **Do not** check the solution until you have attempted this question yourself.

Level 3: Number Theory

1. Bill has cows, pigs and chickens on his farm. The number of chickens he has is three times the number of pigs, and the number of pigs he has is two more than the number of cows. Which of the following could be the total number of these animals?

    A. 14
    B. 15
    C. 16
    D. 17
    E. 18

Solution

* Let's take a guess and say that Bill has 3 cows. Then he has $3 + 2 = 5$ pigs, and $3 \cdot 5 = 15$ chickens. It follows that the total number of animals is $3 + 5 + 15 = 23$. This is too big.

Let's guess next that Bill has 1 cow. Then he has $1 + 2 = 3$ pigs, and $3 \cdot 3 = 9$ chickens. The total number of animals is then $1 + 3 + 9 = 13$. This is too small.

Bill must have 2 cows, $2 + 2 = 4$ pigs, and $3 \cdot 4 = 12$ chickens. Therefore, the total is $2 + 4 + 12 = 18$ animals. Thus, the answer is choice **E**.

Note: We were pretty unlucky to have to take 3 guesses before getting the answer, but even so, not too much time was used.

Before we go on, try to solve this problem the way you might do it in school.

Solution

Algebraic solution: If we let x represent the number of cows, then the number of pigs is $x + 2$, and the number of chickens is $3(x + 2)$. Thus, the total number of animals is

$$x + (x + 2) + 3(x + 2) = x + x + 2 + 3x + 6 = 5x + 8.$$

So, some possible totals are 13, 18, 23, … which we get by substituting 1, 2, 3, … for x. Substituting 2 in for x gives 18 which is answer choice **E**.

Warning: Many students incorrectly interpret "three times the number of pigs" as $3x + 2$. This is incorrect. The number of pigs is $x + 2$, and so "three times the number of pigs" is $3(x + 2) = 3x + 6$.

Pick a Number

A problem may become much easier to understand and to solve by substituting a specific number in for a variable. Just make sure that you choose a number that satisfies the given conditions.

Here are some guidelines when picking numbers.

(1) Pick a number that is simple but not too simple. In general, you might want to avoid picking 0 or 1 (but 2 is usually a good choice).
(2) Try to avoid picking numbers that appear in the problem.
(3) When picking two or more numbers try to make them all different.
(4) Most of the time picking numbers only allows you to eliminate answer choices. So, do not just choose the first answer choice that comes out to the correct answer. If multiple answers come out correct you need to pick a new number and start again. But you only have to check the answer choices that have not yet been eliminated.

(5) If there are fractions in the question a good choice might be the least common denominator (lcd) or a multiple of the lcd.
(6) In percent problems choose the number 100.
(7) If your first attempt does not eliminate 4 of the 5 choices, try to choose a number that's of a different "type." Here are some examples of types:
    (a) A positive integer greater than 1.
    (b) A positive fraction (or decimal) between 0 and 1.
    (c) A negative integer less than -1.
    (d) A negative fraction (or decimal) between -1 and 0.
(8) If you are picking pairs of numbers, try different combinations from (7). For example, you can try two positive integers greater than 1, two negative integers less than -1, or one positive and one negative integer, etc.

Remember that these are just guidelines and there may be rare occasions where you might break these rules. For example, sometimes it is so quick and easy to plug in 0 and/or 1 that you might do this even though only some of the answer choices get eliminated.

Try to answer the following question using this strategy. **Do not** check the solution until you have attempted this question yourself.

LEVEL 1: NUMBER THEORY

2. If z is an odd integer, what is the greatest odd integer less than z ?

    F. $z - 3$
    G. $z - 2$
    H. $z - 1$
    J. $2(z - 1)$
    K. $2(z - 1) - 3$

Solution

Let's set z equal to 5 (note that we must choose an odd integer for z). The greatest odd integer less than 5 is 3. So, write down the number **3** and put a nice big, dark circle around it.

We substitute 5 in for z in each answer choice and we eliminate any choice that does not come out to 3. We get the following:

F. $5 - 3 = 2$
G. $5 - 2 = 3$
H. $5 - 1 = 4$
J. $2(5 - 1) = 2(4) = 8$
K. $2(5 - 1) - 3 = 2(4) - 3 = 8 - 3 = 5$

Since G is the only choice that has become 3, we can eliminate the other four choices, and we conclude that the answer is choice **G**.

Important note: G is **not** the correct answer simply because it is equal to 3. It is correct because all four of the other choices are **not** 3.

Before we go on, try to solve this problem directly (without picking a specific number).

* If z is odd, then 1 less than z is even and 2 less than z is odd. So, $z - 2$ is the greatest odd integer less than z. Thus, the answer is choice **G**.

Change Fractions to Decimals

Decimals are often easier to work with than fractions, especially since you have a calculator. To change a fraction to a decimal you simply perform the division in your calculator.

LEVEL 1: NUMBER THEORY

3. Which of the following groups contains three fractions that are equal?

   A. $\frac{1}{3}, \frac{1}{6}, \frac{1}{9}$

   B. $\frac{2}{3}, \frac{4}{6}, \frac{6}{8}$

   C. $\frac{2}{5}, \frac{4}{25}, \frac{8}{125}$

   D. $\frac{2}{5}, \frac{6}{15}, \frac{10}{25}$

   E. $\frac{2}{5}, \frac{6}{15}, \frac{10}{20}$

Solution

* We begin with choice C, and change each fraction to a decimal by dividing in our calculator.

$$2/5 = 0.4 \quad 4/25 = 0.16$$

Since these decimals disagree there is no reason to continue, and we eliminate choice C. Let's try choice D next.

$$2/5 = 0.4 \quad 6/15 = 0.4 \quad 10/25 = 0.4$$

Since these are all the same, the answer is choice **D**.

Note: We are also using the strategy of starting with the middle answer choice here. There is no actual advantage to starting with choice C in this problem, but there is no disadvantage either. We should always start with the middle choice just so we are in the habit of doing so (unless there is a specific reason not to).

You're doing great! Let's just practice a bit more. Try to solve each of the following problems. Whenever possible, use one of the strategies you just learned. Then, if possible, solve each problem another way. The answers to these problems, followed by full solutions are at the end of this lesson. **Do not** look at the answers until you have attempted these problems yourself. Please remember to mark off any problems you get wrong.

LEVEL 1: NUMBER THEORY

4. Which of the following numbers is between $\frac{1}{9}$ and $\frac{1}{8}$?

    F. 0.10
    G. 0.12
    H. 0.14
    J. 0.16
    K. 0.18

LEVEL 2: NUMBER THEORY

5. If x is 35% of z and y is 60% of z, what is $x + y$ in terms of z?

    A. $0.21z$
    B. $0.45z$
    C. $0.75z$
    D. $0.81z$
    E. $0.95z$

Level 3: Number Theory

6. Which of the following statements is true about odd and/or even numbers?

    F. The sum of any 2 odd numbers is odd.
    G. The sum of any odd number and any even number is even.
    H. The product of any odd number and any even number is odd.
    J. The product of any 2 odd numbers is odd.
    K. The quotient of any 2 odd numbers is odd.

Level 4: Number Theory

7. What is one possible value of x for which $\frac{3}{16} < x < \frac{1}{5}$?

    A. $\frac{29}{160}$
    B. $\frac{15}{80}$
    C. $\frac{31}{160}$
    D. $\frac{16}{80}$
    E. $\frac{33}{160}$

8. If k is divided by 9, the remainder is 7. What is the remainder if $4k$ is divided by 6?

    F. 5
    G. 4
    H. 3
    J. 2
    K. 1

9. The sum of 3 consecutive even integers is m. In terms of m, what is the sum of the 2 greater of these integers?

    A. $m - 3$
    B. $m - 2$
    C. $\frac{2m}{3} - 2$
    D. $\frac{2m}{3}$
    E. $\frac{2m}{3} + 2$

10. If k is a positive integer, which of the following expressions must be an odd integer?

    F. $k + 5$
    G. $\frac{k}{5}$
    H. $5k$
    J. k^5
    K. 5^k

Definitions Used in This Lesson

Definitions of **integers**, **positive integers**, and **consecutive integers** can be found in Lesson 1.

The **even integers** consist of the even numbers from the set of integers:
$$\{\ldots, -4, -2, 0, 2, 4, \ldots\}$$
The **odd integers** consist of the odd numbers from the set of integers:
$$\{\ldots, -5, -3, -1, 1, 3, 5, \ldots\}$$
Consecutive even integers are even integers that follow each other in order. The difference between consecutive even integers is 2. Here are two examples.

    $4, 6, 8$ these are three consecutive integers
    $-2, 0, 2, 4, 6$ these are five consecutive integers

In general, if x is an integer, then $x, x + 2, x + 4, x + 6, \ldots$ are consecutive even integers.

Answers

1. E   6. J
2. G   7. C
3. D   8. G
4. G   9. E
5. E   10. K

Full Solutions

4.

* Solution by changing fractions to decimals: Change the two fractions to decimals by dividing in your calculator. Dividing 1 by 9 gives about 0.1111. Dividing 1 by 8 gives 0.125. Since 0.12 is between these two the answer is choice **G**.

5.

Solution by picking a number: Let's substitute the number 100 in for z (see point 6 above under Picking Numbers). Then x is 35% of 100, which is 35, and y is 60% of 100, which is 60. So, we have $x + y = 35 + 60 = \mathbf{95}$. The answer is clearly choice E, but for the sake of completion let's plug $z = 100$ into each answer choice.

- A. 21
- B. 45
- C. 75
- D. 81
- E. 95

We have confirmed that the answer is choice **E**.

* Algebraic solution: $x = 0.35z$ and $y = 0.60z$. So, we have $x + y = 0.35z + 0.60z = 0.95z$. Therefore, the answer is choice **E**.

Remark: For more practice converting between decimals and percents, see the optional material at the end of Lesson 21.

6.

Solution by picking numbers: Let's start by choosing 2 odd numbers, say 3 and 5. We have $3 + 5 = 8$, an even number. This eliminates choice F. We have $3 \cdot 5 = 15$, an odd number. So, we CANNOT eliminate choice J with these numbers. We have $3 \div 5 = \frac{3}{5}$. This is not an integer, and so in particular, it is not an odd number. This eliminates choice K.

Now let's choose an odd number and an even number, say 3 and 4. We have $3 + 4 = 7$, an odd number. This eliminates choice G. We have $3 \cdot 4 = 12$, an even number. This eliminates choice H.

Since we have eliminated choices F, G, H, and K, the answer is choice **J**.

Notes: (1) Only integers can be even and odd. Nonetheless, the ACT often uses the terminology "odd number" rather than "odd integer."

(2) Real numbers that are not integers CANNOT be even or odd. For example, the number $\frac{3}{5}$ is not an integer, and therefore it is not even or odd ($\frac{3}{5}$ is a rational number or fraction).

As another example $\sqrt{2}$ is neither even nor odd because it is not an integer ($\sqrt{2}$ is an irrational number since it cannot be expressed as a fraction).

* Direct solution: The product of any 2 odd integers is odd, choice **J**.

Notes: (1) The following summarizes how even and odd integers behave with respect to addition and multiplication. We write e for even and o for odd:

$$e + e = e \qquad e \cdot e = e$$
$$e + o = o \qquad e \cdot o = e$$
$$o + e = o \qquad o \cdot e = e$$
$$o + o = e \qquad o \cdot o = o$$

(2) The set of integers is **closed** for addition and subtraction. This means that whenever we add or multiply two integers, we always get an integer. This observation allows us to ask what happens when we add or multiply 2 even or odd integers. The answer to this question is given in Note (1).

(3) The set of integers is also closed for subtraction, and subtraction behaves just like addition. For example, when we subtract an odd integer from another odd integer, we get an even integer (see Note (1)).

(4) The set of integers is **not** closed for division. In other words, when we divide one integer by another integer, we may or may not get another integer. For example, when we divide the integer 3 by the integer 5, we get a number which is not an integer.

7.

* Solution by changing fractions to decimals: We divide 3 by 16, and 1 by 5 in our calculators: $\frac{3}{16} = 0.1875$ $\frac{1}{5} = 0.2$

Now let's start with choice C, and divide 31 by 160 in our calculator to get $\frac{31}{160} = 0.19375$.

Since $0.1875 < 0.19375 < 0.2$, the answer is choice **C**.

8.

Solution by picking a number: Let's choose a positive integer whose remainder is 7 when it is divided by 9. A simple way to find such a k is to add 9 and 7. So, let $k = 16$. Then we have $4k = 4 \cdot 16 = 64$. 6 goes into 64 ten times with a remainder of 4. So, the answer is choice **G**.

Important: To find a remainder you must perform division **by hand** (or use the calculator algorithm below). Dividing one integer by another in your calculator does **not** give you a remainder!

* Note: A slightly simpler choice for k is $k = 7$. Indeed, when 7 is divided by 9 we get 0 with 7 left over. Then $4k = 28$, and the remainder when 28 is divided by 6 is 4, choice **G**.

Notes: (1) In general, we can get a value for k by starting with any multiple of 9 and adding 7. So, $k = 9n + 7$ for some integer n.

(2) The answer to this problem is independent of our choice for k (assuming that k satisfies the given condition, of course). The method just described does **not** show this (see the next solution).

Complete solution: This solution demonstrates the independence of our choice for k. **Do not** use this method on the actual ACT.

The given condition means that we can write k as $k = 9n + 7$ for some integer n. Then

$4k = 4(9n + 7) = 36n + 28 = 36n + 24 + 4 = 6(6n + 4) + 4 = 6z + 4$

where z is the integer $6n + 4$. This shows that when $4k$ is divided by 6 the remainder is 4, choice **G**.

Calculator Algorithm for computing a remainder: Although performing division in your calculator never produces a remainder, there is a simple algorithm you can perform which mimics long division. Let's find the remainder when 64 is divided by 6 using this algorithm.

Step 1: Perform the division in your calculator: $64/6 \approx 10.6666667$
Step 2: Multiply the integer part of this answer by the divisor:
$$10 \cdot 6 = 60$$
Step 3: Subtract this result from the dividend to get the remainder:
$$64 - 60 = 4$$

9.
Solution by picking numbers: Let's let the 3 consecutive even integers be 2, 4, and 6, so that $m = 2 + 4 + 6 = 12$, and the sum of the 2 greater integers is $4 + 6 = \mathbf{10}$. Put a nice big dark circle around the number 10 so that you can find it easily later. We now substitute 12 for m into each answer choice.

   A. $12 - 3 = 9$
   B. $12 - 2 = 10$
   C. $\frac{2 \cdot 12}{3} - 2 = 6$
   D. $\frac{2 \cdot 12}{3} = 8$
   E. $\frac{2 \cdot 12}{3} + 2 = 10$

We can eliminate choices A, C, and D because they came out incorrect.

Now let's try 4, 6, and 8, so that $m = 4 + 6 + 8 = 18$, and the sum of the 2 greater integers is $6 + 8 = \mathbf{14}$. We need check only choices B and E. For choice B we get $18 - 2 = 16$. This is incorrect, and so the answer should be choice E. Let's just confirm that E is correct: $\frac{2 \cdot 18}{3} + 2 = 14$. Indeed, the answer is choice **E**.

* **Algebraic solution:** Let's let the 3 consecutive even integers be x, $x + 2$, and $x + 4$. The sum of the 3 integers is then $x + (x + 2) + (x + 4) = 3x + 6$, and we are given that this sum is equal to m. It follows that $3x + 6 = m$. Subtracting 6 from each side of this equation yields $3x = m - 6$. Dividing by 3, we get $x = \frac{m-6}{3}$. We want to express the sum of $x + 2$ and $x + 4$ in terms of m. We have

$$(x+2)+(x+4) = 2x+6 = \frac{2(m-6)}{3}+6 = \frac{(2m-12)}{3}+6$$
$$= \frac{2m}{3}-\frac{12}{3}+6 = \frac{2m}{3}-4+6 = \frac{2m}{3}+2$$

This is choice **E**.

10.

Solution by picking a number: Let's choose a positive integer value for k, say $k = 2$. We now substitute 2 for k into each answer choice.

  F. 7
  G. $\frac{2}{5}$
  H. 10
  J. 32
  K. 25

We can eliminate choices H and J because they are even integers, and we can eliminate choice G because it is not an integer.

Now let's try $k = 3$. We need check only choices F and K.

  F. 8
  K. 125

We can eliminate choice F because it is even. The answer is therefore choice **K**.

* Direct solution: The product of odd integers is always odd. Since 5 is odd, multiplying 5 by itself multiple times will always yield an odd integer. Therefore, the answer is choice **K**.

Note: See problem 6 for more on sums, products, and quotients of integers.

OPTIONAL MATERIAL

The following questions will test your understanding of definitions used in this lesson. These are **not** in the format of ACT questions.

1. Which of the following numbers are positive integers? Choose all that apply.

$$4 \quad -4 \quad 0 \quad 2\sqrt{64} \quad \sqrt{18} \quad \frac{1.2}{0.3} \quad \frac{2\pi - \pi}{\pi} \quad \sqrt{4} - \sqrt{9} \quad \sqrt{2} - \sqrt{3 - 2\sqrt{2}}$$

2. Which of the following numbers are even integers? Which are odd integers? Choose all that apply. Assume that k is an integer.

$$\frac{1}{4} \quad -3 \quad \frac{.67}{.01} \quad \sqrt{2} \quad 0 \quad 2k \quad 2k+1 \quad 2k-3 \quad k^2$$

3. Find a number k such that $2k$ is an odd integer. Find a number r such that $2r$ is not an integer.

4. Let j, k, m and n be integers with j and k even, and m and n odd. Determine whether each of the following is even or odd.

$$j+k \quad j+m \quad m+n \quad jk \quad jm \quad mn \quad j^2 \quad m^2$$

5. Which of the following positive integers are prime numbers?

$$19 \quad 1 \quad 27 \quad 31 \quad 53 \quad 1643 \quad 3001$$

Answers

1. $4, 2\sqrt{64} = 2 \cdot 8 = 16, \frac{1.2}{0.3} = \frac{12}{3} = 4, \frac{2\pi - \pi}{\pi} = \frac{\pi}{\pi} = 1,$

$$\sqrt{2} - \sqrt{3 - 2\sqrt{2}} = \sqrt{2} - \sqrt{2 - 2\sqrt{2} + 1} = \sqrt{2} - \sqrt{(\sqrt{2} - 1)^2}$$
$$= \sqrt{2} - (\sqrt{2} - 1) = \sqrt{2} - \sqrt{2} + 1 = 1$$

$\sqrt{18} = \sqrt{9 \cdot 2} = \sqrt{9}\sqrt{2} = 3\sqrt{2}$, not an integer
$\sqrt{4} - \sqrt{9} = 2 - 3 = -1$, not positive

2. Even integers: $0, 2k, k^2$ if k is even

Odd integers: $-3, \frac{.67}{.01} = 67, 2k+1, 2k-3, k^2$ if k is odd

3. For example, we can let $k = \frac{1}{2}$ and $r = \frac{1}{4}$. Then $2k = 1$ and $2r = \frac{1}{2}$. Note that k and r are **not** integers.

4. $j + k$ is even, $j + m$ is odd, $m + n$ is even, jk is even, jm is even, mn is odd, j^2 is even, m^2 is odd

Note: See problem 6 from this lesson for more on sums and products of integers.

5. 19, 31, 53, 3001

Note: $1643 = 31 \cdot 53$. So, 1643 is not prime

A little trick for determining if a large integer is prime: Take the square root of the integer and check if the integer is divisible by each prime up to this square root. If not, the number is prime. For example, note that $\sqrt{3001} \approx 54.8$. In your calculator divide 3001 by 2, 3, 5, 7, 11, 13, 17, 19, 23, 29, 31, 37, 41, 43, 47, and 53. Since none of these are integers, 3001 is prime.

LESSON 6
ALGEBRA

Reminder: Before beginning this lesson remember to redo the problems from Lesson 2 that you have marked off. Do not "unmark" a question unless you get it correct.

The Distributive Property

The **distributive property** says that for all real numbers a, b, and c,

$$a(b + c) = ab + ac$$

More specifically, this property says that the operation of multiplication distributes over addition. The distributive property is very important as it allows us to multiply and factor algebraic expressions.

Numeric example: Show that $2(3 + 4) = 2 \cdot 3 + 2 \cdot 4$

Solution: $2(3 + 4) = 2 \cdot 7 = 14$ and $2 \cdot 3 + 2 \cdot 4 = 6 + 8 = 14$.

Geometric Justification: The following picture gives a physical representation of the distributive property for this example.

Note that the area of the light grey rectangle is $2 \cdot 3$, the area of the dark grey rectangle is $2 \cdot 4$, and the area of the whole rectangle is $2(3 + 4)$.

Algebraic examples: Use the distributive property to write each algebraic expression in an equivalent form.

(1) $2(x + 1)$ (2) $x(y - 3)$ (3) $-(x - y)$

Solutions: (1) $2(x + 1) = 2x + 2$

(2) $x(y - 3) = xy - 3x$

(3) $-(x - y) = -x + y$

Try the following ACT math problem where the distributive property can be used.

Level 1: Algebra

1. The expression $x[y + (z - w)]$ is equivalent to

   A. $xy + z - w$
   B. $xy + z + w$
   C. $xy + xz - w$
   D. $xy + xz + xw$
   E. $xy + xz - xw$

Solution

*

$$x[y + (z - w)] = xy + x(z - w) = xy + xz - xw$$

So, the answer is choice **E**.

Notes: (1) We applied the distributive property twice here. First we distributed x to y and $z - w$. Then we distributed x to z and $-w$.

(2) We could easily have done this in a single step by distributing x to y, z, and $-w$ all at once.

(3) This problem can also be solved by using the strategy of picking numbers from Lesson 5. In fact, many of the problems in this section can be solved by picking numbers. The methods presented in this lesson however will generally be much faster.

Factoring

When we use the distributive property in the opposite direction, we usually call it **factoring**.

Examples: (1) $2x + 4y = 2(x + 2y)$

(2) $3x + 5xy = x(3 + 5y)$

(3) $6xy + 9yz = 3y(2x + 3z)$

Try the following ACT math problem that can be solved by factoring.

LEVEL 1: ALGEBRA

2. If $10xz - 15yz = kz(2x - ny)$ where k and n are positive real numbers, what is the value of kn?

   F. 8
   G. 12
   H. 15
   J. 18
   K. 30

Solution

*

$$10xz - 15yz = 5z(2x - 3y)$$

So $k = 5$, $n = 3$, and therefore $kn = 5 \cdot 3 = 15$, choice **H**.

Addition and Subtraction of Polynomials

We add polynomials by simply combining like terms. We can change any subtraction problem to an addition problem by first distributing the minus sign. Let's look at an example.

LEVEL 2: ALGEBRA

3. Which of the following is equivalent to the expression $(-3x^2y + 2xy^2) - (-3x^2y - 2xy^2)$?

   A. 0
   B. $-6x^2y$
   C. $4xy^2$
   D. $6x^2y - 4xy^2$
   E. $-6x^2y + 4xy^2$

Solution

*

$$(-3x^2y + 2xy^2) - (-3x^2y - 2xy^2)$$
$$= -3x^2y + 2xy^2 + 3x^2y + 2xy^2$$
$$= (-3x^2y + 3x^2y) + (2xy^2 + 2xy^2) = 0 + 4xy^2 = 4xy^2$$

This is choice **C**.

Multiplication of Polynomials

Most students are familiar with the mnemonic FOIL to help them multiply two binomials (polynomials with 2 terms) together. As a simple example, we have

$$(x+1)(x-2) = x^2 - 2x + x - 2 = x^2 - x - 2$$

Unfortunately, this method works ONLY for binomials. It does not extend to polynomials with more than 2 terms. Let's demonstrate another way to multiply polynomials with the same example.

We begin by lining up the polynomials vertically:

$$\begin{array}{r} x+1 \\ \underline{x-2} \end{array}$$

We multiply the -2 on the bottom by each term on top, moving from right to left. First note that -2 times 1 is -2:

$$\begin{array}{r} x+1 \\ \underline{x-2} \\ -2 \end{array}$$

Next note that -2 times x is $-2x$:

$$\begin{array}{r} x+1 \\ \underline{x-2} \\ -2x-2 \end{array}$$

Now we multiply the x on the bottom by each term on top, moving from right to left. This time as we write the answers we leave one blank space on the right:

$$\begin{array}{r} x+1 \\ \underline{x-2} \\ -2x-2 \\ \underline{x^2+x} \end{array}$$

Finally, we add:

$$\begin{array}{r} x+1 \\ \underline{x-2} \\ -2x-2 \\ \underline{x^2+x} \\ x^2-x-2 \end{array}$$

Try to use this algorithm to solve the following problem.

LEVEL 2: ALGEBRA

4. The expression $(3x-2)(x+5)$ is equivalent to:

   F. $3x^2 - 7$
   G. $3x^2 - 10$
   H. $3x - 2x - 7$
   J. $3x^2 + 13x - 10$
   K. $3x^2 - 13x - 10$

Solution

*

$$\begin{array}{r} 3x - 2 \\ x + 5 \\ \hline 15x - 10 \\ 3x^2 - 2x \\ \hline 3x^2 + 13x - 10 \end{array}$$

This is choice **J**.

You're doing great! Let's practice a bit more. You may want to review the strategies **Take a Guess** and **Pick a Number** from Lesson 5. The answers to these problems, followed by full solutions are at the end of this lesson. **Do not** look at the answers until you have attempted these problems yourself. Please remember to mark off any problems you get wrong.

LEVEL 1: ALGEBRA

5. If $3y - 18 = 15$, then $y - 6 =$

   A. 30
   B. 20
   C. 15
   D. 10
   E. 5

Level 2: Algebra

6. Which of the following is equivalent to the expression $(3x-2)(2x+1)$?

   F. $6x^2 - 2$
   G. $6x^2 - x - 2$
   H. $6x^2 + x - 2$
   J. $5x^2 - 4$
   K. $3x$

Level 3: Algebra

7. If x is $\frac{3}{5}$ of y and y is $\frac{5}{7}$ of z, what is the value of $\frac{z}{x}$?

   A. $\frac{1}{4}$
   B. $\frac{3}{7}$
   C. $\frac{5}{4}$
   D. $\frac{10}{7}$
   E. $\frac{7}{3}$

8. If $3^x = 11$, then $3^{2x} =$

   F. 5.5
   G. 22
   H. 33
   J. 121
   K. 1331

9. What polynomial must be added to $x^2 + 3x - 5$ so that the sum is $5x^2 - 8$?

   A. $4x^2 - 5x + 6$
   B. $4x^2 - 3x - 3$
   C. $4x^2 + 3x + 3$
   D. $5x^2 - 3x - 3$
   E. $5x^2 + 3x + 6$

10. For all x, $(x^2 - 3x + 1)(x + 2) = ?$

   F. $x^3 - x^2 - 5x + 2$
   G. $x^3 - x^2 - 5x - 2$
   H. $x^3 - x^2 + 5x + 2$
   J. $x^3 + x^2 + 5x + 2$
   K. $x^3 + x^2 - 5x + 2$

Definitions Used in This Lesson

A **polynomial in** x has the form $a_n x^n + a_{n-1} x^{n-1} + \cdots + a_1 x + a_0$ where $a_0, a_1, \ldots, a_n$ are real numbers. **Ex:** $x^2 + 2x - 35$ is a polynomial.

Answers

1. E   6. G
2. H   7. E
3. C   8. J
4. J   9. B
5. E   10. F

Full Solutions

5.
Solution by taking a guess: Let's start with a "random" guess for y, say $y = 10$. So, let's plug 10 in for y in the first equation.

$$3y - 18 = 15$$
$$3 \cdot 10 - 18 = 15$$
$$30 - 18 = 15$$
$$12 = 15$$

It looks as though 10 is a little too small. $y = 11$ should do the trick.

$$3y - 18 = 15$$
$$3 \cdot 11 - 18 = 15$$
$$33 - 18 = 15$$
$$15 = 15$$

So y is, in fact, 11. Thus, $y - 6 = 11 - 6 = 5$, and the answer is **E**.

Algebraic solution: We solve for y algebraically.

$$3y - 18 = 15$$
$$3y = 33$$
$$y = 11$$

So, $y - 6 = 11 - 6 = 5$, and the answer is choice **E**.

*** Solution using the distributive property:** We solve for $y - 6$.
$$3y - 18 = 15$$
$$3(y - 6) = 15$$
$$y - 6 = 5$$

Thus, the answer is choice **E**.

6.
* $(3x - 2)(2x + 1) = 6x^2 + 3x - 4x - 2 = 6x^2 - x - 2$

This is choice **G**.

Note: We can multiply $(3x - 2)$ and $(2x + 1)$ either by using FOIL or by using the algorithm given in this lesson.

7.
* Solution by picking a number: Let's choose a value for z, say $z = 35$ (this seems like a good choice since it is the product of the two denominators). Then

$$y = \frac{5}{7} \cdot 35 = 25 \text{ (the word "of" indicates multiplication)},$$

and $x = \frac{3}{5} \cdot 25 = 15$. Therefore, $\frac{z}{x} = \frac{35}{15} = \frac{7}{3}$, choice **E**.

Recall: To reduce the fraction $\frac{35}{15}$, type 35/15 in your calculator, then press MATH ENTER ENTER.

Algebraic solution: $x = \frac{3y}{5}$ and $y = \frac{5z}{7}$. Solving the last equation for z gives us $z = \frac{7y}{5}$. Then

$$\frac{z}{x} = \frac{\frac{7y}{5}}{\frac{3y}{5}} = \left(\frac{7y}{5}\right) \cdot \left(\frac{5}{3y}\right) = \frac{7}{3}.$$

Thus, the answer is choice **E**.

8.
Solution by guessing: Let's try to guess what x is. $3^2 = 9$, and $3^3 = 27$. So, x is between 2 and 3. Now, $3^{2 \cdot 2} = 3^4 = 81$ and $3^{2 \cdot 3} = 3^6 = 729$. Therefore, the answer is between 81 and 729. Thus, the answer must be choice **J**.

* **Algebraic solution:** $3^{2x} = (3^x)^2 = 11^2 = 121$. Thus, the answer is choice **J**.

Note: For a review of the basic laws of exponents, see Lesson 10.

9.
* **Algebraic solution:** We need to subtract $(5x^2 - 8) - (x^2 + 3x - 5)$. We first eliminate the parentheses by distributing the minus sign:

$$5x^2 - 8 - x^2 - 3x + 5$$

Finally, we combine like terms to get $4x^2 - 3x - 3$, choice **B**.

Remark: Pay careful attention to the minus and plus signs in the solution above. In other words, make sure you are distributing correctly.

10.
* **Algebraic solution:** We multiply the two polynomials.

$$\begin{array}{r} x^2 - 3x + 1 \\ \underline{x + 2} \\ 2x^2 - 6x + 2 \\ \underline{x^3 - 3x^2 + x + 0} \\ x^3 - x^2 - 5x + 2 \end{array}$$

This is choice **F**.

Download additional solutions for free here:

www.satprepget800.com/28LesInt

LESSON 7
GEOMETRY

Reminder: Before beginning this lesson remember to redo the problems from Lesson 3 that you have marked off. Do not "unmark" a question unless you get it correct.

Slope

The **slope** of a line is

$$Slope = m = \frac{rise}{run} = \frac{y_2 - y_1}{x_2 - x_1}$$

Lines with positive slope have graphs that go upwards from left to right. Lines with negative slope have graphs that go downwards from left to right. If the slope of a line is zero, it is horizontal. Vertical lines have **no** slope (also called **infinite slope** or **undefined slope**).

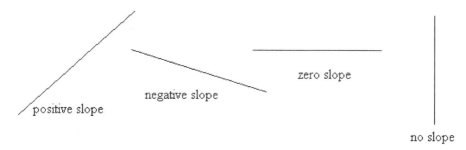

LEVEL 1: GEOMETRY

1. In the standard (x, y) coordinate plane, what is the slope of the line segment joining the points $(3, -5)$ and $(7, 2)$?

    A. $-\frac{7}{4}$
    B. $-\frac{4}{7}$
    C. $\frac{4}{7}$
    D. $\frac{7}{10}$
    E. $\frac{7}{4}$

Solution

* $\frac{2-(-5)}{7-3} = \frac{2+5}{4} = \frac{7}{4}$, choice **E**.

Notes: (1) Here we have $x_1 = 3$, $y_1 = -5$, $x_2 = 7$, and $y_2 = 2$.

(2) We could have also considered the points in the other order to get $\frac{-5-2}{3-7} = \frac{-7}{-4} = \frac{7}{4}$.

(3) A common mistake is to subtract the x-values in the numerator and the y-values in the denominator. This might give $\frac{7-3}{2-(-5)} = \frac{4}{7}$. This would lead to incorrectly choosing choice C.

(4) Make sure that you subtract "in the same direction" for both the numerator and denominator. For example, the following computation is wrong: $\frac{2-(-5)}{3-7} = \frac{7}{-4} = -\frac{7}{4}$. This would lead to incorrectly choosing A.

Before we go on, try to also solve this problem geometrically by plotting the two points.

Solution

Let's plot the two points.

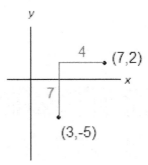

Note that to get from $(3, -5)$ to $(7,2)$ we move up 7 and right 4. Therefore, the answer is $\frac{7}{4}$, choice **E**.

Note: If you cannot see where the 7 and 4 come from visually, then you can formally find the differences: $2 - (-5) = 7$ and $7 - 3 = 4$.

Plug in the Given Point

If the graph of a function or other equation passes through certain points, plug those points into the equation to eliminate answer choices.

Try to answer the following question using this strategy. **Do not** check the solution until you have attempted this question yourself.

LEVEL 3: GEOMETRY

2. Which of the following is an equation of the line in the xy-plane that passes through the point $(0, -3)$ and is parallel to the line $y = -4x + 7$?

   F. $4x + y = -6$
   G. $4x + y = -3$
   H. $4x + y = 3$
   J. $-x + 4y = 6$
   K. $-x + 4y = 3$

Solution

* Since the point $(0, -3)$ lies on the line, if we substitute 0 in for x and -3 for y, we should get a true equation

   F. $4 \cdot 0 - 3 = -6$ or $-3 = -6$ False
   G. $4 \cdot 0 - 3 = -3$ or $-3 = -3$ True
   H. $4 \cdot 0 - 3 = 3$ or $-3 = 3$ False
   J. $-0 + 4(-3) = 6$ or $-12 = 6$ False
   K. $-0 + 4(-3) = 3$ or $-12 = 3$ False

We can eliminate choices F, H, J, and K because they have become false. The answer is therefore choice **G**.

Important note: G is **not** the correct answer simply because it came out true. It is correct because all of the other choices were false.

Before we go on, try to solve this problem using geometry.

Solution

Recall the slope-intercept form for the equation of a line: $y = mx + b$

$(0, -3)$ is the y-intercept of the line. Thus, $b = -3$. The slope of the given line is -4. Since the new line is parallel to this line, its slope is also -4, and the equation of the new line in slope-intercept form is $y = -4x - 3$.

We now add $4x$ to each side of this last equation to get $4x + y = -3$. This is choice **G**.

Notes: (1) The **slope-intercept form of an equation of a line** is $y = mx + b$ where m is the slope of the line and b is the y-coordinate of the y-intercept, ie. the point $(0, b)$ is on the line. Note that this point lies on the y-axis.

(2) Parallel lines have the same slope, and perpendicular lines have slopes that are negative reciprocals of each other.

You're doing great! Let's just practice a bit more. The answers to these problems, followed by full solutions are at the end of this lesson. **Do not** look at the answers until you have attempted these problems yourself. Please remember to mark off any problems you get wrong.

LEVEL 1: GEOMETRY

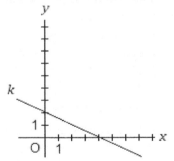

3. What is the equation of line k in the figure above?

    A. $y = -2x + 2$
    B. $y = -2x + 4$
    C. $y = -\frac{1}{2}x + 2$
    D. $y = -\frac{1}{2}x + 4$
    E. $y = 2x + 2$

Level 3: Geometry

4. In parallelogram *CRAB*, which of the following must be true about the measures of ∠*CRA* and ∠*RAB*?

   F. each are 90°
   G. each are less than 90°
   H. each are greater than 90°
   J. they add up to 90°
   K. they add up to 180°

5. The volume of a right circular cylinder is 1024π cubic centimeters. If the height is twice the base radius of the cylinder, what is the base radius of the cylinder?

   A. 2
   B. 4
   C. 6
   D. 8
   E. 16

6. In the figure below, what is the slope of line *m*?

   F. $-\frac{1}{2}$
   G. $\frac{1}{4}$
   H. $\frac{1}{2}$
   J. 2
   K. 4

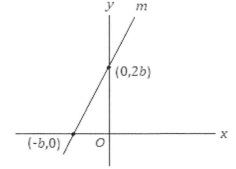

7. In the figure below, line k (not shown) passes through O and intersects PQ between P and Q. Which of the following could not be the slope of line k?

A. 0.01
B. 0.22
C. 0.31
D. 0.39
E. 0.41

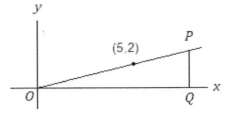

LEVEL 4: GEOMETRY

8. The consecutive vertices of a certain isosceles trapezoid are P, Q, R, and S where $\overline{PQ} \parallel \overline{SR}$. Which of the following are NOT congruent?

F. $\angle P$ and $\angle Q$
G. $\angle R$ and $\angle S$
H. $\overline{PS}$ and $\overline{QR}$
J. $\overline{PQ}$ and $\overline{SR}$
K. $\overline{PR}$ and $\overline{QS}$

9. In the figure below, $PQRS$ is a rhombus. Which of the following statements must be true?

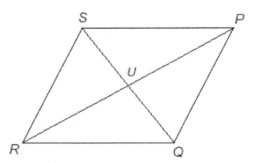

A. The measure of $\angle RUQ$ is 90°.
B. The measure of $\angle SUR$ is less than 90°.
C. The measure of $\angle PQS$ is equal to the measure of $\angle SRP$.
D. The measure of $\angle RUQ$ is less than the measure of $\angle PQS$.
E. The measure of $\angle RUQ$ is less than the measure of $\angle SUR$.

10. A container in the shape of a right circular cylinder has an inside base radius of 5 centimeters and an inside height of 6 centimeters. This cylinder is completely filled with fluid. All of the fluid is then poured into a second right circular cylinder with a larger inside base radius of 7 centimeters. What must be the minimum inside height, in centimeters, of the second container?

    F. $\frac{5}{\sqrt{7}}$
    G. $\frac{7}{5}$
    H. 5
    J. $\frac{150}{49}$
    K. $\frac{25}{6}$

Definitions Used in This Lesson

Definitions of a **triangle**, **quadrilateral**, **rectangle**, **square**, and **circle**, can be found in Lesson 3.

A **parallelogram** is a quadrilateral whose opposite sides are parallel.

Facts about parallelograms:
(1) opposite sides are congruent
(2) opposite angles are congruent
(3) adjacent angles are supplementary
(4) the diagonals bisect each other

Note that rectangles are parallelograms, and therefore squares are also parallelograms.

The **area** of a parallelogram is $A = bh$.

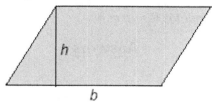

A **rhombus** is a parallelogram with four equal sides.

Facts about rhombuses:
(1) the diagonals are perpendicular
(2) the diagonals bisect the angles

Note that squares are rhombuses.

A **trapezoid** is a quadrilateral with two parallel sides (and two nonparallel sides).

The two parallel sides are called **bases**, and the nonparallel sides are called **legs**.

A trapezoid is **isosceles** if the nonparallel sides are congruent.

Note that isosceles trapezoids have two pairs of congruent angles, and noncongruent angles are supplementary.

isosceles trapezoid   nonisosceles trapezoid

The **area** of a trapezoid is $A = \frac{(b_1+b_2)}{2} h$.

In other words, to compute the area of a trapezoid we take the average of the two bases and multiply by the height.

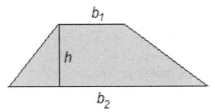

A **cylinder** is a three-dimensional geometric solid bounded by two equal parallel circles and a curved surface formed by moving a straight line so that its ends lie on the circles.

The **volume** of a cylinder is $V = \pi r^2 h$

Answers

1. E   6. J
2. G   7. E
3. C   8. J
4. K   9. A
5. D   10. J

Full Solutions

3.

Solution by plugging in points: Since the point $(0, 2)$ lies on the line, if we substitute 0 in for x, we should get 2 for y. Let's substitute 0 in for x into each answer choice.

    A. 2
    B. 4
    C. 2
    D. 4
    E. 2

We can eliminate choices B and D because they did not come out to 2.

The point $(4, 0)$ also lies on the line. So, if we substitute 4 in for x, we should get 0 for y. Let's substitute 4 in for x in choices A, C, and E.

    A. $-2(4) + 2 = -8 + 2 = -6$
    C. $\left(-\frac{1}{2}\right)(4) + 2 = -2 + 2 = 0$
    E. $2(4) + 2 = 8 + 2 = 10$

We can eliminate choices A and E because they did not come out to 0. Therefore, the answer is choice **C**.

* Solution using the slope-intercept form of an equation of a line: Recall that the slope-intercept form for the equation of a line is

$$y = mx + b.$$

$(0, 2)$ is the y-intercept of the point. Thus, $b = 2$. The slope of the line is $m = \frac{rise}{run} = -\frac{2}{4} = -\frac{1}{2}$. So, the equation of the line is $y = -\frac{1}{2}x + 2$, choice **C**.

Note: To find the slope using the graph we simply note that to get from the y-intercept of the line to the x-intercept of the line we need to move down 2, then right 4.

4.

* Let's draw a picture.

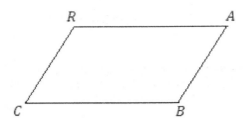

Now note that ∠CRA and ∠RAB are adjacent, and therefore supplementary (see Fact (3) above). So, the answer is choice **K**.

Notes: (1) If you have forgotten that adjacent angles of a parallelogram are supplementary, you can also solve this problem by process of elimination as follows.

Observe that in the picture we just drew that the measure of angle CRA is greater than 90 degrees, and the measure of angle RAB is less than 90 degrees. So, we can eliminate choices F, G, and H.

Since the measure of angle CRA by itself is greater than 90 degrees, we can eliminate choice J. Therefore, the answer is choice **K**.

(2) If you have trouble eliminating choices from the general picture above, try choosing specific angle measures. Here is an example:

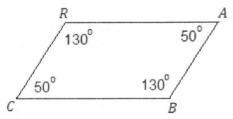

Observe that we had to choose angle measures that sum to 360 (since $CRAB$ is a quadrilateral). We also had to make sure that opposite angles were congruent (since $CRAB$ is a parallelogram).

5.
Solution by starting with choice C: Let's start with choice C, and guess that $r = 6$. Then $h = 12$, so that $V = \pi r^2 h = \pi(6)^2(12) = 432\pi$, too small. Let's try choice D next, and guess that $r = 8$. In this case, $h = 16$, and so $V = \pi r^2 h = \pi(8)^2(16) = 1024\pi$. This is correct, and so the base radius is 8, choice **D**.

* Algebraic solution:
$$V = \pi r^2 h$$
$$1024\pi = \pi r^2 (2r)$$
$$512 = r^3$$
$$8 = r.$$

Therefore, the answer is 8, choice **D**.

6.

Solution by picking a number: Let's choose a value for b, say $b = 3$. Then the two points are $(-3, 0)$ and $(0, 6)$. The slope is $\frac{6-0}{0-(-3)} = \frac{6}{3} = 2$, choice **J**.

Remarks: (1) Here we have used the slope formula $m = \frac{y_2 - y_1}{x_2 - x_1}$.
(2) $0 - (-3) = 0 + 3 = 3$.
(3) We could have also found the slope graphically by plotting the two points and observing that to get from $(-3, 0)$ to $(0, 6)$ we need to move up 6 and right 3. Thus, the slope is $m = \frac{rise}{run} = \frac{6}{3} = 2$.

* Solution using the slope formula: Let's use the formula for slope (as given in Remark (1) above). $\frac{2b-0}{0-(-b)} = \frac{2b}{b} = 2$, choice **J**.

7.

* The slope of line OP is $\frac{2}{5} = 0.4$ (see the Remark below) and the slope of line OQ is 0. Therefore, the slope cannot be greater than 0.4, and the answer is choice **E**.

Remark: (1) If the line k passes through the origin (the point $(0,0)$) and the point (a, b) with $a \neq 0$, then the slope of line k is simply $\frac{b}{a}$.

8.

* Solution: Let's draw a picture

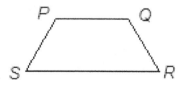

From the picture, we can see that $\overline{PQ}$ and $\overline{SR}$ are not congruent. So, the answer is choice **J**.

Note: The symbol ∥ means "is parallel to."

9.
* The diagonals of a rhombus are perpendicular. Therefore, the measure of ∠RUQ is 90°, choice **A**.

Notes: (1) Since the diagonals of a rhombus are perpendicular, we have $m\angle RUQ = m\angle PUQ = m\angle SUP = m\angle SUR = 90°$. This allows us to eliminate choices B and E.

(2) Once we choose a value for one of the acute angles in the picture, the rest of the angles are determined. For example, let's choose ∠PQS to have measure 50°. The picture will then look as follows.

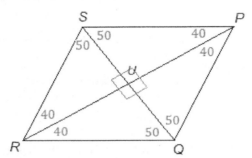

Observe that the diagonals intersect in 90° angles because they are perpendicular. Once we choose the measure of ∠PQS to have measure 50°, we get that the measure of ∠QPR must be $180 - 90 - 50 = 40°$. Since the diagonals of a rhombus bisect the angles, we must have the measure of ∠RQS also equal to 50°. Repeating the previous reasoning allows us to fill in the rest of the angles.

Using this picture, we can eliminate choices C and D.

10.
* The volume of the first cylinder is $V = \pi r^2 h = \pi(5^2)(6) = 150\pi$. The volume of the second cylinder is $V = \pi r^2 h = \pi(7^2)(h) = 49\pi h$. We set the two volumes equal to each other and solve for h.

$$150\pi = 49h\pi$$
$$h = \frac{150}{49}, \text{ choice } \mathbf{J}.$$

OPTIONAL MATERIAL

The following questions will test your understanding of formulas used in this lesson. These are **not** in the format of ACT questions.

1. Find the area of a parallelogram with each of the following bases and heights.

   $b = 2, h = 7$ $b = 1.2, h = 2.5$ $b = x + 1, h = x - 4$ $b = x - 1, h = x^2 + 2$

2. Find the perimeter of a rhombus with side length 3.

3. Find the length of a side of a rhombus with perimeter 20.

4. Find the height of a parallelogram with base 3 and area 15.

5. Find the area of a trapezoid with each of the following bases and heights.

   $b_1 = 3, b_2 = 5, h = 4$ $b_1 = x + 3, b_2 = x + 7, h = x - 1$

6. Find the volume of a cylinder with each of the following base radii and heights.

   $r = h = 2$ $r = 3, h = 4$ $r = \pi, h = 2\pi$ $r = x + 1, h = 2x$

7. Find the height of a cylinder with volume 2π and base radius 5.

8. Find the base radius of a cylinder with volume 100 and height 10.

Answers

1. 14; 3; $(x + 1)(x - 4) = x^2 - 3x - 4$; $(x - 1)(x^2 + 2) = x^3 - x^2 + 2x - 2$
2. $4(3) = 12$
3. $20/4 = 5$
4. $15/3 = 5$
5. 16; $(x + 5)(x - 1) = x^2 + 4x - 5$
6. 8π, 36π, $2\pi^4$, $\pi(x + 1)^2(2x) = 2\pi x(x + 1)^2$
7. $2\pi = \pi(5)^2 h$. So $h = \dfrac{2\pi}{\pi(5)^2} = \dfrac{2}{25}$
8. $100 = \pi r^2(10)$. So $r^2 = \dfrac{100}{10\pi} = \dfrac{10}{\pi}$. So $r = \sqrt{\dfrac{10}{\pi}}$

LESSON 8
COUNTING

Reminder: Before beginning this lesson remember to redo the problems from Lesson 4 that you have marked off. Do not "unmark" a question unless you get it correct.

Writing a List

Sometimes the easiest way to count the number of possibilities is to simply list them all. When doing this it is important that we have a systematic way of forming our list. This will reduce the likelihood of missing something, or listing something twice.

Try to answer the following question by writing a list. **Do not** check the solution until you have attempted this question yourself.

LEVEL 1: COUNTING

1. A menu lists 2 meals and 3 desserts. How many different meal-dessert combinations are possible from this menu?

    A. 5
    B. 6
    C. 8
    D. 9
    E. 12

Solution

Let's make up 2 meals and 3 desserts, say steak and fish for the meals, and cake, pie, and brownie for the desserts. Now let's list all meal-dessert combinations. To save time we will abbreviate each meal and dessert by using its first letter.

sc   sp   sb
fc   fp   fb

We see that there are 6 meal-dessert combinations, choice **B**.

Before we go on, try to solve this problem using a single computation.

Solution

* Solution using the counting principle: $(2)(3) = 6$, choice **B**.

Remark: The **counting principle** says that if one event is followed by a second independent event, the number of possibilities is multiplied. The 2 events here are "choosing a meal," and "choosing a dessert."

Now try to solve each of the following problems by using the strategy you just learned. Then solve each problem with a single computation. The answers to these problems, followed by full solutions are at the end of this lesson. **Do not** look at the answers until you have attempted these problems yourself. Please remember to mark off any problems you get wrong.

LEVEL 1: COUNTING

2. Fred's math class has a homework list of 5 algebra problems and 3 geometry problems. Fred will select one algebra problem and one geometry problem from the list to complete the homework assignment. How many different choices of an algebra problem and a geometry problem are possible?

   F. 2
   G. 8
   H. 15
   J. 125
   K. 243

3. A menu lists 4 meals, 6 drinks, and 3 desserts. How many different ways are there to choose one meal, one drink, and one dessert from this menu?

   A. 13
   B. 18
   C. 22
   D. 27
   E. 72

LEVEL 2: COUNTING

4. Three light bulbs are placed into three different lamps. How many different arrangements are possible for three light bulbs of different colors – one white, one black, and one yellow?

   F. 6
   G. 9
   H. 18
   J. 27
   K. 30

5. A lab technician is testing 4 different liquids. For each test, the technician chooses 2 of the liquids and mixes them together. What is the least number of tests that must be done so that every possible combination of liquids is tested?

   A. 24
   B. 16
   C. 12
   D. 6
   E. 4

6. Four different DVDs are to be stacked in a pile. In how many different orders can the DVDs be placed on the stack?

   F. 10
   G. 16
   H. 24
   J. 27
   K. 256

Level 3: Counting

7. A scientist is testing 5 different liquids. For each test, the scientist chooses 3 of the liquids and mixes them together. What is the least number of tests that must be done so that every possible combination of liquids is tested?

    A. 5
    B. 10
    C. 60
    D. 84
    E. 125

8. Eight different bricks are to be stacked. One brick is chosen for the bottom. In how many different orders can the remaining bricks be stacked?

    F. 27
    G. 35
    H. 1680
    J. 5040
    K. 20,160

9. How many three-digit integers have the hundreds digit equal to 1 or 2, the tens digit equal to 3, 4, or 5 and the units digit (ones digit) equal to 6 or 7 ?

    A. 5
    B. 12
    C. 18
    D. 24
    E. 36

LEVEL 4: COUNTING

10. A desk is to be painted one color and a chair is to be painted a different color. If 6 different colors are available, how many color combinations are possible?

   F. 6
   G. 11
   H. 12
   J. 15
   K. 30

Definitions Used in This Lesson

The **counting principle** says that if one event is followed by a second independent event, the number of possibilities is multiplied.

The **factorial** of a positive integer n, written $n!$, is the product of all positive integers less than or equal to n.

$$n! = 1 \cdot 2 \cdot 3 \cdots n$$

0! is defined to be 1, so that $n!$ is defined for all nonnegative integers n.

A **permutation** is an ordered arrangement of elements from a set.

A **combination** is a subset containing a specific number of the elements of a particular set, selected without regard to the order in which they were chosen.

Answers

1. B   6. H
2. H   7. B
3. E   8. J
4. F   9. B
5. D   10. K

Full Solutions

Note: Full solutions for questions 2 and 3 have been omitted because their solutions are very similar to the solution to question 1.

4.

Solution by writing a list: We list all the possibilities, abbreviating each color by using the first letter.

wby   wyb   bwy   byw   ywb   ybw

We can easily see that there are **6** arrangements, choice **F**.

Solution using the counting principle: There are 3 possible lamps to place the white bulb in. After placing the white bulb, there are 2 lamps to place the black bulb in. Finally, there is 1 lamp left to place the yellow bulb in. By the counting principle we get $(3)(2)(1) = 6$ arrangements, choice **F**.

* Solution using permutations: There are 3 light bulbs, and we are arranging all 3 of them. So there are $_3P_3 = 3! = 1 \cdot 2 \cdot 3 = 6$ arrangements, choice **F**.

Remark: See the optional material at the end of this lesson for a more detailed look at permutations.

5.

Solution by writing a list: We list all the possible mixtures, labeling the liquids 1, 2, 3, and 4.

1, 2   1, 3   1, 4   2, 3   2, 4   3, 4

We can easily see that there are **6** combinations, choice **D**.

* Solution using combinations: We are counting the number of ways to choose 2 of the 4 liquids. This is $_4C_2 = 6$, choice **D**.

Remarks: (1) This is a combination because it does not matter in what order we take the two liquids. We are simply grabbing two of them and mixing them together.

(2) See the optional material at the end of this lesson for a more detailed look at combinations.

6.

Solution by writing a list Let's list all the ways to stack the DVDs. To distinguish the DVDs let's make one red, one blue, one yellow, and one green. As usual, we will abbreviate each DVD's color by using its first letter.

rbyg	rbgy	rybg	rygb	rgby	rgyb
bryg	brgy	byrg	bygr	bgry	bgyr
yrbg	yrgb	ybrg	ybgr	ygrb	ygbr
grby	gryb	gbry	gbyr	gyrb	gybr

We now see that there are 24 arrangements, choice **H**.

Solution using the counting principle: There are 4 possible DVDs for the bottom of the stack. After placing the first DVD, there are 3 possible DVDs that can go on top of the bottom DVD, then 2 DVDs for the next position, and then 1 DVD for the top of the stack. By the counting principle we get $(4)(3)(2)(1) = 24$ arrangements, choice **H**.

* **Solution using permutations:** There are 4 DVDs, and we are arranging all 4 of them. So, there are $_4P_4 = 4! = 1 \cdot 2 \cdot 3 = 24$ arrangements, choice **H**.

Remark: See the optional material at the end of this lesson for a more detailed look at permutations.

7.
Solution by writing a list: We list all of the possibilities. In the following list a * means we are choosing that liquid, and an O means we are not:

```
***OO        *OO**
**O*O        O***O
**OO*        O**O*
*O**O        O*O**
*O*O*        OO***
```

We see that there are 10 combinations, choice **B**.

* **Solution using combinations:** We are counting the number of ways to choose 3 of the 5 liquids. This is $_5C_3 = 10$, choice **B**.

Remark: See the optional material at the end of this lesson for a more detailed look at combinations.

8.
* There are seven bricks left to stack. Therefore, there are
$$7! = (7)(6)(5)(4)(3)(2)(1) = 5040$$
ways to stack these bricks. This is choice **J**.

Remark: In this example it would be unreasonable to form a list.

9.
Solution by writing a list: Let's try to list the numbers in **increasing order**.

136	137	146	147	156	157
236	237	246	247	256	257

And that's it. We see that the answer is 12, choice **B**.

* **Solution using the counting principle:** There are 2 possibilities for the hundreds digit (1 or 2). There are 3 possibilities for the tens digit (3, 4, or 5). There are 2 possibilities for the ones digit (6 or 7).

The counting principle says that we multiply the possibilities to get $2 \cdot 3 \cdot 2 = 12$, choice **B**.

10.
Solution by writing a list: Let's assume the colors are red, blue, green, yellow, purple, and white. We will list all the possibilities in a nice way:

RB, RG, RY, RP, RW
BR, BG, BY, BP, BW
GR, GB, GY, GP, GW
YR, YB, YG, YP, YW
PR, PB, PG, PY, PW
WR, WB, WG, WY, WP

In the above list, we abbreviated each color by using the first letter of its name. The first position is for the desk, and the second for the chair. We see that we have listed 30 possibilities, choice **K**.

* **Solution using the counting principle:** There are 6 ways to choose a color for the desk. Once this color is chosen there are now 5 ways to choose a color for the chair. Therefore, there are $6 \cdot 5 = 30$ possibilities, choice **K**.

Solution using permutations: There are $_6P_2 = 6 \cdot 5 = 30$ ways to choose 2 colors from 6, and place them in a specific order, choice **K**.

Important note: Don't let the word "combinations" in the problem itself trick you. This is **not** a combination in the mathematical sense. If you paint the desk red and the chair blue, then this is a **different** choice from painting the desk blue and the chair red. See the optional material below for a more detailed look at permutations and combinations.

OPTIONAL MATERIAL

Permutations and Combinations

The **factorial** of a positive integer n, written $n!$, is the product of all positive integers less than or equal to n.

$$n! = 1 \cdot 2 \cdot 3 \cdots n$$

0! is defined to be 1, so that $n!$ is defined for all nonnegative integers n.

A **permutation** is just an arrangement of elements from a set. The number of permutations of n things taken r at a time is $_nP_r = \frac{n!}{(n-r)!}$. For example, the number of permutations of {1, 2, 3} taken 2 at a time is $_3P_2 = \frac{3!}{1!} = 6$. These permutations are 12, 21, 13, 31, 23, and 32.

Note that on the ACT you **do not** need to know the permutation formula. You can do this computation very quickly on your graphing calculator. To compute $_3P_2$, type 3 into your calculator, then in the **MATH** menu scroll over to **PRB** and select **nPr** (or press **2**). Then type 2 and press **ENTER**. You will get an answer of 6.

A **combination** is just a subset containing a specific number of the elements of a particular set. The number of combinations of n things taken r at a time is $_nC_r = \frac{n!}{r!(n-r)!}$. For example, the number of combinations of {1, 2, 3} taken 2 at a time is $_3C_2 = \frac{3!}{2!1!} = 3$. These combinations are 12, 13, and 23.

Note that on the ACT you **do not** need to know the combination formula. You can do this computation very quickly on your graphing calculator. To compute $_3C_2$, type 3 into your calculator, then in the **MATH** menu scroll over to **PRB** and select **nCr** (or press **3**). Then type 2 and press **ENTER**. You will get an answer of 3.

Note that 12 and 21 are different permutations, but the same combination.

Example: Compute the number of permutations and combinations of elements from {a, b, c, d} taken (a) 2 at a time, and (b) 4 at a time.

$_4P_2 = \frac{4!}{2!} = \mathbf{12}$, $_4C_2 = \frac{4!}{2!2!} = \mathbf{6}$, $_4P_4 = \frac{4!}{0!} = \mathbf{24}$, $_4C_4 = \frac{4!}{4!0!} = \mathbf{1}$

Notes: (1) The permutations taken 2 at a time are $ab, ba, ac, ca, ad, da, bc, cb, bd, db, cd$, and dc.

(2) The combinations taken 2 at a time are ab, ac, ad, bc, bd, and cd.

Now see if you can list all 24 permutations of $\{a, b, c, d\}$ taken 4 at a time. Note that all 24 of these permutations represent the same combination.

Example: How many committees of 4 people can be formed from a group of 9?

The order in which we choose the 4 people does not matter. Therefore, this is the combination $_9C_4 = \mathbf{126}$.

Download additional solutions for free here:

www.satprepget800.com/28LesInt

LESSON 9
NUMBER THEORY

Reminder: Before beginning this lesson remember to redo the problems from Lessons 1 and 5 that you have marked off. Do not "unmark" a question unless you get it correct.

Complex Numbers

A **complex number** has the form $a + bi$ where a and b are real numbers and $i = \sqrt{-1}$.

Example: The following are complex numbers:

$$5 + 7i \quad \frac{7}{3} + (-6i) = \frac{7}{3} - 6i \quad -2\pi + 5.3i \quad \sqrt{-16} = 4i$$

$0 + 2i = 2i$ This is called a **pure imaginary** number.

$21 + 0i = 21$ This is called a **real number.**

$0 + 0i = 0$ This is **zero.**

Addition and subtraction: We add two complex numbers simply by adding their real parts, and then adding their imaginary parts.

$$(a + bi) + (c + di) = (a + c) + (b + d)i$$

LEVEL 1: COMPLEX NUMBERS

1. For $i = \sqrt{-1}$, the sum $(3 - 7i) + (5 + 4i)$ is

   A. $2 + 11i$
   B. $2 - 3i$
   C. $-2 - 11i$
   D. $8 - 3i$
   E. $8 - 11i$

Solution

* $(3 - 7i) + (5 + 4i) = (3 + 5) + (-7 + 4)i = 8 - 3i$, choice **D**.

100

Multiplication: We can multiply two complex numbers by formally taking the product of two binomials and then replacing i^2 by -1.

$$(a+bi)(c+di) = (ac-bd) + (ad+bc)i$$

LEVEL 3: COMPLEX NUMBERS

2. Which of the following complex numbers is equivalent to $(1+2i)(3-4i)$? (Note: $i = \sqrt{-1}$)

    F. $3-8i$
    G. $3+8i$
    H. $4-2i$
    J. $11+2i$
    K. $11-2i$

Solution

* $(1+2i)(3-4i) = (3+8) + (-4+6)i = 11+2i$, choice **J**.

The **conjugate** of the complex number $a+bi$ is the complex number $a-bi$.

Example: The conjugate of $-3+8i$ is $-3-8i$.

Note that when we multiply conjugates together we always get a real number. In fact, we have

$$(a+bi)(a-bi) = a^2 + b^2$$

Division: We can put the quotient of two complex numbers into standard form by multiplying both the numerator and denominator by the conjugate of the denominator. This is best understood with an example.

LEVEL 4: COMPLEX NUMBERS

3. If the expression $\frac{5+i}{3-2i}$ is rewritten in the form $a+bi$, where a and b are real numbers, what is the value of $b-a$?

    A. 0
    B. 1
    C. 2
    D. 3
    E. 4

Solution

* We multiply the numerator and denominator of $\frac{5+i}{3-2i}$ by $(3+2i)$ to get

$$\frac{(5+i)}{(3-2i)} \cdot \frac{(3+2i)}{(3+2i)} = \frac{(15-2)+(10+3)i}{9+4} = \frac{13+13i}{13} = \frac{13}{13} + \frac{13}{13}i = 1+i$$

So, $a = 1$, $b = 1$, and $b - a = 1 - 1 = 0$, choice **A**.

Now try to solve each of the following problems. The answers to these problems, followed by full solutions are at the end of this lesson. **Do not** look at the answers until you have attempted these problems yourself. Please remember to mark off any problems you get wrong.

LEVEL 1: COMPLEX NUMBERS

4. If $(-5+2i) + (-1-3i) = a+bi$ and $i = \sqrt{-1}$, then what is the value of ab ?

    F. 6
    G. 5
    H. 4
    J. 3
    K. 2

LEVEL 2: COMPLEX NUMBERS

5. When we subtract $4 - 3i$ from $-2 + 7i$ we get which of the following complex numbers?

    A. $2 - 4i$
    B. $-6 + 4i$
    C. $-6 + 10i$
    D. $6 + 4i$
    E. $6 + 10i$

LEVEL 3: COMPLEX NUMBERS

6. For $i = \sqrt{-1}$, $\frac{1}{1+i} \cdot \frac{1-i}{1-i} = ?$

    F. $1+i$
    G. $1-i$
    H. $i-1$
    J. $\frac{1+i}{2}$
    K. $\frac{1-i}{2}$

LEVEL 4: COMPLEX NUMBERS

7. In the complex numbers, where $i^2 = -1$, $(4-3i)^2 =$

    A. 7
    B. 25
    C. $16 - 9i$
    D. $16 + 9i$
    E. $7 - 24i$

8. If $i = \sqrt{-1}$, and $\frac{(3+4i)}{(-5-2i)} = a + bi$, where a and b are real numbers, then what is the value of $29a$?

    F. 23
    G. 14
    H. 9
    J. -14
    K. -23

9. If u and v are real numbers, $i = \sqrt{-1}$, and
$$(v+u) + 6i = 2 - 3ui,$$
then what is uv ?

    A. -9
    B. -8
    C. 2
    D. 8
    E. 9

10. If $(x - 3i)(5 + yi) = 28 - 3i$, which of the following could be the value of $x + y$? (Note: $i = \sqrt{-1}$)

    F. 2
    G. 6
    H. 7
    J. 8
    K. 28

Answers

1. D   6. K
2. J   7. E
3. A   8. K
4. F   9. B
5. C   10. J

Full Solutions

4.
* $(-5 + 2i) + (-1 - 3i) = (-5 - 1) + (2 - 3)i = -6 - i$. So $a = -6$, $b = -1$, and therefore $ab = (-6)(-1) = 6$, choice **F**.

5.
* $(-2 + 7i) - (4 - 3i) = -2 + 7i - 4 + 3i = -6 + 10i$, choice **C**.

6.
* $(1 + i)(1 - i) = 1^2 + 1^2 = 2$. So $\frac{1}{1+i} \cdot \frac{1-i}{1-i} = \frac{1-i}{2}$, choice **K**.

7.
* $(4 - 3i)^2 = (4 - 3i)(4 - 3i) = (16 - 9) + i(-12 - 12) = 7 - 24i$.

This is choice **E**.

8.
* $\frac{(3+4i)}{(-5-2i)} = \frac{(3+4i)}{(-5-2i)} \cdot \frac{(-5+2i)}{(-5+2i)} = \frac{(-15-8)+(6-20)i}{25+4} = \frac{-23-14i}{29} = -\frac{23}{29} - \frac{14}{29}i$

So $29a = 29\left(-\frac{23}{29}\right) = -23$, choice **K**.

9.
* Two complex numbers are equal if their real parts are equal and their imaginary parts are equal. So, we have

$$v + u = 2 \quad \text{and} \quad 6 = -3u.$$

Since $u = \frac{6}{-3} = -2$ (from the second equation), we have that $v - 2 = 2$. Thus, $v = 2 + 2 = 4$. Finally, $uv = (-2)(4) = -8$, choice **B**.

10.
* $(x - 3i)(5 + yi) = (5x + 3y) + (xy - 15)i$. So $5x + 3y = 28$ and $xy - 15 = -3$. So, $xy = 12$. We need to solve the following system of equations:

$$5x + 3y = 28$$
$$xy = 12$$

There are several ways to solve this formally, but we can also just try guessing. We are looking for two numbers that multiply to 12. If we try $x = 2, y = 6$, we see that $5x + 3y = 5(2) + 3(6) = 10 + 18 = 28$.

So, a possible solution to the system is $x = 2, y = 6$, and in this case $x + y = 8$, choice **J**.

Download additional solutions for free here:

www.satprepget800.com/28LesInt

Lesson 10
Algebra

Reminder: Before beginning this lesson remember to redo the problems from Lessons 2 and 6 that you have marked off. Do not "unmark" a question unless you get it correct.

Laws of Exponents

Law	Example
$x^0 = 1$	$3^0 = 1$
$x^1 = x$	$9^1 = 9$
$x^a x^b = x^{a+b}$	$x^3 x^5 = x^8$
$x^a / x^b = x^{a-b}$	$x^{11}/x^4 = x^7$
$(x^a)^b = x^{ab}$	$(x^5)^3 = x^{15}$
$(xy)^a = x^a y^a$	$(xy)^4 = x^4 y^4$
$(x/y)^a = x^a/y^a$	$(x/y)^6 = x^6/y^6$

Now let's practice. Simplify the following expressions using the basic laws of exponents.

1. $5^2 \cdot 5^3$

2. $\dfrac{5^3}{5^2}$

3. $\dfrac{x^5 \cdot x^3}{x^8}$

4. $(2^3)^4$

5. $\dfrac{(xy)^7 (yz)^2}{y^9}$

6. $\left(\dfrac{2}{3}\right)^3 \left(\dfrac{9}{4}\right)^2$

7. $\dfrac{x^4 + x^2}{x^2}$

8. $\dfrac{(x^{10}+x^9+x^8)(y^5+y^4)}{y^4(x^2+x+1)}$

Answers

1. $5^5 = 3125$ 2. $5^1 = 5$ 3. $\dfrac{x^8}{x^8} = 1$ 4. $2^{12} = 4096$

5. $\dfrac{x^7 y^7 y^2 z^2}{y^9} = \dfrac{x^7 y^9 z^2}{y^9} = x^7 z^2$ 6. $\dfrac{2^3}{3^3} \cdot \dfrac{9^2}{4^2} = \dfrac{2^3}{3^3} \cdot \dfrac{(3^2)^2}{(2^2)^2} = \dfrac{2^3}{3^3} \cdot \dfrac{3^4}{2^4} = \dfrac{3^1}{2^1} = \dfrac{3}{2}$

7. $\dfrac{x^2(x^2+1)}{x^2} = x^2 + 1$ 8. $\dfrac{x^8(x^2+x+1)y^4(y+1)}{y^4(x^2+x+1)} = x^8(y+1)$

Logarithms

The word **"logarithm"** just means "exponent." For example, in the exponential equation $9 = 3^2$, the logarithm is 2. The number 3 is called the **base**. We say "2 is the logarithm of 9 when we use a base of 3," and abbreviate this as $2 = \log_3 9$. More generally, the following two equations are equivalent: $y = a^x$ and $x = \log_a y$.

Laws of Logarithms

Law	Example
$\log_b 1 = 0$	$\log_2 1 = 0$
$\log_b b = 1$	$\log_6 6 = 1$
$\log_b x + \log_b y = \log_b(xy)$	$\log_5 7 + \log_5 2 = \log_5 14$
$\log_b x - \log_b y = \log_b(\frac{x}{y})$	$\log_3 21 - \log_3 7 = \log_3 3 = 1$
$\log_b x^n = n\log_b x$	$\log_8 3^5 = 5\log_8 3$

Now let's practice. Simplify the following expressions using the basic laws of logarithms. Assume all unknowns are positive.

1. $\log_2 8$
2. $\log_4 2$
3. $\log_5 \frac{1}{25}$
4. $\log_b \frac{b^2}{b^7}$
5. $\log 10^3$
6. $\log_4 2 + \log_4 8$
7. $\log_{xy} x^2 + \log_{xy} y^2$
8. $\frac{1}{b}\log_a a^b$
9. $\log_5 x - \log_5 \frac{x}{\sqrt{5}}$

Answers

1. 3 (because $2^3 = 8$)
2. $\frac{1}{2}$ (because $4^{\frac{1}{2}} = \sqrt{4} = 2$)
3. -2 (because $5^{-2} = \frac{1}{25}$)
4. $\log_b b^{2-7} = \log_b b^{-5} = -5$
5. $3 \log 10 = 3$ (**Note:** $\log x = \log_{10} x$)
6. $\log_4(2 \cdot 8) = \log_4 16 = 2$
7. $\log_{xy}(x^2 y^2) = \log_{xy}(xy)^2 = 2\log_{xy} xy = 2$
8. $\log_a(a^b)^{\frac{1}{b}} = \log_a a^{b \cdot \frac{1}{b}} = \log_a a = 1$ or $b \cdot \frac{1}{b}\log_a a = \log_a a = 1$
9. $\log_5(x \div \frac{x}{\sqrt{5}}) = \log_5(x \cdot \frac{\sqrt{5}}{x}) = \log_5 \sqrt{5} = \log_5 5^{\frac{1}{2}} = \frac{1}{2}\log_5 5 = \frac{1}{2}$

Now try to solve each of the following problems. The answers to these problems, followed by full solutions are at the end of this lesson. **Do not** look at the answers until you have attempted these problems yourself. Please remember to mark off any problems you get wrong.

LEVEL 1: ALGEBRA

1. $3a^5 \cdot 5a^7$ is equivalent to:

    A. $8a^{12}$
    B. $8a^{35}$
    C. $15a^2$
    D. $15a^{12}$
    E. $15a^{35}$

LEVEL 3: ALGEBRA

2. If $2^x = 3$, then $2^{3x} =$

    F. 6
    G. 9
    H. 27
    J. 81
    K. 243

3. Which of the following expressions is equivalent to $(-x^2y^7)^3$?

    A. $-x^5y^{10}$
    B. $-x^6y^{21}$
    C. $-3x^5y^{10}$
    D. $-3x^6y^{21}$
    E. x^6y^{21}

LEVEL 4: ALGEBRA AND FUNCTIONS

4. Whenever n is an integer greater than 1, $\log_n n^3n^5 = ?$

    F. 2
    G. 8
    H. 12
    J. 15
    K. 30

5. What is the set of all values of k that satisfy the equation $(x^5)^{k^2-9} = 1$ for all nonzero values of x ?

   A. $\{0\}$
   B. $\{3\}$
   C. $\{9\}$
   D. $\{-2, 2\}$
   E. $\{-3, 3\}$

6. If $\dfrac{x^a x^b}{(x^c)^d} = x^2$ for all $x \neq 0$, which of the following must be true?

   F. $a + b - cd = 2$
   G. $\dfrac{a+b}{cd} = 2$
   H. $ab - cd = 2$
   J. $ab - c^d = 2$
   K. $\dfrac{ab}{c^d} = 2$

7. For what real value of y is $\dfrac{2^y 2^9}{(2^4)^8} = \dfrac{1}{32}$ true?

   A. 2
   B. 3
   C. 11
   D. 18
   E. 25

8. Let a and b be nonzero real numbers such that $2^{a+3} = 16b$. Which of the following is an expression for 2^{a+4} in terms of b ?

   F. $\dfrac{1}{24b^3}$
   G. $\dfrac{1}{8b}$
   H. b^5
   J. $2^2 b^3$
   K. $2^5 b$

9. What is the value of $\log_3 81$?

  A. 3
  B. 4
  C. 8
  D. 9
  E. 27

10. The value of $\log_3\left(3^{\frac{21}{4}}\right)$ is between which of the following pairs of consecutive integers?

  F. 0 and 1
  G. 2 and 3
  H. 4 and 5
  J. 5 and 6
  K. 6 and 7

Answers

1. D	6. F
2. H	7. D
3. B	8. K
4. G	9. B
5. E	10. J

Full Solutions

1.
* $3a^5 \cdot 5a^7 = 3 \cdot 5 \cdot a^5 \cdot a^7 = 15a^{5+7} = 15a^{12}$, choice **D**.

Note: This problem (and many of the other problems in this lesson) can also be solved by picking numbers and using your calculator. I leave this solution to the reader.

2.
* **Algebraic solution:** $2^{3x} = (2^x)^3 = 3^3 = 27$, choice **H**.

Solution by estimating: When $x = 1.5$, $2^x = 2^{1.5} \approx 2.8$ which is close to 3. So, the answer should be close to $2^{3x} = 2^{3 \cdot 1.5} = 2^{4.5} \approx 22.6$. Therefore, the most likely answer is 27, choice **H**.

Note: We can continue to use our calculator to get better estimates for x By trial and error, we see that $2^{1.58} \approx 2.99$. We then have $2^{3 \cdot 1.58} \approx 26.7$. So, clearly the answer is 27, choice **H**.

3.
* $(-x^2y^7)^3 = (-1)^3(x^2)^3(y^7)^3 = -1 \cdot x^6 y^{21} = -x^6 y^{21}$, choice **B**.

4.
* $\log_n n^3 n^5 = \log_n n^{3+5} = \log_n n^8 = 8 \log_n n = 8 \cdot 1 = 8$, choice **G**.

5.
* **Quick solution:** We simply need to solve the equation $k^2 - 9 = 0$. This equation has the two solutions $k = \pm 3$, choice **E**.

Notes: (1) Any expression raised to the power of 0 is 1. For example, $(x^5)^0 = 1$ for any x. Conversely, if $a^b = 1$, and $a \neq 0$, then b must be equal to 0.

In this problem, we have $a = x^5$ and $b = k^2 - 9$. So, we must set $k^2 - 9 = 0$.

(2) There are several ways to solve the equation $k^2 - 9 = 0$.

<u>Method 1 (Guess and Check):</u> We can simply guess the numbers that appear in the answer choices. It's easy to check that $3^2 - 9 = 9 - 9 = 0$ and $(-3)^2 - 9 = 9 - 9 = 0$.

<u>Method 2 (Factoring):</u> $k^2 - 9 = (k - 3)(k + 3)$. So we have $k - 3 = 0$ or $k + 3 = 0$. This gives solutions $k = 3$ and $k = -3$.

<u>Method 3 (Square Root Property):</u> We add 9 to each side of the equation to get $k^2 = 9$. We then apply the square root property to get $k = \pm 3$.

See Lesson 18 for more on the square root property and factoring.

6.
* **Solution using laws of exponents:** $\frac{x^a x^b}{(x^c)^d} = \frac{x^{a+b}}{x^{cd}} = x^{a+b-cd}$. So we have $x^{a+b-cd} = x^2$, and therefore $a + b - cd = 2$, choice **F**.

7.
* $\frac{2^y 2^9}{(2^4)^8} = \frac{2^{y+9}}{2^{4 \cdot 8}} = \frac{2^{y+9}}{2^{32}} = 2^{y+9-32} = 2^{y-23}$ and $\frac{1}{32} = \frac{1}{2^5} = 2^{-5}$. So, we have $2^{y-23} = 2^{-5}$, and therefore, $y - 23 = -5$. So, $y = -5 + 23 = 18$, choice **D**.

8.
* $2^{a+4} = 2^{a+3+1} = 2^{a+3} \cdot 2^1 = 16b \cdot 2^1 = 2^4 b \cdot 2^1 = 2^{4+1} b = 2^5 b.$

This is choice **K**.

9.

Calculator solution by changing the base: We use the change of base formula and our calculator to get

$$\log_3 81 = \frac{\log 81}{\log 3} = 4$$

This is choice **B**.

Note: (1) $\log x$ means $\log_{10} x$

(2) To change any logarithm to base 10 use the formula $\log_b a = \frac{\log a}{\log b}$.

Direct calculator solution: Press ALPHA followed by Y=, and then WINDOW. Now select logBASE((or press 5). You can now enter $\log_3 81$ directly, and the display will output 4, choice **B**.

Solution by changing to exponential form: The logarithmic equation $y = \log_3 81$ is equivalent to the exponential equation $3^y = 81$. Since 81 can be written as 3^4, we have $3^y = 3^4$. Therefore, $y = 4$, choice **B**.

* **Quick solution:** The question is asking "3 to what power is 81?" Well 3 to the **fourth** power is 81. So, the answer is 4, choice **B**.

10.
* $\log_3 \left(3^{\frac{21}{4}}\right) = \frac{21}{4} \log_3 3 = \frac{21}{4} = 5.25.$ So, the answer is choice **J**.

OPTIONAL MATERIAL

Negative and Fractional Exponents

Law	Example
$x^{-1} = 1/x$	$3^{-1} = 1/3$
$x^{-a} = 1/x^a$	$9^{-2} = 1/81$
$x^{1/n} = \sqrt[n]{x}$	$x^{1/3} = \sqrt[3]{x}$
$x^{m/n} = \sqrt[n]{x^m} = \left(\sqrt[n]{x}\right)^m$	$x^{9/2} = \sqrt{x^9} = \left(\sqrt{x}\right)^9$

Now let's practice. Rewrite each of the following expressions without negative or fractional exponents.

1. 7^{-1} 2. $\dfrac{5^2}{5^5}$ 3. $\dfrac{x^{-5} \cdot x^{-3}}{x^{-4}}$ 4. $5^{\frac{1}{2}}$

5. $5^{-\frac{1}{2}}$ 6. $7^{-\frac{11}{3}}$ 7. $\dfrac{x^{-\frac{5}{2}} \cdot x^{-1}}{x^{-\frac{4}{3}}}$

Answers

1. $\dfrac{1}{7}$ 2. $5^{-3} = \dfrac{1}{5^3} = \dfrac{1}{125}$ 3. $\dfrac{x^{-8}}{x^{-4}} = x^{-4} = \dfrac{1}{x^4}$ 4. $\sqrt{5}$

5. $\dfrac{1}{5^{\frac{1}{2}}} = \dfrac{1}{\sqrt{5}}$ 6. $\dfrac{1}{7^{\frac{11}{3}}} = \dfrac{1}{\sqrt[3]{7^{11}}}$ 7. $\dfrac{x^{-\frac{7}{2}}}{x^{-\frac{4}{3}}} = x^{-\frac{13}{6}} = \dfrac{1}{x^{\frac{13}{6}}} = \dfrac{1}{\sqrt[6]{x^{13}}}$

Remark for number 5: In high school math classes, teachers will often insist that denominators of fractions be **rationalized**. This means that a legal operation should be performed to remove any radicals from the denominator. If we so choose we can do this in the solution to number 5 by multiplying the numerator and denominator by $\sqrt{5}$ to get $\dfrac{\sqrt{5}}{5}$.

Note that on the ACT there is no need to rationalize denominators of fractions. You can usually just use your calculator to get a decimal approximation.

Challenge problem: Rationalize the denominators in the solutions to questions 6 and 7.

Answers: 6. $\dfrac{\sqrt[3]{7^{22}}}{7^{11}}$ 7. $\dfrac{1}{\sqrt[6]{x^{13}}} = \dfrac{\sqrt[6]{x^{65}}}{x^{13}}$

LESSON 11
GEOMETRY

Reminder: Before beginning this lesson remember to redo the problems from Lessons 3 and 7 that you have marked off. Do not "unmark" a question unless you get it correct.

Draw Your Own Figure

If a problem doesn't have a figure, you may want to draw your own. Sometimes drawing a quick picture of the situation makes the problem very easy, or at least easier.

Try to answer the following question using this strategy. **Do not** check the solution until you have attempted this question yourself.

LEVEL 2: GEOMETRY

1. C is the midpoint of line segment AB, and D and E are the midpoints of AC and CB, respectively. If the length of DE is 7, what is the length of AB?

    A. 3.5
    B. 7
    C. 10.5
    D. 14
    E. 17.5

Solution

* Let's draw a figure.

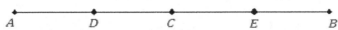

Since the length of DE is 7, the length of AD plus the length of EB is also 7. Therefore, the length of AB is $7 + 7 = 14$, choice **D**.

Parallel Lines Cut by a Transversal

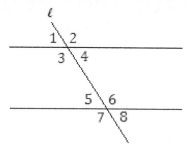

The figure above shows two parallel lines cut by the transversal ℓ.

Angles 1, 4, 5, and 8 all have the same measure. Also, angles 2, 3, 6, and 7 all have the same measure. Any two angles that do not have the same measure are supplementary, that is their measures add to 180°.

Technical notes: (1) Various pairs of these angles are given special names. Angles 3 and 6 are called **alternate interior angles**, angles 1 and 8 are called **alternate exterior angles**, and angles 1 and 5 are called **corresponding angles**. Each of these angle pairs are congruent precisely when the two lines cut by the transversal are parallel.

(2) The following specially named angles do not require a transversal. Angles 1 and 4 are called **vertical angles**. Vertical angles are always congruent.

Angles 1 and 3 form a **linear pair**. Angles that form a linear pair are always **supplementary** (their angle measures sum to 180°).

Exercise: In the figure above, find one more pair of alternate interior angles, one more pair of alternate exterior angles, three more pairs of corresponding angles, three more pairs of vertical angles, and seven more linear pairs.

LEVEL 2: GEOMETRY

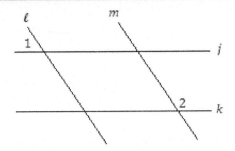

2. In the figure above, lines j and k are parallel and lines ℓ and m are parallel. If the measure of ∠1 is 68°, what is the measure of ∠2 ?

    F. 158°
    G. 112°
    H. 98°
    J.   76°
    K. 68°

Solution

* $m\angle 2 = 180° - m\angle 1 = 180° - 68° = 112°$, choice **G**.

Note: In the figure below we put a "1" on all angles that are congruent to angle 1 (and thus have measure 68°), and a "2" on all angles that are congruent to angle 2 (and thus have measure 112°).

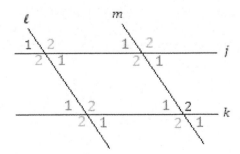

Similarity

Two triangles are **similar** if their angles are congruent. Note that similar triangles **do not** have to be the same size. Also, note that to show that two triangles are similar we need only show that two pairs of angles are congruent. We get the third pair for free because all triangles have angle measures summing to 180 degrees.

Example:

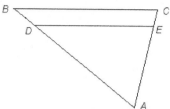

In the figure above, assume that $\overline{BC}$ is parallel to $\overline{DE}$. It then follows that angles ADE and ABC are congruent (corresponding angles). Since triangles ADE and ABC share angle A, the two triangles are similar.

Important Fact: Corresponding sides of similar triangles are in proportion.

So, for example, in the figure above, $\frac{AD}{AB} = \frac{DE}{BC}$.

LEVEL 2: GEOMETRY

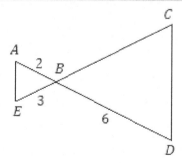

3. In the figure above, $AE \parallel CD$ and segment AD intersects segment CE at B. What is the length of segment CE ?

    A. 3
    B. 4
    C. 7
    D. 11
    E. 12

* $\frac{BC}{BD} = \frac{BE}{BA}$. So $\frac{BC}{6} = \frac{3}{2}$. Thus, $2BC = 18$, and so $BC = \frac{18}{2} = 9$.

It follows that $CE = BC + BE = 9 + 3 = 12$, choice **E**.

Transformations

The following four images demonstrate the four basic geometry transformations that can show up on the ACT.

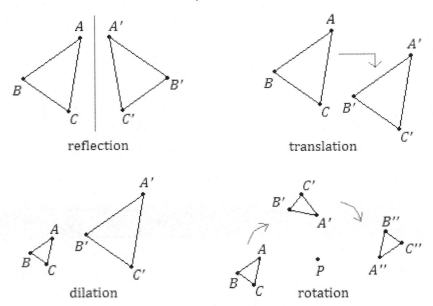

A **reflection** is generally done across a line. In the image above, $\triangle ABC$ is reflected across the vertical line to $\triangle A'B'C'$ (we can also think of $\triangle A'B'C'$ as being reflected across the vertical line to $\triangle ABC$).

A **translation** is a movement which can be horizontal, vertical, or a combination of both. In the image above, $\triangle ABC$ is translated to the right and down to $\triangle A'B'C'$ (we can also think of $\triangle A'B'C'$ as being translated to the left and up to $\triangle ABC$).

A **dilation** is an expansion or contraction. In the image above, $\triangle ABC$ is expanded to $\triangle A'B'C'$ (we can also think of $\triangle A'B'C'$ as being contracted to $\triangle ABC$).

A **rotation** is generally done about a point. In the image above, $\triangle ABC$ is rotated 90° clockwise about P to $\triangle A'B'C'$. Also, $\triangle A'B'C'$ is rotated 90° clockwise about P to $\triangle A''B''C''$. We can also think of $\triangle ABC$ as being rotated 180° clockwise about P to $\triangle A''B''C''$ (we also have the corresponding counterclockwise rotations going the other way).

A rotation 180° about a point is also sometimes called a **point reflection**. So, we can also say that $\triangle ABC$ is reflected in the point P to $\triangle A''B''C''$.

Exercise: Plot the point $(2,3)$ in the standard (x,y) coordinate plane. Find the image of the point when it is (a) reflected in the x-axis, (b) reflected in the y-axis, (c) reflected in the line $y = x$, (d) translated 5 units up and 4 units left, (e) dilated by a factor of 7, (f) rotated clockwise 90°, (g) rotated counterclockwise 90°, and (g) reflected in the origin.

Answers: (a) $(2,-3)$, (b) $(-2,3)$, (c) $(3,2)$, (d) $(-2,8)$, (e) $(14,21)$, (f) $(3,-2)$, (g) $(-3,2)$, (h) $(-2,-3)$

You're doing great! Let's just practice a bit more. Try to solve each of the following problems by using one of the strategies you just learned. Then, if possible, solve each problem another way. The answers to these problems, followed by full solutions are at the end of this lesson. **Do not look at the answers until you have attempted these problems yourself.** Please remember to mark off any problems you get wrong.

LEVEL 2: GEOMETRY

4. Square $FORM$ with center P is shown below. Point K starts at F and is rotated clockwise about point P a total of 540°. After the rotation, K is at the same location as which of the following points?

   F. F
   G. O
   H. R
   J. M
   K. P

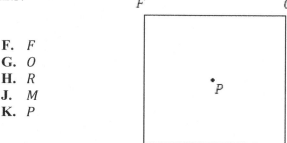

Level 3: Geometry

5. A 36 feet tall tree is casting a shadow 24 feet long. At the same time, a nearby tree is casting a shadow 30 feet long. If the lengths of the shadows are proportional to the heights of the trees, what is the height, in feet, of the taller tree?

   A. 54
   B. 45
   C. 42
   D. 36
   E. 30

6. In the figure below, what is the value of $\frac{ED}{AD}$?

   F. $\frac{1}{7}$
   G. $\frac{1}{4}$
   H. $\frac{2}{5}$
   J. $\frac{1}{2}$
   K. $\frac{6}{7}$

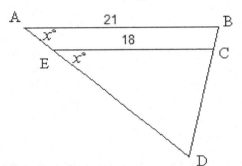

Level 4: Geometry

7. In the figure below, $FROG$ is a trapezoid, Y lies on $\overleftrightarrow{FG}$, and angle measures are as marked. What is the measure of $\angle RGO$?

   A. 19°
   B. 33°
   C. 53.5°
   D. 61°
   E. 73°

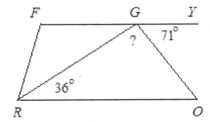

8. The ratio of the side lengths for a triangle is 3 : 7 : 14. In a second triangle similar to the first, the longest side is 11 feet. To the nearest tenth of a foot, what is the length of the shortest side of the second triangle?

   F. 2.2
   G. 2.4
   H. 3.6
   J. 5.5
   K. Cannot be determined from the given information

9. A triangle ΔPQR, is reflected across the y-axis to have the image $\Delta P'Q'R'$ in the standard (x, y) coordinate plane. So, Q reflects to Q'. If the coordinates of Q are (a, b), what are the coordinates of Q' ?

   A. $(a, -b)$
   B. $(-a, b)$
   C. $(-a, -b)$
   D. (b, a)
   E. Cannot be determined from the given information

10. Consider the transformation of the (x, y) coordinate plane that maps each point (a, b) to the point (ca, cb) for some positive constant c. If this transformation maps $(20, 45)$ to $(4, 9)$, then to where does this transformation map the point $(100, 10)$?

    F. $(20, 2)$
    G. $(95, 5)$
    H. $(90, 3)$
    J. $(10, 4.5)$
    K. $(20, 5)$

Answers

1. D	6. K
2. G	7. E
3. E	8. G
4. H	9. B
5. B	10. F

121

Full Solutions

4.

* Since 360° is a full rotation, we can subtract 360° from 540° to get 540° − 360° = 180°. So, we wind up at point R, choice **H**.

Notes: (1) 180° and 540° are called **coterminal angles** because they differ by a multiple of 360°. Any time we add or subtract 360° we get an angle that is coterminal with the original angle.

(2) A rotation by 180° takes a point to the same place whether it is clockwise or counterclockwise. So, in this problem the fact that point K is rotated clockwise isn't needed.

If, however, we were rotating by any angle <u>not</u> coterminal with 180°, then this information would be important. For example, rotating point K 90° clockwise from F takes it to point O, whereas rotating point K 90° counterclockwise from F takes it to point M.

(3) A rotation about P by 180° is the same as a reflection in point P. Notice that if M starts at F, and we reflect it through P, then M ends up at R.

5.

* **Solution by drawing a figure and similar triangles:** We draw two triangles.

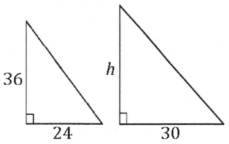

Since we are given that the lengths of the shadows are proportional to the heights of the trees, we have

$$\frac{30}{24} = \frac{h}{36}$$

$$24h = 30 \cdot 36$$

$$h = \frac{30 \cdot 36}{24} = 45$$

This is choice **B**.

6.
* Triangles ECD and ABD are similar, and corresponding sides of similar triangles are in proportion. Therefore,
$$\frac{ED}{AD} = \frac{EC}{AB} = \frac{18}{21} = \frac{6}{7}$$
Thus, the answer is choice **K**

Remarks: (1) To see that triangles ABD and ECD are similar, observe that angles BAD and CED are congruent, and the two triangles share angle D.

(2) When a triangle is inside another similar triangle it may help to draw the individual triangles next to each other, oriented so that congruent angles are in the same direction. See the figures below.

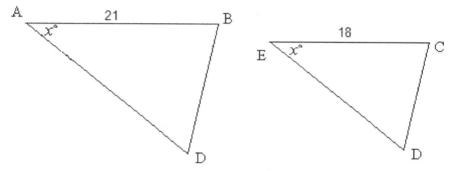

See the optional material below for another common example of this that is a bit more complicated.

7.
* Using transversal $\overline{RG}$, we see that $m\angle FGR = 36°$ (the m here stands for "measure"). So, we have $m\angle RGO = 180 - 36 - 71 = 73°$, choice **E**.

Notes: (1) $\angle GRO$ and $\angle FGR$ are called **alternate interior angles**. When parallel lines are cut by a transversal, the alternate interior angles formed are congruent. This is called the **alternate interior angle theorem**.

It might help to extend the transversal $\overline{RG}$ as follows:

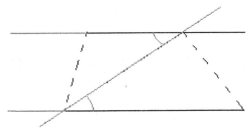

If we ignore the dotted segments in the figure above, we have two parallel lines cut by a transversal, and we see a pair of alternate interior angles that are congruent. There is one other pair of alternate interior angles in the figure. Can you identify it? Can you also identify two pairs of congruent **alternate exterior angles**, and four pairs of congruent **corresponding angles**?

(2) $\angle FGR$, $\angle RGO$, and $\angle YGO$ form a straight line. It follows that the sum of the measures of these three angles is 180°. So, we have

$$m\angle FGR + m\angle RGO + m\angle YGO = 180°.$$

It follows that

$$m\angle RGO = 180° - m\angle FGR - m\angle YGO = 180 - 36 - 71 = 73°.$$

8.
* If we let x be the length of the shortest side of the second triangle, in feet, then we have $\frac{x}{11} = \frac{3}{14}$. So, $14x = 33$, and $x = \frac{33}{14} \approx 2.35714$. Rounded to the nearest foot, this is 2.4, choice **G**.

9.
* **Quick solution:** The only important information here is that the point (a, b) is being reflected in the y-axis. When a point is reflected in the y-axis, the x-coordinate is negated, and the y-coordinate remains the same. So, the answer is $(-a, b)$, choice **B**.

Notes: (1) Below is a picture of a point Q in the first quadrant with coordinates (a, b), and its reflection in the y-axis, Q', with coordinates $(-a, b)$.

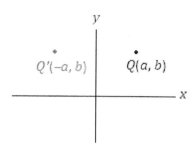

(2) The picture given in note 1 above gives just one of the four possible cases. The point Q could also be in one of the other three quadrants. You may want to draw a picture for each of the other three cases, and in each case, observe that the coordinates of Q' are $(-a, b)$.

(3) If using a and b is confusing, you may want to draw a picture using a specific point. For example, if we let Q be the point $(3,4)$, then it's image when it is reflected in the y-axis is $(-3,4)$.

10.
* To get from the point $(20, 45)$ to $(4, 9)$, we multiply each coordinate by $\frac{1}{5}$. So, we do the same to each coordinate of $(100, 10)$ to get $(20, 2)$, choice **F**.

Notes: (1) Let's do the algebra formally to find c using the first coordinate of each of the given points. We are given that $a = 20$ and $ca = 4$. So, we have $c \cdot 20 = 4$, and therefore, $c = \frac{4}{20} = \frac{1}{5}$.

(2) We can also find c by using the second coordinate of each point. We are given that $b = 45$ and $cb = 9$. So, $c \cdot 45 = 9$, and thus, $c = \frac{9}{45} = \frac{1}{5}$.

(3) Once we know that $c = \frac{1}{5}$, we have $\frac{1}{5} \cdot 100 = 20$ and $\frac{1}{5} \cdot 10 = 2$.

OPTIONAL MATERIAL

Similarity in Right Triangles

Consider the following figure.

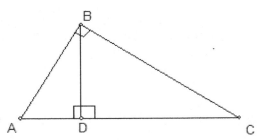

We have a right triangle with an **altitude** drawn from the right angle to the hypotenuse. In this figure, triangles BDC, ADB, and ABC are similar to each other. When solving a problem involving this figure I strongly recommend redrawing all three triangles next to each other so that congruent angles match up. The three figures will look like this.

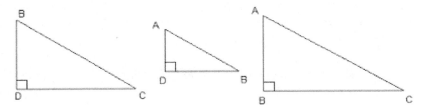

Let's look at two examples.

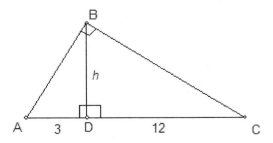

1. Solve for h in the triangle above.

Solution: We redraw the three triangles next to each other so that congruent angles match up.

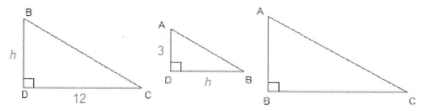

We now set up a ratio, cross multiply, and divide: $\frac{h}{12} = \frac{3}{h}$. So, $h^2 = 36$, and therefore $h = \mathbf{6}$.

Remark: Clearly, we didn't need to redraw the third triangle, but I suggest drawing all three until you get the hang of this.

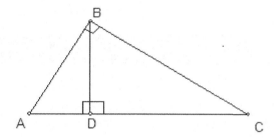

2. In the triangle above, $DC = 3$ and $BC = 6$. What is the value of AC ?

Solution: We redraw the three triangles next to each other so that congruent angles match up.

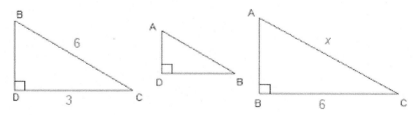

We now set up a ratio, cross multiply, and divide: $\frac{6}{3} = \frac{x}{6}$. So $36 = 3x$, and therefore $x = \mathbf{12}$.

Remark: Here we didn't actually need the second triangle.

Lesson 12
Probability

Reminder: Before beginning this lesson remember to redo the problems from Lessons 4 and 8 that you have marked off. Do not "unmark" a question unless you get it correct.

Simple Probability Principle

To compute a simple probability where all outcomes are equally likely, divide the number of "successes" by the total number of outcomes.

Try to answer the following question using the simple probability principle. **Do not** check the solution until you have attempted this question yourself.

LEVEL 2: PROBABILITY

3, 5, 6, 15, 27, 35, 45, 75

1. A number is to be selected at random from the list above. What is the probability that the number selected will be a multiple of both 3 and 5?

   A. $\frac{1}{8}$
   B. $\frac{1}{4}$
   C. $\frac{3}{8}$
   D. $\frac{1}{2}$
   E. $\frac{5}{8}$

Solution

* The total number of outcomes is 8. The number of "successes" is 3. Therefore, the probability is $\frac{3}{8}$, choice **C**.

Notes: (1) In this problem a "success" is a number that is a multiple of both 3 and 5.

(2) You can check if each number is a "success" by dividing the number by 3 and by 5. If you get an integer in both cases, then the number is a "success." Otherwise it is not. For example, $27/3 = 9$ and $27/5 = 5.4$. Since 5.4 is not an integer, the number 27 is not a "success."

(3) You can check if each number is a "success" more quickly by dividing the number by 15. If you get an integer, then the number is a "success." Otherwise it is not. For example, $27/15 = 1.8$ which is not an integer. Therefore, the number 27 is not a "success."

(4) The "successes" are 15, 45, and 75.

You're doing great! Let's practice a bit more. Try to solve each of the following problems by using the simple probability principle. Then, if possible, solve each problem another way. The answers to these problems, followed by full solutions are at the end of this lesson. **Do not** look at the answers until you have attempted these problems yourself. Please remember to mark off any problems you get wrong.

LEVEL 1: PROBABILITY

2. There are exactly 17 coins in a bag. There are 6 pennies, 4 nickels, 5 dimes, and the rest are quarters. If one coin is selected at random from the bag, what is the probability that the coin is a quarter?

F. $\frac{2}{17}$
G. $\frac{3}{17}$
H. $\frac{4}{17}$
J. $\frac{5}{17}$
K. $\frac{6}{17}$

3. In a jar, there are exactly 56 marbles, each of which is yellow, purple, or blue. The probability of randomly selecting a yellow marble from the jar is $\frac{2}{7}$, and the probability of randomly selecting a purple marble from the jar is $\frac{3}{7}$. How many marbles in the jar are blue?

   A. 8
   B. 12
   C. 16
   D. 20
   E. 24

LEVEL 2: PROBABILITY

4. Of the marbles in a jar, 14 are green. Joseph randomly takes one marble out of the jar. If the probability is $\frac{7}{8}$ that the marble he chooses is green, how many marbles are in the jar?

   F. 8
   G. 10
   H. 12
   J. 14
   K. 16

LEVEL 3: PROBABILITY

5. Shown below, a circular board with a spinner has 3 regions (white, black, and grey) whose areas are in the ratio of $1:3:4$, repectively. The spinner is spun and it lands in one of the three regions at random. What is the probability that the region it lands in is NOT the white region?

   A. $\frac{1}{8}$
   B. $\frac{3}{8}$
   C. $\frac{1}{2}$
   D. $\frac{5}{8}$
   E. $\frac{7}{8}$

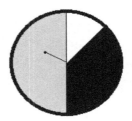

6. There are y bricks in a row. If one brick is to be selected at random, the probability that it will NOT be cracked is $\frac{6}{7}$. In terms of y, how many of the bricks are cracked?

   F. $\frac{y}{7}$
   G. $\frac{5y}{7}$
   H. $\frac{7y}{5}$
   J. $\frac{12y}{7}$
   K. $7y$

7. If the letters A, B, E, R, and Z are to be randomly ordered, what is the probability that the letters will appear in the order Z, E, B, R, A?

   A. $\frac{1}{120}$
   B. $\frac{1}{60}$
   C. $\frac{1}{40}$
   D. $\frac{1}{30}$
   E. $\frac{1}{24}$

8. Set X contains only the integers 0 through 160 inclusive. If a number is selected at random from X, what is the probability that the number selected will be less than 83?

   F. $\frac{83}{160}$
   G. $\frac{83}{161}$
   H. $\frac{82}{160}$
   J. $\frac{82}{161}$
   K. $\frac{84}{161}$

LEVEL 4: PROBABILITY

9. Maria has 6 dresses and 6 scarves, and each dress matches a different scarf. If she chooses one of these dresses and one of these scarves at random, what is the probability that they will NOT match?

   A. $\frac{1}{36}$
   B. $\frac{1}{6}$
   C. $\frac{2}{3}$
   D. $\frac{5}{6}$
   E. $\frac{35}{36}$

10. An urn contains several marbles of which 63 are blue, 15 are red, and the remainder are white. If the probability of picking a white marble from this urn at random is $\frac{1}{3}$, how many white marbles are in the urn?

    F. 6
    G. 15
    H. 30
    J. 39
    K. 45

Definitions Used in This Lesson

Definitions of the **counting principle**, **factorials**, **permutations**, and **combinations** can be found in Lesson 8.

Answers

1. C
2. F
3. C
4. K
5. E

6. F
7. A
8. G
9. D
10. J

Full Solutions

2.

* The number of quarters in the bag is $17 - 6 - 4 - 5 = 2$. Therefore, the probability of selecting a quarter from the bag is $\frac{2}{17}$, choice **F**.

3.

Straightforward solution: The number of yellow marbles in the jar is $(\frac{2}{7})(56) = 16$. The number of purple marbles in the jar is $(\frac{3}{7})(56) = 24$. Therefore, the number of blue marbles in the jar is $56 - 16 - 24 = 16$, choice **C**.

* **Quick solution:** The probability of selecting a blue marble from the jar is $1 - \frac{2}{7} - \frac{3}{7} = \frac{2}{7}$. Therefore, the number of blue marbles in the jar is $(\frac{2}{7})(56) = 16$, choice **C**.

Remark: The probability of a **certain event** is 1. If you add up the probabilities of each possible outcome you get 1.

4.

Solution by starting with choice H: Normally we would start with choice H as our first guess, but it is easy to see that the number of marbles in the jar must be divisible by 8. So, we can eliminate choices G, H, and J right away. So, let's try choice K and guess that there are 16 marbles in the jar. We then have that $\frac{7}{8} \cdot 16 = 14$, which is correct. Thus, the answer is 16, choice **K**.

* **Algebraic solution:** $\frac{7}{8}$ of the total number of marbles is green. If we let x stand for the total, then $\frac{7}{8}x = 14$. We now multiply each side of this equation by $\frac{8}{7}$ to get $x = 14 \cdot \frac{8}{7} = 16$, choice **K**.

5.

Algebraic solution: If we let the area of the white region be x, then the area of the black region is $3x$, and the area of the grey region is $4x$.

The total is then $x + 3x + 4x = 8x$ and the "successes" is $3x + 4x = 7x$.

By the simple probability principle, the desired probability is $\frac{7x}{8x} = \frac{7}{8}$, choice **E**.

* **Quick solution:** $\frac{3+4}{1+3+4} = \frac{7}{8}$, choice **E**.

6.
Solution by picking numbers: Let's choose a value for y, say $y = 7$. Then there are 7 bricks in a row. Since the probability is $\frac{6}{7}$ that a brick is not cracked, the probability is $1 - \frac{6}{7} = \frac{1}{7}$ that a brick is cracked. So $\frac{1}{7} \cdot 7 = 1$ brick is cracked. **Put a nice, big dark circle around the number 1.** We now substitute 7 in for y in each of the answer choices.

    F. 1
    G. 5
    H. $\frac{49}{5}$
    J. 12
    K. 49

Since G, H, J, and K are incorrect we can eliminate them. Therefore, the answer is choice **F**.

Important note: F is **not** the correct answer simply because it is equal to 1. It is correct because all four of the other choices are **not** 1.

Algebraic solution: Let x be the number of cracked bricks. It follows that $\frac{x}{y} = \frac{1}{7}$. Now cross multiply and divide to solve for x. $7x = y$, and therefore $x = \frac{y}{7}$, choice **F**.

*** Quick solution:** We are given that $\frac{6}{7}$ of the total number of bricks are not cracked. Therefore $1 - \frac{6}{7} = \frac{1}{7}$ of the bricks are cracked. The total is y, so that the answer is $\frac{1}{7}y = \frac{y}{7}$, choice **F**.

7.
* The total number of arrangements of the five letters given is $5 \cdot 4 \cdot 3 \cdot 2 \cdot 1 = 120$. Only one of these results in Z, E, B, R, A. Therefore, the probability is $\frac{1}{120}$, choice **A**.

Remark: If you are having trouble counting the total number of arrangements in this problem, go back and review Lesson 8.

8.

* There are a total of 161 integers. There are 83 integers from set X that are less than 83. Therefore, the probability is $\frac{83}{161}$, choice **G**.

Remark: The number of integers from a to b, inclusive, is $b - a + 1$. So, Here, the number of integers from 0 to 160 is $160 - 0 + 1 = 161$, and the number of integers from 0 to 82 is $82 - 0 + 1 = 83$. If you ever forget this little formula, test it out on a small list. For example, let's count the number of integers from 3 to 7, inclusive. They are 3, 4, 5, 6, 7, and we see there are 5 of them. Now, $7 - 3 = 4$ which is not the correct amount, but $7 - 3 + 1 = 5$ which is the correct amount.

9.

* By the counting principle there are $6 \cdot 6 = 36$ dress/scarf combinations. 6 of these combinations are matching. Therefore, there are $36 - 6 = 30$ nonmatching combinations. So, the probability the dress and scarf will not match is $\frac{30}{36} = \frac{5}{6}$, choice **D**.

10.

* **Quick solution:** There are $63 + 15 = 78$ marbles that are not white. Also $1 - \frac{1}{3} = \frac{2}{3}$ of the marbles are not white. So, $\frac{2}{3}$ of the total number of marbles is 78. Therefore $\frac{1}{3}$ of the total number of marbles is $\frac{78}{2} = 39$, choice **J**.

Algebraic solution: Let x be the total number of marbles. Then we have $\frac{2}{3}x = 63 + 15 = 78$. So, $x = 78(\frac{3}{2}) = 117$. The number of white marbles is then $(\frac{1}{3})(117) = 39$, choice **J**.

Download additional solutions for free here:

www.satprepget800.com/28LesInt

Lesson 13
Number Theory

Reminder: Before beginning this lesson remember to redo the problems from Lessons 1, 5, and 9 that you have marked off. Do not "unmark" a question unless you get it correct.

Scientific Notation

We use **scientific notation** to write very large and very small numbers in a convenient way. A number written in scientific notation has the form $a.\boldsymbol{b} \times 10^c$, where a is a nonzero digit, $\boldsymbol{b}$ is a string of digits, and c is an integer.

Example 1: Change the number 317,000 from decimal notation to scientific notation.

Solution: Note that this number has a "hidden" decimal point at the end of the number. We move that decimal point **5** places to the left, and place it between the 3 and the 1. We also drop any zeroes at the end of the number. So, we get $317{,}000 = \boldsymbol{3.17} \times \boldsymbol{10^5}$.

Notes: (1) We placed the decimal point right after the leftmost nonzero digit, which in this case is 3.

(2) The exponent is 5 because we had to move the decimal point 5 places to the **left**.

Example 2: Change the number 0.0000057 from decimal notation to scientific notation.

Solution: This time we move that decimal point **6** places to the right, and place it between the 5 and the 7. We also drop any zeroes at the beginning of the number. So, we get $0.0000057 = \boldsymbol{5.7} \times \boldsymbol{10^{-6}}$.

Notes: (1) We placed the decimal point right after the leftmost nonzero digit, which in this case is 5.

(2) The exponent is -6 because we had to move the decimal point 6 places to the **right**.

Example 3: Change the number 2.73×10^{11} from scientific notation to decimal notation.

Solution: We move the decimal point 11 places to the right to get $2.73 \times 10^{11} = \mathbf{273,000,000,000}$.

Note: We moved the decimal point to the right because the exponent is positive.

Example 4: Change the number 8.937×10^{-4} from scientific notation to decimal notation.

Solution: We move the decimal point 4 places to the left to get $8.937 \times 10^{-4} = \mathbf{0.0008937}$.

Note: We moved the decimal point to the left because the exponent is negative.

Arithmetic Sequences

An **arithmetic sequence** is a sequence of numbers such that the difference d between consecutive terms is constant. The number d is called the **common difference** of the arithmetic sequence.

Here is a simple example of an arithmetic sequence: $1, 3, 5, 7, 9, 11, \ldots$ In this example, the common difference is $d = 2$.

Arithmetic sequence formula: $a_n = a_1 + (n-1)d$

In the above formula, a_n is the nth term of the sequence. For example, a_1 is the first term of the sequence.

Example: In the arithmetic sequence $1, 3, 5, 7, 9, 11, \ldots$ note that $a_1 = 1$ and $d = 2$. Therefore, $a_n = 1 + (n-1)(2) = 1 + (2n-2) = 2n-1$.

Geometric Sequences

A **geometric sequence** is a sequence of numbers such that the quotient r between consecutive terms is constant. The number r is called the **common ratio** of the geometric sequence.

Here is a simple example of a geometric sequence: $1, 2, 4, 8, 16, 32, \ldots$ In this example the common ratio is $r = 2$.

Geometric sequence formula: $g_n = g_1 \cdot r^{n-1}$

In the above formula, g_n is the nth term of the sequence. For example, g_1 is the first term of the sequence.

Example: In the geometric sequence 1, 2, 4, 8, 16, 32, ... note that $g_1 = 1$ and $r = 2$. Therefore, $g_n = 1 \cdot 2^{n-1} = 2^{n-1}$.

Now try to solve each of the following problems. The answers to these problems, followed by full solutions are at the end of this lesson. Please **do not** look at the answers until you have attempted each of these problems yourself. Remember to mark off any problems you get wrong.

LEVEL 1: NUMBER THEORY

1. The number 0.000 000 000 000 025 is equivalent to which of the following expressions?

    A. 2.5×10^{15}
    B. 2.5×10^{14}
    C. 2.5×10^{-13}
    D. 2.5×10^{-14}
    E. 2.5×10^{-15}

2. The first term is 2 in the geometric sequence 2, 4, 8, 16,.... What is the EIGHTH term of the geometric sequence?

    F. 32
    G. 64
    H. 128
    J. 256
    K. 512

3. The first term of a sequence is 23. Each term after the first is 7 less than the previous term. What is the first negative number in the sequence?

    A. -1
    B. -2
    C. -3
    D. -5
    E. -7

LEVEL 2: NUMBER THEORY

4. $\frac{9.2 \times 10^{-5}}{2.3 \times 10^{-13}} = ?$

   F. 4.0×10^8
   G. 4.0×10^{-8}
   H. 4.0×10^{-18}
   J. 4.2×10^{18}
   K. 4.2×10^8

5. In scientific notation, $530{,}000{,}000 + 900{,}000{,}000 = ?$

   A. 1.43×10^{-10}
   B. 1.43×10^{-9}
   C. 1.43×10^8
   D. 1.43×10^9
   E. 1.43×10^{10}

6. The first term of an arithmetic sequence is 7 and the common difference is 3. What is the fifth term of the sequence?

   F. -5
   G. -2
   H. 16
   J. 19
   K. 22

$$20, 59, 30, 89, 45, \ldots$$

7. In the sequence above, 20 is the first term and each term thereafter is obtained by using the following rules.

   – If the previous term is even, multiply it by 3, then subtract 1.
   – If the previous term is odd, add 1 to it, then divide by 2.

   What is the eighth term of the sequence?

   A. 12
   B. 23
   C. 35
   D. 70
   E. 201

Level 3: Number Theory

8. It is estimated that the earth is 4.5 billion years old. When written in scientific notation, which of the following expressions is equal to the number of years used to estimate the age of the earth?

   F. 4.5×10^6
   G. 9.0×10^6
   H. 4.5×10^9
   J. 45×10^9
   K. 90×10^9

Level 4: Number Theory

9. A tennis ball is dropped from 567 centimeters above the ground and after the fourth bounce it rises to a height of 7 centimeters. If the height to which the tennis ball rises after each bounce is always the same fraction of the height reached on its previous bounce, what is this fraction?

   A. $\frac{1}{81}$
   B. $\frac{1}{27}$
   C. $\frac{1}{9}$
   D. $\frac{1}{3}$
   E. $\frac{1}{2}$

10. The first term of the sequence below is 4, and each term after the first is four times the preceding term. Which of the following expressions represents the nth term of the sequence?

    $$4, 16, 64, \ldots$$

    F. $4n$
    G. $(n-1)^4$
    H. n^4
    J. 4^{n-1}
    K. 4^n

Answers

1. D
2. J
3. D
4. F
5. D
6. J
7. C
8. H
9. D
10. K

Full Solutions

1.

* We move the decimal point to the right 14 places, and so we get 2.5×10^{-14}, choice **D**.

2.

* The common ratio for this geometric sequence is 2. So, we get to the next term by multiplying the previous term by 2. So, the first eight terms of the sequence are 2, 4, 8, 16, 32, 64, 128, 256, and the answer is **J**.

3.

* Let's write out the sequence: 23, 16, 9, 2, −5, … The first negative number is −5, choice **D**.

4.

* $\frac{9.2 \times 10^{-5}}{2.3 \times 10^{-13}} = \frac{9.2}{2.3} \times \frac{10^{-5}}{10^{-13}} = 4.0 \times 10^{8}$, choice **F**.

Notes: (1) In general, we have $\frac{a \times b}{c \times d} = \frac{a}{c} \times \frac{b}{d}$.

We used this rule to get from the first expression to the second.

(2) To compute $\frac{10^{-5}}{10^{-13}}$, we subtract the exponents. In this case, we have $-5 - (-13) = -5 + 13 = 8$.

For a complete review of the laws of exponents, see Lesson 10.

5.

* $530{,}000{,}000 + 900{,}000{,}000 = 1{,}430{,}000{,}000 = 1.43 \times 10^{9}$. This is choice **D**.

Note: To convert 1,430,000,000 to scientific notation, we need to move the decimal point to the left 9 places. This is why the exponent is 9.

6.
* $a_5 = a_1 + (n-1)d = 7 + 4 \cdot 3 = 7 + 12 = 19$, choice **J**.

Notes: (1) We used the arithmetic sequence formula here.

(2) When we apply the formula, we are simply adding the number 3 (the common difference) to the number 7 four times.

7.
* The sixth term of the sequence is $\frac{45+1}{2} = \frac{46}{2} = 23$.
The seventh term of the sequence is $\frac{23+1}{2} = \frac{24}{2} = 12$.
The eighth term of the sequence is $3 \cdot 12 - 1 = 36 - 1 = 35$, choice **C**.

8.
* 4.5 billion $= 4{,}500{,}000{,}000 = 4.5 \times 10^9$, choice **H**.

Note: To convert 4,500,000,000 to scientific notation, we need to move the decimal point to the left 9 places. This is why the exponent is 9.

9.
* **Solution by starting with choice C:** Let's begin with choice C and divide 567 by 9 four times to get 0.0864197531, which is much too small. So, we can eliminate choices A, B, and C. We next try choice D. If we divide 567 by 3 four times we get 7 so that the correct answer is choice **D**.

Note: We could have also multiplied 7 by 3 four times to get 567.

An algebraic solution: We want to solve the following equation.

$$567x^4 = 7$$
$$x^4 = \frac{7}{567} = \frac{1}{81}$$
$$x = \frac{1}{3}$$

Thus, the answer is choice **D**.

10.
* **Solution by picking numbers:** Let's choose a value for n, say $n = 3$. We see that the 3rd term of the sequence is **64**. **Put a nice big circle around this number.** Now substitute $n = 3$ into each answer choice.

     F. 12
     G. 16
     H. 81
     J. 16
     K. 64

Since F, G, H and J are incorrect we can eliminate them. Therefore, the answer is choice **K**.

* Quick solution: We can rewrite the sequence as $4^1, 4^2, 4^3,\ldots$

Note that the 1st term is 4^1, the 2nd term is 4^2, the 3rd term is 4^3, etc. Thus, the nth term is is 4^n, choice **K**.

Download additional solutions for free here:

www.satprepget800.com/28LesInt

LESSON 14
ALGEBRA

Reminder: Before beginning this lesson remember to redo the problems from Lessons 2, 6, and 10 that you have marked off. Do not "unmark" a question unless you get it correct.

Systems of Linear Equations

There are many ways to solve a system of linear equations. We will use an example to demonstrate several different methods.

LEVEL 5: ALGEBRA

1. If $2x + 3y = 7$ and $5y + 3x = 5$, what is the value of x?

    A. -10
    B. -5
    C. 10
    D. 20
    E. 25

* **The elimination method:** We begin by making sure that the two equations are "lined up" properly. We do this by placing the equations vertically, and rewriting the left-hand side of the second equation with the x term first.

$$2x + 3y = 7$$
$$3x + 5y = 5$$

We will now multiply each side of the first equation by 5, and each side of the second equation by -3.

$$5(2x + 3y) = (7)(5)$$
$$-3(3x + 5y) = (5)(-3)$$

Do not forget to distribute correctly on the left. Add the two equations.

$$10x + 15y = 35$$
$$-9x - 15y = -15$$
$$x = 20$$

This is choice **D**.

144

Remarks: (1) We chose to use 5 and -3 because multiplying by these numbers makes the y column "match up," so that when we add the two equations in the next step the y term vanishes. We could have also used -5 and 3.

(2) If we wanted to find y instead of x we would multiply the two equations by 3 and -2 (or -3 and 2). In general, if you are looking for only one variable, try to eliminate the one you are **not** looking for.

(3) We chose to multiply by a negative number so that we could add the equations instead of subtracting them. We could have also multiplied the first equation by 5, the second by 3, and subtracted the two equations, but a computational error is more likely to occur this way.

The substitution method: We solve the second equation for y and substitute into the first equation.

$5y = 5 - 3x$ implies $y = \frac{5-3x}{5} = \frac{5}{5} - \frac{3x}{5} = 1 - \frac{3x}{5}$. So now using the first equation we have

$$2x = 7 - 3y = 7 - 3\left(1 - \frac{3x}{5}\right) = 7 - 3 + \frac{9x}{5} = 4 + \frac{9x}{5}.$$

Multiply each side of this equation by 5 to get rid of the denominator on the right. So, we have $10x = 20 + 9x$, and therefore, $x = 20$, choice **D**.

Remark: If we wanted to find y instead of x we would solve one of the equations for x and substitute into the other equation.

The graphing calculator method: We begin by solving each equation for y.

$$3y = 7 - 2x \qquad\qquad 5y = 5 - 3x$$
$$y = \frac{7}{3} - \frac{2x}{3} \qquad\qquad y = 1 - \frac{3x}{5}$$

In your graphing calculator press the Y= button, and enter the following.

Y1 = 7/3 −2X/3
Y2 = 1 − 3X/5

Now press ZOOM 6 to graph these two lines in a standard window. It looks like the point of intersection of the two lines is off to the right. So, we will need to extend the viewing window.

Press the WINDOW button, and change Xmax to 50 and Ymin to -20. Then press 2nd TRACE (which is CALC) 5 (or select INTERSECT). Then press ENTER 3 times. You will see that the x-coordinate of the point of intersection of the two lines is 20, choice **D**.

Remark: The choices made for Xmax and Ymin were just to try to ensure that the point of intersection would appear in the viewing window. Many other windows would work just as well.

Plugging in answer choices: We can substitute each answer choice (starting with C) into each equation for x, and solve for y. When we get the same y value, we have found the answer. I leave the details of this solution to the reader.

Matrices

A **matrix** is simply an array of numbers. Here are some examples:

$$A = \begin{bmatrix} 0 & 1 \\ 3 & 2 \end{bmatrix} \quad B = \begin{bmatrix} 1 & -2 \\ 2 & 3 \\ 0 & -1 \end{bmatrix} \quad C = \begin{bmatrix} 1 & 2 & 0 \\ 0 & 3 & 6 \end{bmatrix}$$

A is a 2×2 matrix because it has 2 rows and 2 columns. Similarly, B is a 3×2 matrix and C is a 2×3 matrix.

Two matrices are **equal** if they have the same size, and all of their entries are equal. For example, if $\begin{bmatrix} x & y \\ z & w \end{bmatrix} = \begin{bmatrix} 0 & 1 \\ 3 & 2 \end{bmatrix}$, then $x = 0$, $y = 1$, $z = 3$, and $w = 2$.

We add two matrices of the same size by adding entry by entry. For example,

$$\begin{bmatrix} 1 & -2 \\ 2 & 3 \\ 0 & -1 \end{bmatrix} + \begin{bmatrix} 2 & 1 \\ 3 & 0 \\ 5 & -2 \end{bmatrix} = \begin{bmatrix} 3 & -1 \\ 5 & 3 \\ 5 & -3 \end{bmatrix}$$

We multiply a matrix by a real number (called a **scalar**) by multiplying each entry by that number. For example,

$$3 \begin{bmatrix} 2 & -5 & 3 \\ 1 & -1 & -2 \end{bmatrix} = \begin{bmatrix} 6 & -15 & 9 \\ 3 & -3 & -6 \end{bmatrix}$$

Example:

$$2 \begin{bmatrix} 2 & 3 \\ 5 & -2 \end{bmatrix} + 5 \begin{bmatrix} 1 & 0 \\ 2 & 2 \end{bmatrix} = \begin{bmatrix} 4 & 6 \\ 10 & -4 \end{bmatrix} + \begin{bmatrix} 5 & 0 \\ 10 & 10 \end{bmatrix} = \begin{bmatrix} 9 & 6 \\ 20 & 6 \end{bmatrix}$$

We can multiply two matrices together if the number of columns of the first matrix is equal to the number of rows of the second matrix. For example, if we consider the matrices A, B, and C above, we can multiply A times C because A has 2 columns and C has 2 rows. Here are the products we **can** form:

$$AA \quad AC \quad BA \quad BC \quad CB$$

And here are the products we **cannot** form:

$$AB \quad BB \quad CA \quad CC$$

Now how do we actually multiply two matrices? This is a bit complicated and requires just a little practice. For each row of the first matrix and each column of the second matrix, we add up the products entry by entry. Let's compute the product AC as an example.

$$AC = \begin{bmatrix} 0 & 1 \\ 3 & 2 \end{bmatrix} \cdot \begin{bmatrix} 1 & 2 & 0 \\ 0 & 3 & 6 \end{bmatrix} = \begin{bmatrix} x & y & z \\ u & v & w \end{bmatrix}$$

Since x is in the first row and first column, we use the first row of A and the first column of C to get $x = \begin{bmatrix} 0 & 1 \end{bmatrix} \begin{bmatrix} 1 \\ 0 \end{bmatrix} = 0 \cdot 1 + 1 \cdot 0 = 0 + 0 = 0$.

Since u is in the second row and first column, we use the second row of A and the first column of C to get $y = \begin{bmatrix} 3 & 2 \end{bmatrix} \begin{bmatrix} 1 \\ 0 \end{bmatrix} = 3 \cdot 1 + 2 \cdot 0 = 3$.

See if you can follow this procedure to compute the values of the remaining entries. The final product is

$$AC = \begin{bmatrix} 0 & 3 & 6 \\ 3 & 12 & 12 \end{bmatrix}$$

Note: The product of a **2 × 2** matrix and a **2 × 3** matrix is a 2 × 3 matrix.

More generally, the product of an $m \times n$ matrix and an $n \times p$ marix is an $m \times p$ matrix. Observe that the inner most numbers (both n) must agree, and the resulting product has dimensions given by the outermost numbers (m and p).

The **determinant** of the 2 × 2 matrix $\begin{bmatrix} a & b \\ c & d \end{bmatrix}$ is

$$\begin{vmatrix} a & b \\ c & d \end{vmatrix} = ad - bc$$

For example, let's compute the determinant of matrix A above.

$$|A| = \begin{vmatrix} 0 & 1 \\ 3 & 2 \end{vmatrix} = 0 \cdot 2 - 1 \cdot 3 = 0 - 3 = -3$$

Consider the following system of equations:

$$ax + by = c$$
$$dx + ey = f$$

The **augmented matrix** of this system is the matrix

$$\begin{bmatrix} a & b & | & c \\ d & e & | & f \end{bmatrix}$$

In other words, the entries of the matrix are the **coefficients** in the equations. We simply disregard the variables.

LEVEL 2: ALGEBRA

2. Which of the following augmented matrices represents the system of linear equations below?

$$7x + y = 4$$
$$5x - 3y = -2$$

F. $\begin{bmatrix} 7 & 1 & | & -4 \\ 5 & -3 & | & 2 \end{bmatrix}$

G. $\begin{bmatrix} 7 & 1 & | & 4 \\ 5 & -3 & | & -2 \end{bmatrix}$

H. $\begin{bmatrix} 7 & 0 & | & 4 \\ 5 & -3 & | & -2 \end{bmatrix}$

J. $\begin{bmatrix} 7 & -1 & | & 4 \\ 5 & -3 & | & -2 \end{bmatrix}$

K. $\begin{bmatrix} 7 & 5 & | & 4 \\ 1 & -3 & | & -2 \end{bmatrix}$

Solution

* It should be clear that the answer is choice **G**.

You're doing great! Let's just practice a bit more. Try to solve each of the following problems. **Do not** look at the answers until you have attempted these problems yourself. Please remember to mark off any problems you get wrong.

Level 2: Algebra

3. What is the sum of the solutions of the 2 equations below?
$$6x = 15$$
$$2y + 3 = 11$$

   A. $1\frac{1}{5}$
   B. $6\frac{1}{2}$
   C. 7
   D. 8
   E. $15\frac{1}{2}$

4. The system of equations below has one solution (a, b). What is the value of a ?
$$x + 2y = 3$$
$$x + y = 1$$

   F. -2
   G. -1
   H. 0
   J. 3
   K. 7

Level 3: Algebra

5. What value of k satisfies the matrix equation below?
$$5\begin{bmatrix} 2 & 0 & 1 \\ 3 & 1 & 2 \end{bmatrix} - 3\begin{bmatrix} 3 & 2 & 0 \\ k & 1 & 2 \end{bmatrix} = \begin{bmatrix} 1 & -6 & 5 \\ 9 & 2 & 4 \end{bmatrix}$$

   A. -2
   B. -1
   C. 0
   D. 1
   E. 2

6. The system of equations below has 1 solution (c, d). What is the value of d?

$$2c + 3d = 12$$
$$3c - d = -4$$

   F. -4
   G. -2
   H. 0
   J. 2
   K. 4

Level 4: Algebra

7. Which of the following (x, y) pairs is the solution for the system of equations $\frac{1}{3}x - \frac{1}{6}y = 7$ and $\frac{1}{5}y - \frac{1}{5}x = 8$?

   A. $(-36, -57)$
   B. $(12, 43)$
   C. $(\frac{101}{5}, \frac{307}{5})$
   D. $(82, 122)$
   E. $(122, 82)$

8. Given that $d \begin{bmatrix} 1 & 3 \\ 2 & 4 \end{bmatrix} = \begin{bmatrix} a & b \\ c & 7 \end{bmatrix}$ for some real number d, what is $4ab$?

   F. $\frac{7}{4}$
   G. $\frac{7}{2}$
   H. $\frac{49}{4}$
   J. $\frac{147}{4}$
   K. 49

LEVEL 5: ALGEBRA

9. For what positive real value of b, if any, is the determinant of the matrix $\begin{bmatrix} 2 & b \\ b & 7 \end{bmatrix}$ equal to b^2 ?

   A. 2
   B. 7
   C. $\sqrt{7}$
   D. $\sqrt{14}$
   E. There is no such value of b.

10. Which of the following matrices is equal to the matrix product $\begin{bmatrix} -7 & 3 \\ 2 & -1 \end{bmatrix} \cdot \begin{bmatrix} 2 \\ -3 \end{bmatrix}$

    F. $\begin{bmatrix} -14 & -9 \\ 4 & 3 \end{bmatrix}$
    G. $\begin{bmatrix} -14 & -9 \\ 3 & 4 \end{bmatrix}$
    H. $\begin{bmatrix} -14 & 4 \\ -6 & 3 \end{bmatrix}$
    J. $\begin{bmatrix} -23 \\ 7 \end{bmatrix}$
    K. $\begin{bmatrix} -5 \\ 1 \end{bmatrix}$

Answers

1. D
2. G
3. B
4. G
5. E
6. K
7. D
8. J
9. C
10. J

Full Solutions

3.
* From the first equation, we have $x = \frac{15}{6} = 2.5$.

We subtract 3 from each side of the second equation to get $2y = 8$. Dividing each side of this last equation by 2 yields $y = 4$.

Finally, $x + y = 2.5 + 4 = 6.5 = 6\frac{1}{2}$, choice **B**.

4.

* Solution using the elimination method: We subtract the second equation from the first

$$\begin{array}{r} x + 2y = 3 \\ \underline{x + y = 1} \\ y = 2 \end{array}$$

Now we can substitute $y = 2$ into either equation to find x. Let's use the second equation: $x + 2 = 1 \implies x = 1 - 2 = -1$, choice **G**.

Notes: (1) Technically we are supposed to replace x by a and y by b first. The solution then looks like this:

$$\begin{array}{r} a + 2b = 3 \\ \underline{a + b = 1} \\ b = 2 \end{array}$$

$a + 2 = 1 \implies a = 1 - 2 = -1$, choice **G**.

(2) We can find x without solving for y first by multiplying the second equation by -2, and then adding the two equations:

$$\begin{array}{r} x + 2y = 3 \\ \underline{-2x - 2y = -2} \\ -x = 1 \end{array}$$

So, $x = -1$.

Solution by starting with choice H: If we guess that $a = 0$, then we have $b = 1$ from the second equation, and $2b = 3$, or equivalently, $b = \frac{3}{2}$ from the first equation. Since the two values for b are different, 0 is not the answer, and we can eliminate choice H.

Let's try G next and guess that $a = -1$. Then both equations give us $b = 2$. Since they both agree, the answer is choice **G**.

5.

* Quick solution: We need only find the entry in the second row and first column.

$$5 \cdot 3 - 3k = 9$$
$$15 - 3k = 9$$
$$-3k = -6$$
$$k = 2$$

This is choice **E**.

Note: For completeness, let's do the whole computation on the left:

$$5\begin{bmatrix} 2 & 0 & 1 \\ 3 & 1 & 2 \end{bmatrix} - 3\begin{bmatrix} 3 & 2 & 0 \\ k & 1 & 2 \end{bmatrix} = \begin{bmatrix} 10 & 0 & 5 \\ 15 & 5 & 10 \end{bmatrix} - \begin{bmatrix} 9 & 6 & 0 \\ 3k & 3 & 6 \end{bmatrix}$$
$$= \begin{bmatrix} 1 & -6 & 5 \\ 15-3k & 2 & 4 \end{bmatrix}$$

So we have

$$\begin{bmatrix} 1 & -6 & 5 \\ 15-3k & 2 & 4 \end{bmatrix} = \begin{bmatrix} 1 & -6 & 5 \\ 9 & 2 & 4 \end{bmatrix}$$

In particular, we must have $15 - 3k = 9$. So, $k = 2$, choice **E**.

6.

* **Solution using the elimination method:** We multiply each side of the first equation by 3, and each side of the second equation by -2.

$$3(2c + 3d) = (12)(3)$$
$$-2(3c - d) = (-4)(-2)$$

Do not forget to distribute correctly on the left. Add the two equations.

$$\begin{aligned} 6c + 9d &= 36 \\ \underline{-6c + 2d} &= \underline{8} \\ 11d &= 44 \end{aligned}$$

So $d = \frac{44}{11} = 4$, choice **K**.

Solution by starting with choice H: If we guess that $d = 0$, then we have $c = 6$ from the first equation, and $c = -\frac{4}{3}$ form the second equation. Since the two values for c are different, 0 is not the answer, and we can eliminate choice H.

Let's try K next and guess that $d = 4$. Then both equations give us $c = 0$. Since they both agree, the answer is choice **K**.

7.

* Solution using the elimination method: Let's begin by multiplying the first equation by 6 and the second equation by 5 to get rid of the denominators. So, we have

$$2x - y = 42$$
$$y - x = 40$$

Let's rewrite $y - x$ as $-x + y$ and add the two equations.

$$2x - y = 42$$
$$\underline{-x + y = 40}$$
$$x = 82$$

Let's substitute $x = 82$ into the second equation in the solution to get $y - 82 = 40$. Adding 82 gives $y = 40 + 82 = 122$.

So, the answer is $(82, 122)$, choice **D**.

Solution by plugging in the points: Let's begin plugging the answer choices into the given equations. Choice C looks to be difficult, so let's start with choice B.

$$\frac{1}{3}x - \frac{1}{6}y = \frac{1}{3}(12) - \frac{1}{6}(43) = 4 - \frac{43}{6} \neq 7$$

So, we can eliminate choice B.

Let's try D next.

$$\frac{1}{3}x - \frac{1}{6}y = \frac{1}{3}(82) - \frac{1}{6}(122) = \frac{2 \cdot 82}{6} - \frac{122}{6} = \frac{164 - 122}{6} = \frac{42}{6} = 7$$

$$\frac{1}{5}y - \frac{1}{5}x = \frac{1}{5}(122) - \frac{1}{5}(82) = \frac{122 - 82}{5} = \frac{40}{5} = 8$$

So, the answer is choice **D**.

8.
*

$$d\begin{bmatrix} 1 & 3 \\ 2 & 4 \end{bmatrix} = \begin{bmatrix} d & 3d \\ 2d & 4d \end{bmatrix}$$

So, we have

$$\begin{bmatrix} d & 3d \\ 2d & 4d \end{bmatrix} = \begin{bmatrix} a & b \\ c & 7 \end{bmatrix}$$

Equating the entries in row 2, column 2, we have $4d = 7$, and so $d = \frac{7}{4}$.

It follows that $a = d = \frac{7}{4}$, $b = 3d = \frac{21}{4}$, and so $4ab = 4\left(\frac{7}{4}\right)\left(\frac{21}{4}\right) = \frac{147}{4}$, choice **J**.

9.
* The determinant of the matrix is $2 \cdot 7 - b \cdot b = 14 - b^2$. So, we need $14 - b^2 = b^2$. At this point we can either plug in the answer choices or solve the equation algebraically.

<u>Method 1 (starting with choice C)</u>: Let's start with choice C and substitute $\sqrt{7}$ in for b. The left-hand side of the equation then becomes

$$14 - \sqrt{7}^2 = 14 - 7 = 7.$$

Since $7 = \sqrt{7}^2 = b^2$, the answer is choice **C**.

<u>Method 2 (algebraic solution)</u>: Let's solve the equation for b.

$$14 - b^2 = b^2$$
$$14 = 2b^2$$
$$7 = b^2$$

So $b = \pm\sqrt{7}$.

Since the question asks for the positive real value of b, the answer is $\sqrt{7}$, choice **C**.

Notes: (1) We get from the first equation to the second equation by adding b^2 to each side. Note that $b^2 + b^2 = 2b^2$.

(2) We get from the second equation to the third equation by dividing each side by 2. Note that $\frac{14}{2} = 7$.

(3) We solve the equation $b^2 = 7$ by using the **square root property**.

See Lesson 18 for more on the square root property.

10.
*
$$\begin{bmatrix} -7 & 3 \\ 2 & -1 \end{bmatrix} \cdot \begin{bmatrix} 2 \\ -3 \end{bmatrix} = \begin{bmatrix} (-7)(2) + (3)(-3) \\ (2)(2) + (-1)(-3) \end{bmatrix} = \begin{bmatrix} -23 \\ 7 \end{bmatrix}$$

This is choice **J**.

OPTIONAL MATERIAL

Solving Systems of Equations with Your Calculator

As usual, we assume you are using a TI-84 calculator or something equivalent. Let's solve a simple system of equations using our calculator.

$$x - y = 10$$
$$x + y = 40$$

Begin by pushing the MATRIX button (which is 2ND x^{-1}). Scroll over to EDIT and then select [A] (or press 1). We will be inputting a 2 × 3 matrix, so press 2 ENTER 3 ENTER. We then begin entering the numbers 1, −1, and 10 for the first row, and 1, 1, and 40 for the second row. To do this we can simply type 1 ENTER −1 ENTER 10 ENTER 1 ENTER 1 ENTER 40 ENTER.

Note: What we have just done was create the **augmented matrix** for the system of equations. This is simply an array of numbers which contains the coefficients of the variables together with the right-hand sides of the equations. (See problem 2 above, for example.)

Now push the QUIT button (2ND MODE) to get a blank screen. Press MATRIX again. This time scroll over to MATH and select rref((or press B). Then press MATRIX again and select [A] (or press 1) and press ENTER.

Note: What we have just done is put the matrix into **reduced row echelon form**. In this form, we can read off the solution to the original system of equations.

Warning: Be careful to use the rref(button (2 r's), and not the ref button (which has only one r).

Your display will show the following.

$$[\,[1\ 0\ 25]$$
$$[0\ 1\ 15]\,]$$

The first line is interpreted as $x = 25$ and the second line as $y = 15$.

Let's now look at a harder example.

$$2x = 7 - 3y$$
$$5y = 5 - 3x$$

First notice that the equations are not "lined up" properly. We fix this by adding $3y$ to each side of the first equation, and adding $3x$ to each side of the second equation.

$$2x + 3y = 7$$
$$3x + 5y = 5$$

Now we press MATRIX, scroll over to EDIT, select [A], input 2 ENTER 3 ENTER followed by 2 ENTER 3 ENTER 7 ENTER 3 ENTER 5 ENTER 5 ENTER. We then push QUIT followed by MATRIX, we scroll over to MATH and select rref(. We press MATRIX again, select [A] and press ENTER. We get the following.

$$[\,[1\ 0\ 20]$$
$$[0\ 1\ -11]\,]$$

In other words, $x = 20$ and $y = -11$

Now you try this one yourself.

$$3x = 3 + 7y$$
$$2y = 5 - 5x$$

Answer: $x = 1, y = 0$

Notes: (1) Make sure that all the variables are on the left-hand sides of the equations, the constants are on the right-hand sides of the equations, and the variables are all lined up correctly (first column x's, second column y's).

(2) This procedure is known in higher mathematics as **Gauss-Jordan Reduction**.

This method works equally well on larger systems of equations. Try to solve the following system using your calculator.

$$2x + 3y - 4z = 2$$
$$x - y + 5z = 6$$
$$3x + 2y - z = 4$$

Answer: $x = -.4, y = 3.6, z = 2$

www.Get800TestPrep.com

Lesson 15
Geometry

Reminder: Before beginning this lesson remember to redo the problems from Lessons 3, 7, and 11 that you have marked off. Do not "unmark" a question unless you get it correct.

The Pythagorean Theorem

The Pythagorean Theorem says that if a right triangle has legs of lengths a and b, and a hypotenuse of length c, then $c^2 = a^2 + b^2$.

Try to answer the following question using the Pythagorean Theorem. **Do not** check the solution until you have attempted this question yourself.

Level 3: Geometry

1. In right triangle ABC below, what is the length of side AB?

   A. $\sqrt{18}$
   B. 6
   C. 8
   D. 16
   E. 64

Solution

* We use the Pythagorean Theorem: $c^2 = a^2 + b^2 = 23 + 41 = 64$. Therefore, $AB = c = 8$, choice **C**.

Distance

There are two methods for finding the distance between two points.

Method 1: Plot the two points, draw a right triangle, and use the Pythagorean Theorem.

Method 2: Use the **distance formula**:

The distance between the two points (s, t) and (u, v) is given by

158

$d = \sqrt{(u-s)^2 + (v-t)^2}$, or equivalently, $d^2 = (u-s)^2 + (v-t)^2$

Example: Let's find the distance between the points $(2,-4)$ and $(-4,4)$.

Solution using a right triangle: Let's plot the two points and form a right triangle.

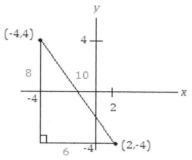

We got the length of the left leg by subtracting $4 - (-4) = 4 + 4 = 8$, and we got the length of the bottom leg by $2 - (-4) = 2 + 4 = 6$. We now use the Pythagorean Theorem: $c^2 = 6^2 + 8^2 = 36 + 64 = 100$. So, $c = \mathbf{10}$.

Remarks: (1) If you recognize that 6, 8, 10 is a multiple of the **Pythagorean triple** 3, 4, 5 (just multiply each number by 2), then you do not need to use the Pythagorean Theorem.

(2) 3, 4, 5 and 5, 12, 13 are the two most common Pythagorean triples.

* Solution using the distance formula:

$d = \sqrt{(-4-2)^2 + (4-(-4))^2} = \sqrt{(-6)^2 + 8^2} = \sqrt{36 + 64} = \sqrt{100} = \mathbf{10}.$

Special Right Triangles

It's useful to know how to draw the following two special triangles.

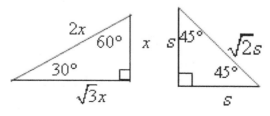

Now try to answer the following question. **Do not** check the solution until you have attempted this question yourself.

LEVEL 4: GEOMETRY

2. In the triangle below, $QR = 8$. What is the area of $\triangle PQR$?

F. $32\sqrt{3}$
G. 32
H. $16\sqrt{3}$
J. 16
K. $8\sqrt{3}$

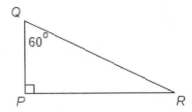

Solution

* Using the special 30, 60, 90 triangle, we can label each side with its length as follows.

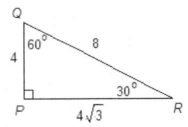

The area is then $A = \frac{1}{2}bh = \frac{1}{2}(4\sqrt{3})(4) = 8\sqrt{3}$, choice **K**.

Note: The hypotenuse of a 30, 60, 90 triangle is always twice the length of the side opposite the 30 degree angle.

Also, if we always think of a side as going with its opposite angle, there will never be any confusion, even if our picture is facing a different direction than we are used to. This is actually good advice for any triangle problem. Always think of a side in terms of its opposite angle and vice versa.

We can also solve this problem using basic trigonometry. Let's do this now.

Important note: Trigonometry will be covered in Lesson 19. If you have trouble understanding the following solution now, you may want to come back to review it after completing Lesson 19.

Solution

Let's label the sides of the triangle.

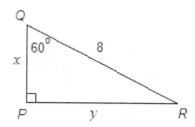

We have $\cos 60° = \frac{\text{ADJ}}{\text{HYP}} = \frac{x}{8}$. So $x = 8 \cos 60°$.

We also have $\sin 60° = \frac{\text{OPP}}{\text{HYP}} = \frac{y}{8}$. So $y = 8 \sin 60°$.

The area of the triangle is

$$\tfrac{1}{2} xy = \tfrac{1}{2} \cdot 8 \cos 60° \cdot 8 \sin 60° = 32 \cdot \tfrac{1}{2} \cdot \tfrac{\sqrt{3}}{2} = 8\sqrt{3}$$

This is choice **K**.

Notes: (1) We can do the computation $\tfrac{1}{2} \cdot 8 \cos 60° \cdot 8 \sin 60°$ right in our calculator to get approximately 13.8564.

We could then put the answer choices in our calculator to see which choice matches that decimal approximation. We see $8\sqrt{3} \approx 13.8564$. So, the answer is choice K.

(2) We could use the special 30, 60, 90 triangle to get

$$\cos 60° = \frac{\text{ADJ}}{\text{HYP}} = \tfrac{1}{2} \quad \text{and} \quad \sin 60° = \frac{\text{OPP}}{\text{HYP}} = \tfrac{\sqrt{3}}{2}$$

So, we have $\tfrac{1}{2} \cdot 8 \cos 60° \cdot 8 \sin 60° = \tfrac{1}{2} \cdot 8 \cdot \tfrac{1}{2} \cdot 8 \cdot \tfrac{\sqrt{3}}{2} = 8\sqrt{3}$, choice K.

(3) When doing trigonometry, we can substitute any value for x in the picture of the 30, 60, 90 triangle that we like, because the x's always cancel. For example, with $x = 1$, we get the picture on the right.

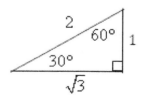

You're doing great! Let's just practice a bit more. Try to solve each of the following problems. The answers to these problems, followed by full solutions are at the end of this lesson. **Do not** look at the answers until you have attempted these problems yourself. Please remember to mark off any problems you get wrong.

LEVEL 2: GEOMETRY

3. The lengths of two sides of right triangle shown below are given in centimeters. The midpoint of $\overline{PR}$ is how many centimeters from R ?

    A. 11
    B. 14
    C. 24
    D. 28
    E. 42

    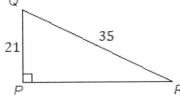

4. If a rectangle measures 63 centimeters by 84 centimeters, what is the length, in centimeters, of a diagonal of the rectangle?

    F. 55
    G. 67
    H. 73.5
    J. 105
    K. 147

5. Square $FORM$, shown below, has side length 7 feet. What is the length, in feet, of $\overline{FR}$?

    A. 49
    B. 28
    C. $7\sqrt{2}$
    D. 7
    E. $2\sqrt{7}$

    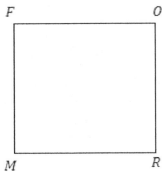

162

LEVEL 3: GEOMETRY

6. In the figure below, what is the area of square *ABCD* ?

   F. 9
   G. 64
   H. 73
   J. $\sqrt{55}$
   K. $\sqrt{73}$

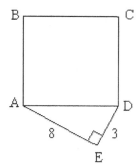

7. A chord 48 meters long is 10 meters from the center of a circle, as shown below. What is the <u>diameter</u> of the circle?

   A. 13
   B. 17
   C. 26
   D. 39
   E. 52

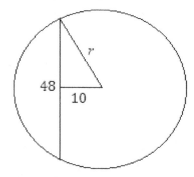

LEVEL 4: GEOMETRY

8. A 50-foot ladder is leaning against a vertical wall so that the base of the ladder is 20 feet away from the base of the wall. To the nearest foot, how far up the wall does the ladder reach?

   F. 45
   G. 46
   H. 47
   J. 48
   K. 49

9. An airplane is flying at a height of 3 miles above the ground. The angle of depression from the airplane to the airport is 60°, as shown in the figure below. What is the distance from the airplane to the airport, in miles?

A. $\frac{\sqrt{3}}{3}$
B. $\frac{\sqrt{3}}{2}$
C. $\sqrt{3}$
D. 6
E. $3\sqrt{3}$

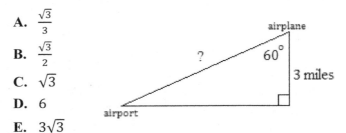

10. What is the area of a square whose diagonal has length $6\sqrt{2}$?

F. 12
G. $12\sqrt{2}$
H. 18
J. 24
K. 36

Answers

1. C
2. K
3. B
4. J
5. C
6. H
7. E
8. G
9. D
10. K

Full Solutions

3.

Solution using the Pythagorean Theorem: We have

$$PR^2 = QR^2 - PQ^2 = 1225 - 441 = 784.$$

So, $PR = \sqrt{784} = 28$.

It follows that the midpoint of PR is $\frac{28}{2} = 14$ cm from R, choice **B**.

Notes: (1) The Pythagorean Theorem $c^2 = a^2 + b^2$ can be written in the form $b^2 = c^2 - a^2$.

In this problem, instead of writing $PR^2 + PQ^2 = QR^2$, we used this new form to write $PR^2 = QR^2 - PQ^2$. Using this form just saves us one step of algebra.

(2) The **midpoint** of a line segment lies midway between the two points of the segment, and thus it splits the segment in half.

* **Solution using a Pythagorean triple:** $21 = 7 \cdot 3$ and $35 = 7 \cdot 5$. It follows that $PR = 7 \cdot 4 = 28$. So, the answer is $\frac{28}{2} = 14$, choice **B**.

Notes: (1) The Pythagorean triple we started with here is 3, 4, 5. Any multiple of a Pythagorean triple is also a Pythagorean triple. Here we multiplied by 7 to get the Pythagorean triple 63, 84, 105.

(2) We divide 28 by 2, because we want only half the length of PR (the midpoint of PR splits the segment in half).

4.
* Let's draw a picture.

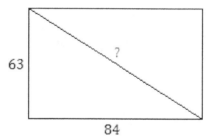

Since $63 = 21 \cdot 3$ and $84 = 21 \cdot 4$, it follows that the length of the diagonal in the figure is $21 \cdot 5 = 105$, choice **J**.

Notes: (1) We started with the Pythagorean triple 3, 4, 5 here. Any multiple of a Pythagorean triple is also a Pythagorean triple. We multiplied this triple by 21 to get the Pythagorean triple 21, 28, 35.

(2) We could also use the Pythagorean Theorem together with our calculator to get that the length of the diagonal is $\sqrt{63^2 + 84^2} = 105$.

5.
The picture looks like this:

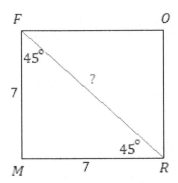

* **Solution using a 45, 45, 90 triangle:** Since all sides of a square have equal length, when we draw a diagonal of a square an isosceles right triangle is formed. An isosceles right triangle is the same as a 45, 45, 90 triangle. So, the diagonal has length $7\sqrt{2}$, choice **C**.

Solution using the Pythagorean Theorem: The length of a diagonal of the square is $\sqrt{7^2 + 7^2} = \sqrt{2 \cdot 7^2} = \sqrt{2} \cdot \sqrt{7^2} = \sqrt{2} \cdot 7 = 7\sqrt{2}$, choice **C**.

6.

* **Solution using the Pythagorean Theorem:** Let x be the length of a side of the square. So $AD = x$. We now use the Pythagorean Theorem.

$$x^2 = 8^2 + 3^2 = 64 + 9 = 73.$$

But x^2 is precisely the area of the square. Therefore, the answer is 73, choice **H**.

7.

* **Solution using a Pythagorean triple:** We have a right triangle with legs $10 = 2 \cdot 5$ and $24 = 2 \cdot 12$. Using the Pythagorean triple 5, 12, 13, we have $r = 2 \cdot 13 = 26$. So, the diameter of the circle is $2 \cdot 26 = 52$, choice **E**.

Notes: (1) To the right is a picture illustrating the solution.

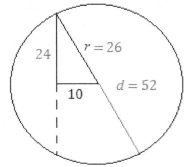

(2) We can also use the Pythagorean Theorem to get r:

$$r^2 = 10^2 + 24^2 = 100 + 576 = 676.$$

So, $r = \sqrt{676} = 26$.

8.
* Let's draw a picture and use the Pythagorean theorem.

$$x^2 = 50^2 - 20^2 = 2500 - 400 = 2100$$

So, $x = \sqrt{2100} \approx 45.826$.

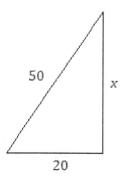

To the nearest foot, this is 46, choice **G**.

Note: We have used the Pythagorean Theorem in the form $b^2 = c^2 - a^2$. See problem 3 for details.

9.
* **Solution using a 30, 60, 90 triangle:** The question is asking for the hypotenuse of the triangle, which is $2 \cdot 3 = 6$, choice **D**.

10.
The picture looks like this:

Solution using a 45, 45, 90 triangle: Since all sides of a square have equal length, an isosceles right triangle is formed. An isosceles right triangle is the same as a 45, 45, 90 triangle. So, the length of a side of the triangle is 6. The area of the square is then $6 \cdot 6 = 36$, choice **K**.

Solution using the Pythagorean Theorem: Since all sides of a square have equal length, an isosceles right triangle is formed. If we let x be the length of a side of the square, then by the Pythagorean Theorem

$$x^2 + x^2 = \left(6\sqrt{2}\right)^2$$
$$2x^2 = 36 \cdot 2$$
$$x^2 = 36$$
$$x = 6$$

Thus, the area of the square is $6 \cdot 6 = 36$, choice **K**.

Remark: We did a bit more work than we had to here. The area of the square is $A = x^2$. We already found that $x^2 = 36$. There was no need to solve this equation for x.

* **Solution using an area formula:** The area of a square is $A = \frac{d^2}{2}$, where d is the length of a diagonal of the square. Therefore, in this problem

$$A = \frac{d^2}{2} = \frac{(6\sqrt{2})^2}{2} = \frac{72}{2} = 36, \text{ choice } \mathbf{K}.$$

OPTIONAL MATERIAL

CHALLENGE QUESTION: GEOMETRY

Derive the area formula $A = \frac{d^2}{2}$ using the more well-known area formula $A = (\text{side})^2$.

Solution to Challenge Question

We begin by drawing a picture.

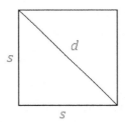

Solution using the Pythagorean Theorem: $d^2 = s^2 + s^2 = 2s^2$. So, $A = s^2 = \frac{d^2}{2}$.

* **Solution using a 45, 45, 90 right triangle:** Note that a 45, 45, 90 triangle is formed in the figure above. Thus, $d = \sqrt{2}s$. Therefore, $s = \frac{d}{\sqrt{2}}$, and $A = s^2 = \left(\frac{d}{\sqrt{2}}\right)^2 = \frac{d^2}{2}$.

Lesson 16
Logic and Sets

Reminder: Before beginning this lesson remember to redo the problems from Lessons 4, 8, and 12 that you have marked off. Do not "unmark" a question unless you get it correct.

The Contrapositive

A statement of the form "if p, then q" is known as a **conditional** statement. An example of such a statement is "If you are a cat, then you have fur." Another common way to say this is "All cats have fur."

There are 3 other statements that often come up in association with a conditional statement. Let's use the example above to illustrate.

Conditional: If you are a cat, then you have fur.
Converse: If you have fur, then you are a cat.
Inverse: If you are not a cat, then you do not have fur.
Contrapositive: If you do not have fur, then you are not a cat.

The most important thing to know for the ACT is that the contrapositive is logically equivalent to the original conditional statement! The converse and inverse are not.

For example, suppose the conditional statement "All cats have fur" is true. You may want to rewrite this as "If you are a cat, then you have fur." It follows that "If you do not have fur, then you are not a cat" is also true.

In particular, if you are given the statement "Skittles does not have fur," you can infer "Skittles is not a cat."

Note that neither the converse nor the inverse is logically equivalent to the original conditional statement, but they are equivalent to each other.

Try to answer the following question using the contrapositive. **Do not** check the solution until you have attempted this question yourself.

Level 2: Logic

All of Jim's friends can ski.

1. If the statement above is true, which of the following statements must also be true?

    A. If John cannot ski, then he is not Jim's friend
    B. If Jeff can ski, then he is not Jim's friend.
    C. If Joseph can ski, then he is Jim's friend.
    D. If James is Jim's friend, then he cannot ski.
    E. If Jordan is not Jim's friend, then he cannot ski.

Solution

* The given statement can be written in conditional form as "If you are Jim's friend, then you can ski." The contrapositive of this statement is "If you cannot ski, then you are not Jim's friend. Replacing "you" with "John" gives the correct answer as choice **A**.

Quantifiers

There are two quantifiers.

The first one is "**For all**," or just "all." Another way to say this is "**Every**."

The second one is "**There exists**." Another way to say this is "**Some**."

The most important thing to know about these quantifiers is how to negate them. You can "pass a *not* through a quantifier by changing the quantifier." Let's look at an example.

The negation of the statement "All pigs have wings" is the statement "Not all pigs have wings." Now let's pass the "not" through the quantifier to get "Some pigs do not have wings." So, the negation of "All pigs have wings" is "Some pigs do not have wings." Similarly, the negation of "Some pigs have wings" is "All pigs do not have wings," or equivalently "No pigs have wings."

The Principle of Double Negation

Note that the negation of the statement "Some pigs have wings" is "All pigs do not have wings." If we negate this statement again, we get "Not every pig does not have wings." So, we see that "Some pigs have wings" is equivalent to "Not every pig does not have wings."

Similarly, the statement "All pigs have wings" is equivalent to "There does not exist a pig that does not have wings."

To summarize, if we apply negation before and after the quantifier, and change the quantifier, we get a statement equivalent to the original.

Sets and Venn diagrams

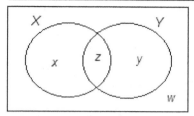

The figure above is a Venn diagram featuring two sets X and Y. Set X has $x + z$ elements, set Y has $y + z$ elements, there are z elements common to X and Y and there are w elements that are in neither X nor Y. Note that x is the number of elements in **only** X and y is the number of elements in **only** Y.

Besides using a Venn diagram, another option is to use the following formula:

Total = X + Y − Both + Neither

Example: There are 30 students in a music class. Of these students, 10 play the piano, 15 play the guitar, and 3 play both the piano and the guitar. How many students in the class do not play either of these two instruments?

Substituting these numbers into the formula, we have

$$30 = 10 + 15 - 3 + N.$$

So, $N = 30 - 22 = \mathbf{8}$.

Alternatively, the Venn diagram would look like this.

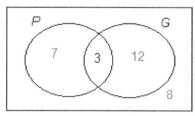

Note that we place the 3 first, then subtract $10 - 3$ to get 7, and $15 - 3$ to get 12. Finally, $30 - 7 - 3 - 12 = \mathbf{8}$.

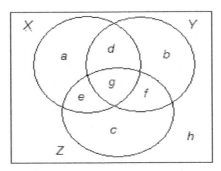

The figure above is a Venn diagram featuring three sets X, Y and Z. Set X has $a + d + e + g$ elements, set Y has $b + d + f + g$ elements, and set Z has $c + e + f + g$ elements. There are $d + g$ elements common to X and Y, there are $e + g$ elements common to X and Z, and there are $f + g$ elements common to Y and Z. Note that a is the number of elements in only X, b is the number of elements in only Y, c is the number of elements in only Z, and g is the number of elements common to X, Y and Z. Finally, h is the number of elements outside of X, Y and Z.

Try to answer the following question. **Do not** check the solution until you have attempted this question yourself.

LEVEL 2: SETS

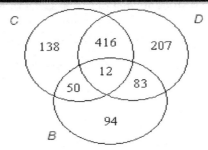

2. 1000 students were polled to determine which of the following animals they had as pets: cats (C), dogs (D), or birds (B). The Venn diagram above shows the results of the poll. How many students said they have exactly 2 of the 3 types of animals?

    F. 133
    G. 416
    H. 439
    J. 549
    K. 561

Solution

* 416 of the students have cats and dogs only.
50 of the students have cats and birds only.
83 of the students have dogs and birds only.

$$416 + 50 + 83 = 549.$$

This is choice **J**.

Try to solve each of the following problems. The answers to these problems, followed by full solutions are at the end of this lesson. **Do not** look at the answers until you have attempted these problems yourself. Please remember to mark off any problems you get wrong.

LEVEL 3: LOGIC AND SETS

3. Let set A consist of the positive multiples of 15 that are less than 70, and let set B consist of the positive multiples of 9 that are less than 70. How many numbers do sets A and B have in common?

   A. 0
   B. 1
   C. 2
   D. 3
   E. 4

4. In a survey, 62 cat owners were asked about two brands of cat food, Brand X and Brand Y. Of the people surveyed, 26 used Brand X, 11 used Brand Y, and 4 used both brands. How many of the people surveyed didn't use either brand of cat food?

   F. 15
   G. 26
   H. 27
   J. 28
   K. 29

5. Let *A* and *B* be two sets of numbers such that every number in *B* is also in *A*. Which of the following CANNOT be true?

   A. If 1 is not in *A*, then 1 is not in *B*.
   B. 2 is in *A*, but not in *B*.
   C. 3 is in *B*, but not in *A*.
   D. 4 is in neither *A* nor *B*.
   E. 5 is in both *A* and *B*.

LEVEL 4: LOGIC AND SETS

If a beverage is listed in menu *A*, it is also listed in menu *B*.

6. If the statement above is true, which of the following statements must also be true?

   F. If a beverage is listed in menu *B*, it is also in menu *A*.
   G. If a beverage is not listed in menu *A*, it is not listed in menu *B*.
   H. If a beverage is not listed in menu *B*, it is not listed in menu *A*.
   J. If a beverage is not listed in menu *B*, it is in menu *A*.
   K. If a beverage is listed in menu *B*, it is not listed in menu *A*.

Some birds in Bryer Park are ducks.

7. If the statement above is true, which of the following statements must also be true?

   A. Every duck is in Bryer Park.
   B. If a bird is not a duck, it is in Bryer Park.
   C. Every bird in Bryer Park is a duck.
   D. All birds in Bryer Park are not ducks.
   E. Not every bird in Bryer Park is not a duck.

8. Set *A* has *a* members, set *B* has *b* members, and set *C* consists of all members that are either in set *A* or set *B* with the exception of the *d* members that are common to both ($d > 0$). Which of the following represents the number of members in set *C* ?

   F. $a + b + d$
   G. $a + b - d$
   H. $a + b + 2d$
   J. $a + b - 2d$
   K. $2a + 2b - 2d$

9. 1000 pet owners were polled to determine which of the following animals they had as pets: cats (C), dogs (D), or birds (B). The Venn diagram below shows the results of the poll except that two of the numbers are missing. If the total number of pet owners polled that said they had dogs as pets is equal to the total number of pet owners polled that said they had birds as pets, how many of the pet owners polled said they have cats as pets?

   A. 169
   B. 335
   C. 380
   D. 501
   E. 513

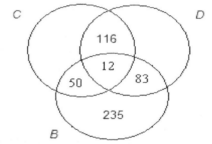

LEVEL 5: LOGIC AND SETS

10. In Dr. Steve's math class, 10 students have dogs and 15 students have cats. If a total of 19 students have only one of these animals, how many students have both dogs and cats?

    F. 1
    G. 2
    H. 3
    J. 4
    K. 6

Answers

1. A   6. H
2. J   7. E
3. B   8. J
4. K   9. E
5. C   10. H

Full Solutions

3.
Solution by listing:

$A = \{15, 30, \mathbf{45}, 60\} \quad B = \{9, 18, 27, 36, \mathbf{45}, 54, 63\}.$

The only number that sets A and B have in common is 45. Therefore, the answer is 1, choice **B**.

* Solution using the least common multiple: The least common multiple of 15 and 9 is 45. So, the numbers that sets A and B have in common are the multiples of 45 less than 70. There is only one such number, 45 itself. So, the answer is 1, choice **B**.

Note: If you are having trouble finding the least common multiple of 15 and 9, see Lesson 17 or the solution to problem 2 from Lesson 1.

4.
* Solution using the formula "Total = X + Y − Both + Neither":

Total = 62, X = 26, Y = 11, and Both = 4.

$62 = 26 + 11 - 4 + \text{Neither} = 33 + \text{Neither}.$

Therefore, Neither = $62 - 33 = 29$, choice **K**.

Solution using a Venn diagram: We draw a Venn diagram

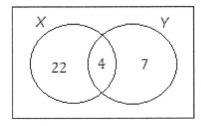

Note that when we draw the diagram we begin with the intersection. This is given to be 4. Now, $26 - 4 = 22$, and $11 - 4 = 7$. Finally, we have

$62 - 22 - 4 - 7 = 29$, choice **K**.

5.

* The given statement can be written in conditional form as "If you are a number in set B, then you are in set A." In particular, if 3 is in B, then 3 is in A. So, the statement in choice **C** cannot be true.

6.

* Simply observe that the statement in choice H is the contrapositive of the given statement. So, the answer is choice **H**.

7.

* **Solution using the principle of double negation:** We negate the statement before and after the quantifier, and change the quantifier "some" to "every" to get choice **E**.

8.

Solution by picking numbers: Let's let $A = \{1, 2\}$ and $B = \{2, 3, 4\}$. Then it follows that $C = \{1, 3, 4\}$. We have $a = 2$, $b = 3$, and $d = 1$. The number of members in set C is **3**.

Now let's check each answer choice, and eliminate any choice that does not come out to 3.

> F. $2 + 3 + 1 = 6$
> G. $2 + 3 - 1 = 4$
> H. $2 + 3 + 2 = 7$
> J. $2 + 3 - 2 = 3$
> K. $4 + 6 - 2 = 8$

Since F, G, H, and K came out incorrect we can eliminate them. Therefore, the answer is choice **J**.

* **Solution using the formula "Total = $X + Y -$ Both + Neither":** The total number of members that are in either set A or set B is $a + b - d$. We need to subtract off the number of members common to both. We get $a + b - d - d = a + b - 2d$, choice **J**.

Remark: It is easy to get tricked in this question. When you add $a + b$ you are counting the number of members common to A and B **twice** (one time for each set). So, we've overcounted by d elements. This is why we have to subtract d to get the total. Note that after we subtract d once, the common elements are still included in the total. We need to subtract d **again** to actually get rid of the common elements.

9.

* The total number of pet owners polled that said they had birds as pets is $235 + 50 + 83 + 12 = 380$. Therefore, the total number of pet owners polled that said they had dogs as pets is 380. So, the missing number in the upper right circle is $380 - 116 - 83 - 12 = 169$. So, the missing number in the upper left is

$$1000 - 169 - 235 - 116 - 50 - 83 - 12 = 335.$$

Thus, the number of pet owners polled that said they have cats as pets is $335 + 50 + 116 + 12 = 513$, choice **E**.

10.

Solution by starting with choice H: Let's start with choice H and guess that 3 students have both dogs and cats. Then $10 - 3 = 7$ students have just dogs, and $15 - 3 = 12$ students have just cats. So, $7 + 12 = 19$ students have only one of these animals. This is correct, and so the answer is 3, choice **H**.

Solution using the formula: We will use the formula Total $= C + D - B$, where C is the number of students that have cats, D is the number of students that have dogs, and B is the number of students that have both. We are given that $C = 10$, $D = 15$, and Total $= 19 + B$ (see the **note** below). So, we have $19 + B = 10 + 15 - B$. Solving for B, we have the following:

$$19 + B = 10 + 15 - B$$
$$19 + B = 25 - B$$
$$2B = 25 - 19$$
$$2B = 6$$
$$B = 3$$

This is choice **H**.

Note: We have used the fact here that the total number of students under consideration is equal to the number of students that have only one of the animals plus the number of students that have both animals.

* **Quick solution:** If we add the number of students that have dogs and the number of students that have cats we get $10 + 15 = 25$. Note that in this total we have counted the students that have both dogs and cats twice. So, if we subtract off the number of students that have only one of these animals we get that $2B = 25 - 19 = 6$, where B is the number of students that have both dogs and cats. So, $B = 3$, choice **H**.

Remark: With a little bit of practice you can do this last computation very quickly in your head (or using your calculator). $\frac{25-19}{2} = 3$.

Algebraic solution: I include this solution for completeness. Let x be the number of students with only cats, z the number of students with only dogs, and y the number of students with both dogs and cats. We are given the following system of equations:

$$x + y = 10$$
$$y + z = 15$$
$$x + z = 19$$

There are several ways to solve this system of equations. One quick way is to add the first two equations, and then subtract the third equation.

$$x + 2y + z = 25$$
$$\underline{x + z = 19}$$
$$2y = 6$$
$$y = 3$$

Exercises: (1) For each of the methods above draw Venn diagrams illustrating each situation.

(2) Try to solve the system of equations given in the algebraic solution in other ways. For example, you can subtract the second equation from the first and then add the third equation. You can also do Gauss–Jordan reduction, etc.

Download additional solutions for free here:

www.satprepget800.com/28LesInt

LESSON 17
NUMBER THEORY

Reminder: Before beginning this lesson remember to redo the problems from Lessons 1, 5, 9, and 13 that you have marked off. Do not "unmark" a question unless you get it correct.

Remainders in Disguise

To solve a problem that asks to find or use a remainder always begin with a number that is evenly divisible.

Try to answer the following question using this strategy. **Do not** check the solution until you have attempted this question yourself.

LEVEL 2: NUMBER THEORY

1. Starting with a blue tile, colored tiles are placed in a row according to the pattern blue, green, yellow, orange, red, purple. If this pattern is repeated, what is the color of the 73rd tile?

    A. Blue
    B. Green
    C. Yellow
    D. Orange
    E. Red

Solution

* We first find an integer as close as possible to 73 that is divisible by 6 (there are six colors in the pattern). We can check this in our calculator. We find that 72 is divisible by 6. Thus, the 72nd tile is purple. So, the 73rd tile is blue, choice **A**.

Notes: (1) Observe that we are cycling through 6 colors. Each of the colors represents a remainder upon division by 6. Blue corresponds with a remainder of 1, green with a remainder of 2, and so on. Note that when we divide by 6, we CANNOT get 6 as a remainder. Purple corresponds with a remainder of 0.

(2) We can use the calculator algorithm introduced in the solution to problem 8 from Lesson 5. Here are the steps for this example:

Step 1: Perform the division in your calculator: $73/6 \approx 12.1666667$
Step 2: Multiply the integer part of this answer by the divisor:
$$12 \cdot 6 = 72$$
Step 3: Subtract this result from the dividend to get the remainder:
$$73 - 72 = \mathbf{1}$$

A remainder of 1 corresponds with a blue tile, choice A.

Prime Factorization

The Fundamental Theorem of Arithmetic: Every integer greater than 1 can be written "uniquely" as a product of primes.

The word "uniquely" is written in quotes because prime factorizations are only unique if we agree to write the primes in increasing order.

For example, 6 can be written as $2 \cdot 3$ or as $3 \cdot 2$. But these two factorizations are the same except that we changed the order of the factors. To make things as simple as possible we always agree to use the **canonical representation**. The word "canonical" is just a fancy name for "natural," and the most natural way to write a prime factorization is in increasing order of primes. So, the canonical representation of 6 is $2 \cdot 3$.

As another example, the canonical representation of 18 is $2 \cdot 3 \cdot 3$. We can tidy this up a bit by rewriting $3 \cdot 3$ as 3^2. So, the canonical representation of 18 is $2 \cdot 3^2$.

If you are new to factoring, you may find it helpful to draw a factor tree.

For example, here is a factor tree for 18:

$$
\begin{array}{c}
18 \\
\swarrow \searrow \\
\boxed{2} \quad 9 \\
\swarrow \searrow \\
\boxed{3} \quad \boxed{3}
\end{array}
$$

To draw this tree, we started by writing 18 as the product 2 · 9. We put a box around 2 because 2 is prime, and does not need to be factored anymore. We then proceeded to factor 9 as 3 · 3. We put a box around each 3 because 3 is prime. We now see that we are done, and the prime factorization can be found by multiplying all the boxed numbers together. Remember that we will usually want the canonical representation, so write the final product in increasing order of primes.

By the Fundamental Theorem of Arithmetic above it does not matter how we factor the number – we will always get the same canonical form. For example, here is a different factor tree for 18:

Quick Exercise: Write each of the following numbers as a product of prime factors (in canonical form).

6   7   9   13   21   30   44   693   67,500   384,659   9,699,690

Answers

$6 = 2 \cdot 3$, $7 = 7$, $9 = 3^2$, $13 = 13$, $21 = 3 \cdot 7$, $30 = 2 \cdot 3 \cdot 5$, $44 = 2^2 \cdot 11$, $693 = 3^2 \cdot 7 \cdot 11$, $67,500 = 2^2 \cdot 3^3 \cdot 5^4$, $384,659 = 11^3 \cdot 17^2$, $9,699,690 = 2 \cdot 3 \cdot 5 \cdot 7 \cdot 11 \cdot 13 \cdot 17 \cdot 19$

GCD and LCM

The **greatest common divisor (gcd)** of a set of positive integers is the largest positive integer that each integer in the set is divisible by. The **least common multiple (lcm)** of a set of positive integers is the smallest positive integer that is divisible by each integer in the set.

Example 1: Find the gcd and lcm of {9, 15}.

Method 1: The factors of 9 are 1, 3 and 9. The factors of 15 are 1, 3, 5 and 15. So the common factors of 9 and 15 are 1 and 3. So, $\gcd(9,15) = $ **3**.

The multiples of 9 are 9, 18, 27, 36, 45, 54, 63,... and the multiples of 15 are 15, 30, 45,... We can stop at 45 because 45 is also a multiple of 9. So lcm(9,15) = **45**.

Method 2: The prime factorizations of 9 and 15 are $9 = 3^2$ and $15 = 3 \cdot 5$. To find the gcd, we multiply together the smallest powers of each prime from both factorizations, and for the lcm, we multiply the highest powers of each prime. So gcd(9,15) = **3** and lcm(9,15) = $3^2 \cdot 5$ = **45**.

Note: If you have trouble seeing where the gcd and lcm are coming from here, it may help to insert the "missing" primes. In this case, 5 is missing from the factorization of 9. So, it might help to write $9 = 3^2 \cdot 5^0$. Now we can think of the gcd as $3^1 \cdot 5^0 = 3$.

Method 3: On your TI-84 calculator press MATH, scroll right to NUM. For the gcd press 9, type 9, 15 and press ENTER. You will see an output of **3**. For the lcm press 8, type 9, 15 and press ENTER for an output of **45**.

Example 2: Find the gcd and lcm of {100, 270}.

The prime factorizations of 100 and 270 are $100 = 2^2 \cdot 5^2$ and $270 = 2 \cdot 3^3 \cdot 5$. So,

$\gcd(100, 270) = 2 \cdot 5 =$ **10** and $\text{lcm}(100, 270) = 2^2 \cdot 3^3 \cdot 5^2 =$ **2700**.

Note: If we insert the "missing" primes in the prime factorization of 100 we get $100 = 2^2 \cdot 3^0 \cdot 5^2$. So we can think of the gcd as

$$2^1 \cdot 3^0 \cdot 5^1 = 10.$$

You're doing great! Let's just practice a bit more. Try to solve each of the following problems. The answers to these problems, followed by full solutions are at the end of this lesson. **Do not** look at the answers until you have attempted these problems yourself. Please remember to mark off any problems you get wrong.

LEVEL 1: NUMBER THEORY

2. What is the least common multiple of 3, 6, 7, 14, and 21 ?

    F. 168
    G. 126
    H. 84
    J. 42
    K. 28

3. What is the greatest common divisor of 10, 15, 25, and 45 ?

    A. 1
    B. 3
    C. 5
    D. 10
    E. 15

LEVEL 2: NUMBER THEORY

4. What is the least common denominator when adding the fractions $\frac{x}{2}, \frac{y}{5}, \frac{z}{25}$, and $\frac{w}{35}$?

    F. 50
    G. 70
    H. 175
    J. 350
    K. 8750

LEVEL 3: NUMBER THEORY

5. What is the largest positive integer value of k for which 7^k divides 98^{15} ?

    A. 2
    B. 7
    C. 15
    D. 28
    E. 30

6. Lisa is making a bracelet. She starts with 3 yellow beads, 5 purple beads, and 4 white beads, in that order, and repeats the pattern until there is no more room on the bracelet. If the last bead is purple, which of the following could be the total number of beads on the bracelet?

   F. 81
   G. 85
   H. 87
   J. 88
   K. 93

LEVEL 4: NUMBER THEORY

7. If m and n are positive integers such that the greatest common factor of m^3n and m^2n^2 is 175, then which of the following could m equal?

   A. 5
   B. 7
   C. 25
   D. 35
   E. 175

8. What is the least positive integer greater than 3 that leaves a remainder of 3 when divided by both 6 and 9?

   F. 6
   G. 18
   H. 21
   J. 54
   K. 57

9. In the repeating decimal $0.\overline{123456} = 0.123456123456123\ldots$ where the digits 123456 repeat, which digit is in the 2000th place to the right of the decimal?

   A. 1
   B. 2
   C. 3
   D. 4
   E. 5

10. When the positive integer k is divided by 8 the remainder is 5. When the positive integer m is divided by 8 the remainder is 7. What is the remainder when the product km is divided by 4 ?

F. 0
G. 1
H. 2
J. 3
K. 4

Definitions Used in This Lesson

Definitions of the **integers**, the **positive integers, consecutive integers, divisibility, least common multiple,** and **greatest common divisor** can be found in Lesson 1.

Answers

1. A
2. J
3. C
4. J
5. E

6. J
7. A
8. H
9. B
10. J

Full Solutions

2.

Solution by plugging in answer choices: Begin by looking at choice K since it is the least. 28 is not divisible by 21, and so we can eliminate choice K.

Let's check choice J next. We use our calculator to compute the following:

$$\frac{42}{3} = 14 \quad \frac{42}{6} = 7 \quad \frac{42}{7} = 6 \quad \frac{42}{14} = 3 \quad \frac{42}{21} = 2$$

Since these are all integers, the answer is choice **J**.

* **Quick calculator solution:** Your calculator can only do two at a time. So, compute $\text{lcm}(3,6) = 6$, $\text{lcm}(6,7) = 42$, $\text{lcm}(42,14) = 42$, and then $\text{lcm}(42,21) = 42$, choice **J**.

3.

Solution by plugging in answer choices: Begin by looking at choice E since it is the greatest. 25 is not divisible by 15, and so we can eliminate E.

Similarly, 15 is not divisible by 10, and so we can eliminate choice D.

Let's check choice C next. We use our calculator to compute the following:

$$\frac{10}{5} = 2 \quad \frac{15}{5} = 3 \quad \frac{25}{5} = 5 \quad \frac{45}{5} = 9$$

Since these are all integers, the answer is choice **C**.

Note that the three given integers are all divisible by 1, but choice A is not the answer because 5 is greater.

* Quick calculator solution: Your calculator can only do two at a time. So, compute $\gcd(10, 15) = 5$, $\gcd(5, 25) = 5$, and then $\gcd(5, 45) = 5$, choice **C**.

Direct solution: $10 = 2 \cdot 5$, $15 = 3 \cdot 5$, $25 = 5^2$, $45 = 3^2 \cdot 5$. So $\gcd(10, 15, 25, 45) = 5$, choice **C**.

4.

* Direct solution: We want the least common multiple of 2, 5, 25, and 35. This is $2 \cdot 5^2 \cdot 7 = 350$, choice **J**.

Notes: (1) The **least common denominator** of a set of fractions is simply the lcm (least common multiple) of the denominators of those fractions.

In this question, the set of denominators is $\{2, 5, 25, 35\}$, and so we are looking for $\text{lcm}(2, 5, 25, 35)$.

(2) To compute $\text{lcm}(2, 5, 25, 35)$, use any of the three methods given in Example 1 above.

Note that if we use the calculator method (method 3), then we have to do two at a time. So, we compute $\text{lcm}(2, 5) = 10$, $\text{lcm}(10, 25) = 50$, and then $\text{lcm}(50, 35) = 350$.

5.

Direct solution: The prime factorization of 98 is $98 = 2 \cdot 7^2$. Therefore,

$$98^{15} = (2 \cdot 7^2)^{15} = 2^{15}(7^2)^{15} = 2^{15} \cdot 7^{30}.$$

From this prime factorization, it should be clear that 7^{30} divides 98^{15}, but 7^{31} does not, choice **E**.

For a review of the basic laws of exponents used here see Lesson 10.

* **Solution by starting with choice E:** Pull out your calculator. Since the question has the word **"largest"** in it, we will start with the largest answer choice which is choice E, and we will divide 98^{15} by 7^{30}. We type 98^15 / 7^30 into our calculator and the output is an integer. So, the answer is choice **E**.

Note that all five answer choices give an integer, but 30 is the largest positive integer that works.

6.

* There are 12 beads before the sequence begins repeating. The 4th, 5th, 6th, 7th and 8th bead are each purple. So, when we divide the total number of beads by 12 the remainder should be a number between 4 and 8, inclusive. Since 84 is divisible by 12, 88 gives a remainder of 4 when divided by 12. So, the answer is choice **J**.

7.

* $175 = 5^2 \cdot 7$. So, we can let $m = 5$, choice **A**.

Notes: (1) If we let $m = 5$ and $n = 7$, then we have $m^3 n = 5^3 \cdot 7$ and $m^2 n^2 = 5^2 \cdot 7^2$. It follows that the greatest common factor of these two numbers is $5^2 \cdot 7 = 175$.

(2) "greatest common factor" (or gcf) is the same thing as "greatest common divisor" (or gcd).

8.

* We first find the least common multiple of 6 and 9, which is 18. We now simply add the remainder: $18 + 3 = 21$, choice **H**.

Note: To compute $\text{lcm}(6, 9)$, use any of the three methods given in Example 1 above.

9.

* Since there are exactly 6 digits before repeating we look for the remainder when 2000 is divided by 6. To do this, we first find an integer as close to 2000 as possible that is divisible by 6. We check this in our calculator.

$$2000/6 \approx 333.333$$
$$1999/6 \approx 333.167$$
$$1998/6 = 333$$

So, 1998 is divisible by 6 and therefore 2000 gives a remainder of 2 when divided by 6. So, the digit in the 2000th place is the same as the digit in the second place to the right of the decimal point. This is 2, choice **B**.

10.

* Solution by picking numbers: Let's choose a positive integer k whose remainder is 5 when it is divided by 8. A simple way to find such a k is to add 8 and 5. So, let $k = 13$. Similarly, let's let $m = 8 + 7 = 15$. Then we have $km = 13 \cdot 15 = 195$. 4 goes into 195 forty-eight times with a remainder of 3, choice **J**.

Note: We can make this problem even simpler by choosing $k = 5$ and $m = 7$. It then follows that $km = 5 \cdot 7 = 35$, and the remainder when we divide this product by 4 is **3**. See problem 8 in Lesson 5 for more information.

Algebraic solution: The given conditions mean that we can write k and m as $k = 8s + 5$ and $m = 8t + 7$ for some integers s and t. Then
$$km = (8s + 5)(8t + 7)$$
$$= 64st + 56s + 40t + 35$$
$$= 4(16st) + 4(14s) + 4(10t) + 4(8) + 3$$
$$= 4(16st + 14s + 10t + 8) + 3$$
$$= 4z + 3$$
where z is the integer $16st + 14s + 10t + 8$. This shows that when km is divided by 4 the remainder is 3, choice **J**.

Note: See problem 8 in Lesson 5 for more information and additional solutions for this type of problem.

OPTIONAL MATERIAL

The following questions will test your understanding of definitions used in this lesson. These are **not** in the format of ACT questions.

1. Which of the following integers are divisible by 6? Choose all that apply: 1   12   9   6   0   −5   −18   100   −3

2. Which of the following integers are divisors of 24? Choose all that apply: 1   2   0   −5   3   −8   24   48   −12   −24   −48

3. Find the gcd and lcm of each set of positive integers.

{4, 6}   {12, 180}   {2, 3, 5}   {14, 21, 77}   {720, 2448, 5400}

Answers

1. 12, 6, 0, −18
2. 1, 2, 3, −8, 24, −12, −24
3. gcd(4, 6) = 2   lcm(4, 6) = 12
   gcd(12, 180) = 12   lcm(12, 180) = 180,
   gcd(2, 3, 5) = 1   lcm(2, 3, 5) = 30
   gcd(14, 21, 77) = 7   lcm(14, 21, 77) = 462,
   gcd(720, 2448, 5400) = 72   lcm(720, 2448, 5400) = 183,600

Further Explanation

1. 12 is divisible by 6 because $12 = 6 \cdot 2$.
6 is divisible by 6 because $6 = 6 \cdot 1$.
0 is divisible by 6 because $0 = 6 \cdot 0$.
−18 is divisible by 6 because $-18 = 6(-3)$.

2. 1 is a divisor of 24 because $24 = 1 \cdot 24$.
−24 is a divisor of 24 because $24 = (-24)(-1)$.
0 is **not** a divisor of 24 because $0 \cdot k = 0 \neq 24$ for all integers k.

3. $4 = 2^2, 6 = 2 \cdot 3$
   $12 = 2^2 \cdot 3, 180 = 2^2 \cdot 3^2 \cdot 5$
   $14 = 2 \cdot 7, 21 = 3 \cdot 7, 77 = 7 \cdot 11$
   $720 = 2^4 \cdot 3^2 \cdot 5, 2448 = 2^4 \cdot 3^2 \cdot 17, 5400 = 2^3 \cdot 3^3 \cdot 5^2$

LESSON 18
ALGEBRA

Reminder: Before beginning this lesson remember to redo the problems from Lessons 2, 6, 10, and 14 that you have marked off. Do not "unmark" a question unless you get it correct.

Square Root Property

The **square root property** says that if $x^2 = a^2$, then $x = \pm a$.

For example, the equation $x^2 = 16$ has the two solutions $x = 4$ and $x = -4$.

Important note: Using the square root property is different from taking a square root. We apply the square root property to an equation of the form $x^2 = a^2$ to get two solutions, whereas when we take the positive square root of a number we get just one answer.

For example, when we take the positive square root of 16 we get 4, i.e. $\sqrt{16} = 4$. But when we apply the square root property to the equation $x^2 = 16$, we have seen that we get the two solutions $x = 4$ and $x = -4$.

Example: Solve the equation $(x-5)^2 = 3$ using the square root property.

Solution: When we apply the square root property we get $x - 5 = \pm\sqrt{3}$. We then add 5 to each side of this last equation to get the two solutions $x = 5 \pm \sqrt{3}$.

Solving Quadratic Equations

A quadratic equation has the form $ax^2 + bx + c = 0$.

Let's use a simple example to illustrate the various methods for solving such an equation.

LEVEL 3: ALGEBRA

1. In the quadratic equation $x^2 - 2x = 15$, find the positive solution for x.

   A. 1
   B. 2
   C. 3
   D. 4
   E. 5

Solution by starting with choice C: Let's start with choice C and guess that $x = 3$. Then $3^2 - 2 \cdot 3 = 9 - 6 = 3$. This is too small.

Let's try choice E next and guess that $x = 5$. In this case, we get $5^2 - 2 \cdot 5 = 25 - 10 = 15$. This is correct. So, the answer is choice **E**.

Solution by factoring: We bring everything to the left-hand side of the equation to get $x^2 - 2x - 15 = 0$. We then factor the left-hand side to get $(x - 5)(x + 3) = 0$. So, $x - 5 = 0$ or $x + 3 = 0$. It follows that $x = 5$ or $x = -3$. Since we want the positive solution for x, the answer is 5, choice **E**.

Solution by using the quadratic formula: As in the last solution we bring everything to the left-hand side of the equation to get

$$x^2 - 2x - 15 = 0.$$

We identify $a = 1$, $b = -2$, and $c = -15$.

$$x = \frac{-b \pm \sqrt{b^2 - 4ac}}{2a} = \frac{2 \pm \sqrt{4 + 60}}{2} = \frac{2 \pm \sqrt{64}}{2} = \frac{2 \pm 8}{2} = 1 \pm 4.$$

So, we get $x = 1 + 4 = 5$ or $x = 1 - 4 = -3$. Since we want the positive solution for x, the answer is 5, choice **E**.

Graphical solution: In your graphing calculator press the Y= button, and enter the following.

$$Y1 = X^{\wedge}2 - 2X - 15$$

Now press ZOOM 6 to graph the parabola in a standard window. Then press 2nd TRACE (which is CALC) 2 (or select ZERO), move the cursor just to the left of the second x-intercept and press ENTER. Now move the cursor just to the right of the second x-intercept and press ENTER again.

Press ENTER once more, and you will see that the x-coordinate of the second x-intercept is 5, choice **E**.

The Discriminant

As we just saw in the third solution to problem 1, the quadratic equation $ax^2 + bx + c = 0$ can be solved using the quadratic formula:

$$x = \frac{-b \pm \sqrt{b^2 - 4ac}}{2a}$$

The expression under the square root is called the discriminant of the quadratic equation. In other words, the **discriminant** of the quadratic equation $ax^2 + bx + c = 0$ is defined as

$$\Delta = b^2 - 4ac$$

Although computing the discriminant of a quadratic equation does not give the roots (solutions) of the equation, it does give us a lot of information about the nature of the roots and the graph of the equation.

If **Δ = 0** (i.e., the discriminant is 0), then the quadratic formula simplifies to $x = -\frac{b}{2a}$, and we see that there is just one solution to the quadratic equation.

Graphically, this means that the graph of the function $y = ax^2 + bx + c$ is a parabola that intersects the x-axis at one point.

Additionally, if the coefficients a and b are integers, then the unique solution will be a rational number.

Example: Find the discriminant of $x^2 + 6x + 9 = 0$. Then describe the nature of the roots of the equation, and describe the graph of the function $y = x^2 + 6x + 9$.

Solution: In this question, we have $a = 1$, $b = 6$, and $c = 9$. So, the discriminant is

$$\Delta = b^2 - 4ac = 6^2 - 4(1)(9) = 36 - 36 = 0.$$

It follows that the roots of the quadratic equation are equal (in other words, there is really just one root) and rational (a fraction, where the numerator and denominator are both integers).

The graph of the function $y = x^2 + 6x + 9$ is an upward facing parabola that intersects the x-axis at one point.

Notes: (1) The unique rational root of this quadratic equation is

$$x = -\frac{b}{2a} = -\frac{6}{2} = -3.$$

This means that the only x-intercept of the parabola is the point $(-3, 0)$. In this case, this point also happens to be the vertex of the parabola.

(2) The discriminant does not tell us if the parabola opens upwards or downwards. However, this is easy to determine simply by looking at the value of a.

If $a > 0$ (i.e. a is a positive number), then the parabola opens upwards.

If $a < 0$ (i.e. a is a negative number), then the parabola opens downwards.

In this problem, we know that the parabola opens upwards because $a = 1 > 0$.

(3) It is very easy to also find the y-intercept of the parabola. We simply substitute 0 in for x into the equation. So, we get $y = 9$. It follows that the y-intercept of the parabola is the point $(0, 9)$.

(4) Now that we know the x-intercepts, y-intercept, and vertex of the parabola, and we know that the parabola opens upwards, it's very easy to sketch the graph. I leave it to the reader to draw a nice sketch.

If $\Delta > 0$ (i.e., the discriminant is positive), we wind up with a positive number under the square root in the quadratic formula. The square root of a positive number is a real number. We therefore wind up with the two real solutions

$$x = \frac{-b \pm \sqrt{b^2 - 4ac}}{2a}$$

Graphically, this means that the graph of the function $y = ax^2 + bx + c$ is a parabola that intersects the x-axis at two points.

If the discriminant also happens to be a perfect square (such as 1, 4, 9, 16, etc.), then both solutions will be rational numbers.

If $\Delta < 0$ (i.e., the discriminant is negative), we wind up with a negative number under the square root in the quadratic formula. The square root of a negative number is an imaginary number. We therefore get two complex solutions.

Graphically, this means that the graph of the function $y = ax^2 + bx + c$ is a parabola that does not intersect the x-axis.

The following picture gives a sample graph of each of the three cases we just discussed.

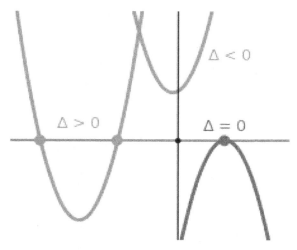

Advanced Factoring

Recall from Lesson 6 that the **distributive property** says that for all real numbers a, b, and c, $a(b + c) = ab + ac$

When we use the distributive property in the opposite direction, we usually call it **factoring**: $ab + ac = a(b + c)$

Here are some more sophisticated techniques for factoring:

The Difference of Two Squares: $a^2 - b^2 = (a - b)(a + b)$

Examples: (1) $x^2 - 9 = (x - 3)(x + 3)$

(2) $4x^2 - 25y^2 = (2x - 5y)(2x + 5y)$

(3) $36 - 49x^2y^2 = (6 - 7xy)(6 + 7xy)$

Trinomial Factoring: $x^2 - (a + b)x + ab = (x - a)(x - b)$

Examples: (1) $x^2 - 5x + 6 = (x - 2)(x - 3)$

(2) $x^2 - 2x - 35 = (x - 7)(x + 5)$

(3) $x^2 + 14x + 33 = (x + 3)(x + 11)$

LEVEL 3: ALGEBRA

2. Which of the following is equivalent to the following expression?
$$16b^2 - 4a^2$$
   F. $(4b - 2a)^2$
   G. $(4b + 2a)^2$
   H. $(b - a)(16b + 4a)$
   J. $(4b - 2a)(4b + 2a)$
   K. $4b - 2a$

Solution

$16b^2 - 4a^2 = (4b - 2a)(4b + 2a)$, choice **J**.

Notes: (1) The positive square root of $16b^2$ is $4b$, and the positive square root of $4a^2$ is $2a$.

(2) This problem can also be solved by picking numbers. I leave this solution to the reader.

Sum and Product of Roots of a Quadratic Function

Let r and s be the roots of the quadratic equation $x^2 + bx + c = 0$. Then
$$b = -(r + s) \quad \text{and} \quad c = rs.$$

Try to answer the following question using these formulas. **Do not** check the solution until you have attempted this question yourself.

LEVEL 3: ALGEBRA

3. What is the sum and product of the two solutions of the equation $x^2 - 3x + 8 = 0$?

   A. sum = -3, product = 8
   B. sum = 3, product = 8
   C. sum = 3, product = -8
   D. sum = -8, product = -3
   E. sum = 8, product = 3

Solution

* We have $b = -3$ and $c = 8$. So, the sum is $-b = -(-3) = 3$ and the product is $c = 8$, choice **B**.

Remark: In plain English, the product of the solutions is equal to the constant term (in this case 8), and the sum of the solutions is the negative of the coefficient of x (in this case, the coefficient of x is -3, and therefore the sum of the solutions is $-(-3) = 3$).

LEVEL 2: ALGEBRA

$$ax - bx + cx - dx$$

4. For all real numbers a, b, c, and d, the expression above can be written as the product of x and which of the following?

   F. $-a + b - c + d$
   G. $-a + b - c - d$
   H. $-a - b - c - d$
   J. $a - b + c - d$
   K. $a + b + c + d$

LEVEL 3: ALGEBRA

5. Which of the following best describes the nature of the roots of the equation $x^2 + 8x + 7 = 0$?

   A. real, rational, unequal
   B. real, irrational, unequal
   C. real, rational, equal
   D. real, irrational, equal
   E. complex

6. Which of the following expressions is a factor of the polynomial $x^2 - x - 90$?

   F. $x - 7$
   G. $x - 8$
   H. $x - 9$
   J. $x - 10$
   K. $x - 11$

LEVEL 4: ALGEBRA

7. Which of the following best describes the graph of the function $y = x^2 + 4x + 8 = 0$?

   A. an upward facing parabola that intersects the x-axis twice
   B. an upward facing parabola that intersects the x-axis once
   C. an upward facing parabola that does not intersect the x-axis
   D. a downward facing parabola that intersects the x-axis once
   E. a downward facing parabola that does not intersect the x-axis

8. Which of the following expressions is a factor of $x^3 - 125$?

   F. $x - 5$
   G. $x + 5$
   H. $x + 125$
   J. $x^2 + 25$
   K. $x^2 - 5x + 25$

9. In the equation below, n and k are constants. If the equation is true for all values of x, what is the value of k ?

   $$(x - n)(x - 9) = x^2 - 4nx + k$$

   A. 3
   B. 6
   C. 9
   D. 27
   E. 54

LEVEL 5: ALGEBRA

10. You are given the following system of equations.
$$dx + ey = f$$
$$y = x^2$$
where d, e, and f are integers. For which of the following will there be more than one (x, y) solution, with real-number coordinates for the system?

F. $e^2 + 4df < 0$
G. $e^2 - 4df < 0$
H. $d^2 + 4ef < 0$
J. $e^2 - 4df > 0$
K. $d^2 + 4ef > 0$

Answers

1. E
2. J
3. B
4. J
5. A

6. J
7. C
8. F
9. D
10. K

Full Solutions

4.
* $ax - bx + cx - dx = x(a - b + c - d)$. So, the answer is choice **J**.

5.
* We have $a = 1$, $b = 8$, and $c = 7$. So, the discriminant is
$$\Delta = b^2 - 4ac = 8^2 - 4(1)(7) = 64 - 28 = 36.$$
Since the discriminant is positive, it follows that the two roots of the quadratic equation are distinct real numbers. Furthermore, since 36 is a perfect square ($6^2 = 36$), the roots are rational. It follows that the answer is choice **A**.

Notes: (1) In this example, we can easily find the two roots of the equation by factoring:
$$x^2 + 8x + 7 = 0$$
$$(x + 1)(x + 7) = 0$$
$$x + 1 = 0 \quad \text{or} \quad x + 7 = 0$$
$$x = -1 \quad \text{or} \quad x = -7$$

So, the two roots are -1 and -7.

(2) The graph of the function $y = x^2 + 8x + 7$ is an upward facing parabola that intersects the x-axis at two points. We know that the parabola opens upwards because $a = 1 > 0$.

6.
* Quick solution: $x^2 - x - 90 = (x - 10)(x + 9)$. So $x - 10$ is a factor and the answer is choice **J**.

Solution using the factor theorem: $10^2 - 10 - 90 = 100 - 100 = 0$. So $x - 10$ is a factor of $x^2 - x - 90$, choice **J**.

Note: The **factor theorem** says that r is a root of the polynomial $p(x)$ if and only if $x - r$ is a factor of the polynomial.

In this question, the polynomial is $p(x) = x^2 - x - 90$, and we saw that $p(10) = 0$. So 10 is a root of the polynomial, and therefore by the factor theorem, $x - 10$ is a factor of the polynomial.

7.
* We have $a = 1$, $b = 4$, and $c = 8$. So, the discriminant is

$$\Delta = b^2 - 4ac = 4^2 - 4(1)(8) = 16 - 32 = -16.$$

Since the discriminant is negative, it follows that the two roots of the quadratic equation are distinct complex numbers, and therefore the graph of the function is an upward facing parabola that does not intersect the x-axis, choice **C**.

Notes: (1) In this example, we can find the two complex solutions of the quadratic equation by using the quadratic formula or by completing the square. I leave it as an exercise to show that the two solutions are $-2 + 2i$ and $-2 - 2i$.

(2) Notice that the two solutions are complex conjugates of each other. This will always happen when the discriminant is negative. For more information on complex conjugates, see Lesson 9.

(3) We know that the parabola opens upwards because $a = 1 > 0$.

8.
* Solution using the factor theorem: $5^3 - 125 = 125 - 125 = 0$. So, $x - 5$ is a factor of $x^3 - 125$, choice **F**.

Note: See the solution to problem 6 for a description of the factor theorem.

In this question, the polynomial is $p(x) = x^3 - 125$, and we saw that $p(5) = 0$. So, 5 is a root of the polynomial, and therefore by the factor theorem, $x - 5$ is a factor of the polynomial.

9.
* **Quick solution:** The left-hand side is 0 when $x = 9$ and $x = n$. The coefficient of x is the negative of the sum of these roots, and so $4n = n + 9$, or $3n = 9$. So, $n = 3$. The constant term is the product of these roots, so that $k = 9 \cdot 3 = 27$, choice **D**.

Solution by picking numbers: Let's plug in some simple values for x.

$x = 0$: $9n = k$
$x = 9$: $0 = 81 - 36n + k$

Substituting $9n$ for k in the second equation yields $0 = 81 - 27n$, so that $27n = 81$, and $n = \frac{81}{27} = 3$. Finally, $k = 9n = 9 \cdot 3 = 27$, choice **D**.

Algebraic solution: Multiply out the left-hand side (FOIL) to get
$$x^2 - 9x - nx + 9n = x^2 - (9 + n)x + 9n.$$
Setting the coefficient of x on the left equal to the coefficient of x on the right yields $-(9 + n) = -4n$, or $9 + n = 4n$, or $3n = 9$. So, $n = 3$. Equating the constant terms on left and right yields $9n = k$. Substituting 3 in for n gives $k = 9 \cdot 3 = 27$, choice **D**.

10.
* By the second equation, we have $y = x^2$, so we can replace y by x^2 in the first equation to get
$$dx + ex^2 = f.$$
Writing this quadratic equation in general form gives the following.
$$ex^2 + dx - f = 0.$$
So, we have $a = e$, $b = d$, and $c = -f$. Thus, the discriminant is
$$\Delta = b^2 - 4ac = d^2 - 4e(-f) = d^2 + 4ef.$$
We want the quadratic equation to have two real solutions. Therefore, the discriminant must be positive. So, we must have $d^2 + 4ef > 0$, choice **K**.

OPTIONAL MATERIAL

Completing the Square

Completing the square is a technique with many useful applications. We complete the square on an expression of the form $x^2 + bx$

To complete the square, we simply take half of b, and then square the result. In other words, we get $\left(\frac{b}{2}\right)^2$.

The expression $x^2 + bx + \left(\frac{b}{2}\right)^2$ is always a perfect square. In fact,

$$x^2 + bx + \left(\frac{b}{2}\right)^2 = \left(x + \frac{b}{2}\right)^2$$

For example, let's complete the square in the expression $x^2 + 6x$.

Well half of 6 is 3, and when we square 3 we get 9. So, the new expression is $x^2 + 6x + 9$ which factors as $(x + 3)^2$.

Important notes: (1) When we complete the square we usually get an expression that is <u>not</u> equal to the original expression. For example, $x^2 + 6x \neq x^2 + 6x + 9$.

(2) The coefficient of x^2 <u>must</u> be 1 before we complete the square. So, for example, we cannot complete the square on the expression $2x^2 + 32x$.

But we can first factor out the 2 to get $2(x^2 + 16x)$, and then complete the square on the expression $x^2 + 16x$ to get $2(x^2 + 16x + 64)$.

Note that we increased the expression by $2 \cdot 64 = 128$.

Example: In the quadratic equation $x^2 - 2x = 15$, find the positive solution for x by completing the square.

Solution

We take half of -2, which is -1, and square this number to get 1. We then add 1 to each side of the equation to get $x^2 - 2x + 1 = 15 + 1$. This is equivalent to $(x - 1)^2 = 16$. We now apply the square root property to get $x - 1 = \pm 4$. So $x = 1 \pm 4$. This yields the two solutions $1 + 4 = 5$, and $1 - 4 = -3$. We want the positive solution for x, so the answer is **5**.

LESSON 19
TRIGONOMETRY

Reminder: Before beginning this lesson remember to redo the problems from Lessons 3, 7, 11, and 15 that you have marked off. Do not "unmark" a question unless you get it correct.

Right Triangle Trigonometry

Let's consider the following right triangle, and let's focus our attention on angle A.

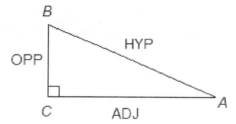

Note that the **hypotenuse** is ALWAYS the side opposite the right angle.

The other two sides of the right triangle, called the **legs**, depend on which angle is chosen. In this picture we chose to focus on angle A. Therefore, the opposite side is BC, and the adjacent side is AC.

It is worth memorizing how to compute the three basic trig functions:

$$\sin A = \frac{\text{OPP}}{\text{HYP}} \qquad \cos A = \frac{\text{ADJ}}{\text{HYP}} \qquad \tan A = \frac{\text{OPP}}{\text{ADJ}}$$

Many students find it helpful to use the word SOHCAHTOA. You can think of the letters here as representing sin, opp, hyp, cos, adj, hyp, tan, opp, adj.

Example: Compute the three basic trig functions for each of the angles (except the right angle) in the triangle below.

203

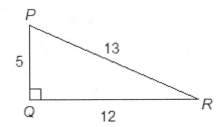

Solution:

$$\sin P = \frac{12}{13} \quad \cos P = \frac{5}{13} \quad \tan P = \frac{12}{5}$$
$$\sin R = \frac{5}{13} \quad \cos R = \frac{12}{13} \quad \tan R = \frac{5}{12}$$

LEVEL 2: TRIGONOMETRY

1. If $0 \leq x \leq 90°$ and $\sin x = \frac{5}{13}$, then $\cos x =$

   A. $\frac{5}{12}$
   B. $\frac{12}{5}$
   C. $\frac{12}{13}$
   D. $\frac{13}{12}$
   E. $\frac{13}{5}$

Solution

* Let's draw a picture. We begin with a right triangle and label one of the angles x.

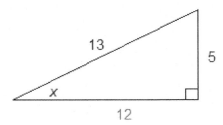

Since $\sin x = \frac{\text{OPP}}{\text{HYP}}$, we label the leg opposite to x with a 5 and the hypotenuse with 13. We can use the Pythagorean triple 5, 12, 13 to see that the other side is 12.

Finally, $\cos x = \frac{\text{ADJ}}{\text{OPP}} = \frac{12}{13}$, choice **C**.

Notes: (1) The most common Pythagorean triples are 3, 4, 5 and 5, 12, 13. Two others that may come up are 8, 15, 17 and 7, 24, 25.

(2) If you don't remember the Pythagorean triple 5, 12, 13, you can use the Pythagorean Theorem:

Here we have $5^2 + b^2 = 13^2$. Therefore $25 + b^2 = 169$. Subtracting 25 from each side of this equation gives $b^2 = 169 - 25 = 144$. So, $b = 12$.

(3) The equation $b^2 = 144$ would normally have two solutions: $b = 12$ and $b = -12$. But the length of a side of a triangle cannot be negative, so we reject -12.

Radian Measure

One full rotation of a circle is 360°. All other rotations are in proportion to the full rotation. For example, half of a rotation of a circle is $\frac{360}{2} = 180°$.

In addition to degree measure, another way to measure rotations of a circle is to divide the arc length of the circle by the radius of the circle. This is called **radian** measure. For example, one full rotation of a circle is $\frac{2\pi r}{r} = 2\pi$ radians, and so half of a rotation of a circle is π radians.

So, we just showed that $180° = \pi$ radians.

We can convert between degree measure and radian measure by using the following simple ratio:

$$\frac{\text{degree measure}}{180°} = \frac{\text{radian measure}}{\pi}$$

Example 1: Convert 60° to radians.

Solution: $\frac{60°}{180°} = \frac{x}{\pi} \Rightarrow x = \frac{60\pi}{180} = \frac{\pi}{3}$ radians.

Shortcut: We can convert from degrees to radians by multiplying the given angle by $\frac{\pi}{180}$.

Example 2: Convert $\frac{\pi}{4}$ radians to degrees.

Solution: $\frac{x°}{180°} = \frac{\pi/4}{\pi} \Rightarrow x = \frac{180}{4} = \mathbf{45°}$.

Shortcut: We can convert from radians to degrees by multiplying the given angle by $\frac{180}{\pi}$.

If the angle has π in the numerator, we can simply replace π by 180.

You're doing great! Let's just practice a bit more. Try to solve each of the following problems. The answers to these problems, followed by full solutions are at the end of this lesson. **Do not** look at the answers until you have attempted these problems yourself. Please remember to mark off any problems you get wrong.

LEVEL 2: TRIGONOMETRY

2. For right triangle ΔPQR shown below, what is $\cos R$?

    F. $\frac{a}{b}$
    G. $\frac{a}{c}$
    H. $\frac{c}{a}$
    J. $\frac{b}{c}$
    K. $\frac{c}{b}$

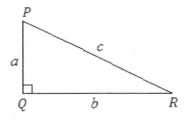

3. The measure of $\angle ABC$ is 150°. What is the measure of $\angle ABC$ in radians?

    A. $\frac{3}{5\pi}$
    B. $\frac{6}{5\pi}$
    C. $\frac{\pi}{6}$
    D. $\frac{5\pi}{6}$
    E. $\frac{5\pi}{3}$

4. In △PQR below, which of the following trigonometric expressions has value $\frac{5}{12}$?

F. tan R
G. tan P
H. sin R
J. sin P
K. cos R

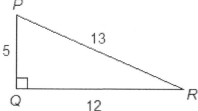

LEVEL 3: TRIGONOMETRY

5. In △CAT, ∠A is a right angle. Which of the following is equal to tan T ?

A. $\frac{CA}{CT}$
B. $\frac{CA}{AT}$
C. $\frac{CT}{CA}$
D. $\frac{CT}{AT}$
E. $\frac{AT}{CA}$

6. The hypotenuse of right triangle △ABC is 15 inches long, and $\cos A = \frac{1}{5}$. How many inches long is $\overline{BC}$ (note that $\overline{BC}$ is the side opposite ∠A) ?

F. $\frac{1}{6\sqrt{6}}$
G. $\frac{1}{2\sqrt{6}}$
H. 3
J. $2\sqrt{6}$
K. $6\sqrt{6}$

7. For right triangle $\triangle PQR$ shown below, $\sin P = \frac{8}{9}$. What is the value of $\cos R$?

   A. $\frac{8}{\sqrt{17}}$
   B. $\frac{8}{9}$
   C. $\frac{9}{8}$
   D. $\frac{\sqrt{17}}{9}$
   E. $\frac{9}{\sqrt{17}}$

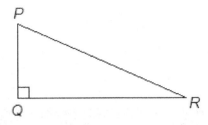

8. Given that $\cos^2 x = \frac{5}{16}$, what is $\sin^2 x$?

   F. $\frac{11}{16}$
   G. $\frac{16}{11}$
   H. $\frac{5}{11}$
   J. $\frac{11}{5}$
   K. $\frac{16}{5}$

LEVEL 4: TRIGONOMETRY

9. A line through the origin and $(3, 5)$ is shown in the standard (x, y) coordinate plane below. The acute angle between the line and the positive x-axis has measure θ. What is the value of $\cos \theta$?

   A. $\frac{3}{5}$
   B. $\frac{5}{3}$
   C. $\frac{3}{\sqrt{34}}$
   D. $\frac{\sqrt{34}}{3}$
   E. $\frac{5}{\sqrt{34}}$

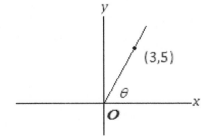

10. A 7-foot ladder is leaning against a wall such that the angle relative to the level ground is 70°. Which of the following expressions involving cosine gives the distance, in feet, from the base of the ladder to the wall?

F. $\dfrac{7}{\cos 70°}$

G. $\dfrac{\cos 70°}{7}$

H. $\dfrac{1}{7\cos 70°}$

J. $7 \cos 70°$

K. $\cos(7 \cdot 70°)$

Answers

1. C
2. J
3. D
4. F
5. B
6. K
7. B
8. F
9. C
10. J

Full Solutions

2.
* $\cos R = \dfrac{\text{ADJ}}{\text{HYP}} = \dfrac{b}{c}$, choice **J**.

3.
* **Quick solution:** $150 \cdot \dfrac{\pi}{180} = \dfrac{5\pi}{6}$, choice **D**.

Solution by setting up a ratio: $\dfrac{150°}{180°} = \dfrac{x}{\pi} \Rightarrow x = \dfrac{150\pi}{180} = \dfrac{5\pi}{6}$, choice **D**.

4.
* Since 5 labels the side *opposite* angle R, and 12 labels the side *adjacent* to angle R, we have $\tan R = \dfrac{\text{OPP}}{\text{ADJ}} = \dfrac{5}{12}$, and the answer is choice **F**.

5.
* **Solution by drawing a picture:** Let's draw a picture.

209

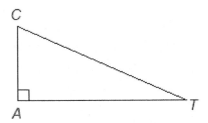

Now just note that $\tan T = \dfrac{\text{OPP}}{\text{ADJ}} = \dfrac{CA}{AT}$, choice **B**.

6.
* Let's draw a picture.

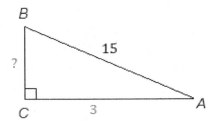

Since $\cos A = \dfrac{1}{5}$, we have $\dfrac{AC}{15} = \dfrac{1}{5}$, and so $AC = \dfrac{15}{5} = 3$. We now use the Pythagorean Theorem to get $BC^2 = 15^2 - 3^2 = 225 - 9 = 216$. So, we have $BC = \sqrt{216} = \sqrt{36 \cdot 6} = \sqrt{36} \cdot \sqrt{6} = 6\sqrt{6}$, choice **K**.

Note: If you are uncomfortable simplifying square roots, you can simply use your calculator to approximate the square root of 216 as 14.7, and then approximate the answer choices in your calculator to see which one matches up.

7.
Basic trig solution: Let's add some information to the picture.

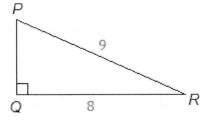

Notice that since $\sin P = \dfrac{\text{OPP}}{\text{HYP}}$, we label the side opposite angle P with 8 and the hypotenuse with 9.

Now observe that $\cos R = \frac{\text{ADJ}}{\text{HYP}} = \frac{8}{9}$, choice **B**.

* Solution using a cofunction identity: Since $m\angle P + m\angle R = 90°$, $\cos R = \sin P = \frac{8}{9}$, choice **B**.

Note: See the Optional Material below for the identity used here.

8.
* Solution using a Pythagorean identity: We use the Pythagorean identity
$$\cos^2 x + \sin^2 x = 1$$
to get $\sin^2 x = 1 - \cos^2 x = 1 - \frac{5}{16} = \frac{11}{16}$, choice **F**.

Notes: (1) $\cos^2 x$ is an abbreviation for $(\cos x)^2$. In other words, we evaluate $\cos x$ first, and then square the result. Similarly, $\sin^2 x$ is an abbreviation for $(\sin x)^2$.

(2) We can perform the computation $1 - \frac{5}{16}$ right in our TI-84 calculator by typing $1 - 5/16$ MATH ENTER ENTER. The output will say $\frac{11}{16}$.

(3) We can also do the computation $1 - \frac{5}{16}$ quickly by hand as follows:
$$1 - \frac{5}{16} = \frac{16}{16} - \frac{5}{16} = \frac{16-5}{16} = \frac{11}{16}$$

Calculator solution: We can solve for x in our calculator. We first take the square root of $\frac{5}{16}$, then press 2ND COS (for $\cos^{-1} x$) 2ND (-) (for ANS) and press ENTER. This gives a value of x (approximately 0.9776). Next press SIN ANS, and then square the result. The output will say 0.6875. Press MATH ENTER ENTER to change this to the fraction $\frac{11}{16}$, choice **F**.

9.
*** Let's form a right triangle, as shown in the figure on the right. Notice that to plot the point $(3, 5)$ we start at the origin, and move 3 units to the right, and then 5 units up. This is how we get the lengths of the legs of the triangle.

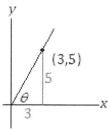

We can use the Pythagorean Theorem to get that the length of the hypotenuse of the triangle is $\sqrt{3^2 + 5^2} = \sqrt{9 + 25} = \sqrt{34}$.

Finally, we have $\cos\theta = \frac{\text{ADJ}}{\text{HYP}} = \frac{3}{\sqrt{34}}$, choice **C**.

10.
* Let's draw a picture.

Observe that the side labelled 7 represents the ladder, and we let x denote the distance from the base of the ladder to the wall.

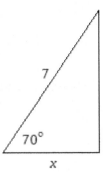

We have $\cos 70° = \frac{\text{ADJ}}{\text{HYP}} = \frac{x}{7}$. Multiplying each side of this equation by 7 gives us

$$x = 7\cos 70°$$

This is choice **J**.

OPTIONAL MATERIAL

Trigonometric Identities

Quotient Identity:

$$\tan x = \frac{\sin x}{\cos x}$$

Negative Identities:

$$\cos(-x) = \cos x \qquad \sin(-x) = -\sin x \qquad \tan(-x) = -\tan x$$

Cofunction Identities:

$$\sin(90° - x) = \cos x \qquad \cos(90° - x) = \sin x$$

Pythagorean Identity: $\qquad \cos^2 x + \sin^2 x = 1$

LESSON 20
STATISTICS

Reminder: Before beginning this lesson remember to redo the problems from Lessons 4, 8, 12, and 16 that you have marked off. Do not "unmark" a question unless you get it correct.

Turn to Lesson 4 and review the strategy **Change Averages to Sums**. Then try to answer the following questions using this strategy whenever possible. **Do not** check the solutions until you have attempted these questions yourself.

LEVEL 1: STATISTICS

1. The average (arithmetic mean) of four numbers is 50. If three of the numbers are 42, 52 and 62, what is the fourth number?

   A. 22
   B. 44
   C. 48
   D. 52
   E. 88

   List A: 58, 35, 72, 46, 49
   List B: 70, 53, 11, 20, 68

2. The median of the numbers in list B is how much greater than the median of the numbers in list A?

   F. 2
   G. 4
   H. 7
   J. 7.6
   K. 8

3. For which of the following lists of 5 numbers is the average (arithmetic mean) less than the median?

   A. 2, 2, 4, 5, 5
   B. 2, 3, 4, 6, 7
   C. 2, 2, 4, 6, 6
   D. 2, 3, 4, 5, 6
   E. 2, 3, 4, 5, 10

LEVEL 2: STATISTICS

4. The average of 7 distinct scores has the same value as the median of the 7 scores. The sum of the 7 scores is 126. What is the sum of the 6 scores that is NOT the median?

   F. 18
   G. 52
   H. 96
   J. 108
   K. 118

$$15, 17, 3, 19, 2, 5, 22, 36, b$$

5. If b is the median of the 9 numbers listed above, which of the following could be the value of b ?

   A. 17
   B. 18
   C. 19
   D. 20
   E. 21

6. For which of the following lists of 6 numbers is the mode NOT equal to the average (arithmetic mean)?

   F. 2, 3, 3, 3, 3, 4
   G. 2, 4, 4, 4, 5, 5
   H. 3, 3, 3, 3, 5, 6
   J. 4, 4, 5, 5, 5, 7
   K. 5, 6, 6, 6, 6, 7

LEVEL 3: STATISTICS

7. The average of x, y, z, and w is 12 and the average of z and w is 7. What is the average of x and y?

   A. 48
   B. 38
   C. 34
   D. 20
   E. 17

8. The list of numbers 17, A, B, 36, 41, 52 has a mode of 17 and a median of 30. What is the mean of the list, to the nearest whole number?

   F. 28
   G. 30
   H. 31
   J. 32
   K. 34

LEVEL 4: STATISTICS

List A: 7, a, b, c
List B: 2, 3, 6, a, b, c

9. If the average (arithmetic mean) of the 4 numbers in list A is 10, what is the average of the 6 numbers in list B?

   A. 44
   B. 22
   C. 11
   D. $\frac{22}{3}$
   E. $\frac{11}{3}$

LEVEL 5: STATISTICS

$$\frac{1}{x^3}, \frac{1}{x^2}, \frac{1}{x}, x, x^2, x^3$$

10. If $-1 < x < 0$, what is the median of the six numbers in the list above?

    F. $\frac{1}{x}$
    G. x^2
    H. $\frac{x^2(x+1)}{2}$
    J. $\frac{x(x^2+1)}{2}$
    K. $\frac{x^2+1}{2x}$

215

Definitions Used in This Lesson

Definitions of **average (arithmetic mean)**, and **median** can be found in Lesson 4.

The **mode** of a set of numbers is the number that occurs most frequently. There can be more than one mode if more than one number occurs with the greatest frequency.

Answers

1. B
2. G
3. A
4. J
5. A

6. H
7. E
8. H
9. D
10. J

Full solutions to these problems are available for free download here:

www.satprepget800.com/28LesInt

OPTIONAL MATERIAL

CHALLENGE QUESTION: STATISTICS

Let $x_1, x_2, \ldots, x_n$ be a list of numbers with average a. Show that the average of $x_1, x_2, \ldots, x_n, a$ is also a.

Solution to Challenge Question

For the original list, the Average is a and the Number is n, so that the Sum is $x_1 + x_2 + \cdots + x_n = an$. Add a to each side of this equation to get $x_1 + x_2 + \cdots + x_n + a = an + a$. Then factor a on the right-hand side to get $x_1 + x_2 + \cdots + x_n + a = a(n+1)$. Finally divide by $n+1$, and we have $\frac{x_1 + x_2 + \cdots + x_n + a}{n+1} = a$.

The left-hand side of this last equation is precisely the average of the new list of numbers, and we have shown that this average is equal to a.

Lesson 21
Number Theory

Reminder: Before beginning this lesson remember to redo the problems from Lessons 1, 5, 9, 13, and 17 that you have marked off. Do not "unmark" a question unless you get it correct.

Setting Up a Ratio

Step 1: Identify two key words and write them down one over the other.
Step 2: Next to each of these key words write down the numbers, variables or expressions that correspond to each key word in two columns.
Step 3: Draw in 2 division symbols and an equal sign.
Step 4: Cross multiply and divide.

Try to answer the following question using this strategy. **Do not** check the solution until you have attempted this question yourself.

Level 1: Number Theory

1. The sales tax on a $5.00 hat is $0.40. At this rate, what would be the sales tax on a $9.00 hat?

    A. $0.36
    B. $0.72
    C. $0.80
    D. $0.96
    E. $1.44

Solution

* This is a simple ratio. We begin by identifying 2 key words that tell us what 2 things are being compared. In this case, such a pair of key words is "hat" and "tax."

hat	5	9
tax	0.40	x

Choose the words that are most helpful to you.

Notice that we wrote in the hat prices next to the word hat, and the tax prices next to the word tax. Also, notice that the tax for a $5 hat is written under the number 5, and the (unknown) tax for a $9 hat is written under the 9. Now draw in the division symbols and equal sign, cross multiply and divide the corresponding ratio to find the unknown quantity x.

$$\frac{5}{0.40} = \frac{9}{x}$$
$$5x = (9)(0.40)$$
$$5x = 3.6$$
$$x = \frac{3.6}{5} = 0.72$$

So, the tax on a $9 hat is $0.72, choice **B**.

Percent Change

Memorize the following simple formula for percent change problems.

$$Percent\ Change = \frac{Change}{Original} \times 100$$

Note that this is the same formula for both a percent increase and a percent decrease problem.

Try to answer the following question using this strategy. **Do not** check the solution until you have attempted this question yourself.

LEVEL 2: NUMBER THEORY

2. In September, Maria could type 30 words per minute. In October, she could type 42 words per minute. By what percent did Maria's speed increase from September to October?

    F. 12%
    G. 18%
    H. 30%
    J. 40%
    K. 42%

Solution

* This is a percent increase problem. So, we will use the formula for percent change. The **original** value is 30. The new value is 42, so that the **change** is 12. Using the percent change formula, we get that the percent increase is $\frac{12}{30} \times 100 = 40\%$, choice **J**.

Warning: Do not accidently use the new value for "change" in the formula. The **change** is the positive difference between the original and new values.

Now try to solve each of the following problems involving ratios and percents. The answers to these problems, followed by full solutions are at the end of this lesson. **Do not** look at the answers until you have attempted these problems yourself. Please remember to mark off any problems you get wrong.

LEVEL 2: NUMBER THEORY

3. 30 percent of 50 is 10 percent of what number?

    A. 10
    B. 70
    C. 100
    D. 130
    E. 150

4. A room has 1700 square feet of surface that needs to be painted. If 3 gallons of paint will cover 710 square feet, what is the least whole number of gallons that must be purchased in order to have enough paint to cover the entire surface?

    F. 4
    G. 5
    H. 6
    J. 7
    K. 8

LEVEL 3: NUMBER THEORY

5. The ratio of the number of boys to the number of girls in a park is 3 to 5. What percent of the children in the park are girls?

    A. 12.5%
    B. 37.5%
    C. 60%
    D. 62.5%
    E. 70%

6. What percent of 60 is 24?

    F. 15%
    G. 20%
    H. 40%
    J. 45%
    K. 60%

7. During a sale at a retail store, if a customer buys one t-shirt at full price, the customer is given a 40 percent discount on a second t-shirt of equal or lesser value. If John buys two t-shirts that have full prices of $70 and $90, by what percent is the total cost of the two t-shirts reduced during the sale?

    A. 17.5%
    B. 28%
    C. 40%
    D. 42%
    E. 60%

LEVEL 4: NUMBER THEORY

8. A mixture is made by combining a green liquid and a purple liquid so that the ratio of the green liquid to the purple liquid is 19 to 6 by weight. How many liters of the purple liquid are needed to make a 370-liter mixture?

    F. 14.8
    G. 29.6
    H. 88.8
    J. 192.4
    K. 281.2

9. If the ratio of two positive integers is 5 to 4, which of the following statements about these integers CANNOT be true?

   A. Their sum is an odd integer.
   B. Their sum is an even integer.
   C. Their product is divisible by 7.
   D. Their product is an even integer.
   E. Their product is an odd integer.

10. What number k must be added to both the numerator and the denominator of the fraction $\frac{5}{19}$ to make the resulting fraction equal to $\frac{6}{13}$?

    F. 8
    G. 7
    H. 6
    J. 5
    K. 4

Definitions Used in This Lesson

Percent means out of 100.

A **ratio** is a relationship between two quantities, normally expressed as the quotient of one divided by the other. The ratio of a to b can be written a/b, $\frac{a}{b}$, or $a:b$.

Answers

1. B   6. H
2. J   7. A
3. E   8. H
4. K   9. E
5. D   10. G

Full Solutions

3.
* 30 percent of 50 is equal to $(0.3)(50) = 15$. So, the question now becomes "15 is 10% of what number?" Well, 15 is 10% of 150, choice **E**.

221

Algebraic solution: We begin by changing the English symbol to a mathematical equation. The word "percent" means "out of 100," the word "of" means "·," the word "is" means "=," and we replace the word "what" by the variable x.

$$\frac{30}{100} \cdot 50 = \frac{10}{100} \cdot x$$

$$\frac{15}{1} = \frac{x}{10}$$

Now cross multiply to get $x = 150$, choice **E**.

    4.
* This is a simple ratio. We begin by identifying 2 key words. In this case, such a pair of key words is "square feet" and "gallons."

square feet	1700	710
gallons	x	3

Now simply cross multiply and divide the corresponding ratio to find the unknown quantity x.

$$\frac{1700}{x} = \frac{710}{3}$$

$$5100 = 710x$$

$$x \approx 7.183$$

So, we will need 8 gallons to cover the entire surface. Thus, the answer is choice **K**.

Note: If we round the answer to the nearest integer we get the **incorrect** number 7 – rounding is not correct here because we need **more** than 7 gallons of paint to cover the surface.

    5.
We can represent the number of boys in the park by $3x$ and the number of girls in the park by $5x$ for some number x. Then the total number of children in the park is $8x$, which we set equal to 100. Now $8x = 100$ implies that $x = \frac{100}{8} = 12.5$. Since we want the percent of the children in the park that are girls, we need to find $5x = 5(12.5) = 62.5$, choice **D**.

Important note: After you find x make sure you look at what the question is asking for. A common error is to give an answer of 12.5%. But the number of girls is **not** equal to x. It is equal to $5x$.

* **Alternate solution:** We set up a ratio of the number of girls in the park to the total number of children in the park.

$$\begin{array}{ccc} \text{girls} & 5 & x \\ \text{total} & 8 & 100 \end{array}$$

$$\frac{5}{8} = \frac{x}{100}$$
$$8x = 500$$
$$x = \frac{500}{8} = 62.5, \text{ choice } \mathbf{D}.$$

6.
* The word "what" indicates an unknown, let's call it x. The word percent means "out of 100" or "divided by 100." The word "of" indicates multiplication, and the word "is" indicates an equal sign. So, we translate the given sentence into an algebraic equation as follows.

$$\frac{x}{100} \cdot 60 = 24$$

So, $x = 24(\frac{100}{60}) = 40$, choice **H**.

7.
* **Solution using the percent change formula:** This is a percent decrease problem. So, we will use the formula for percent change. The **original** cost of the two t-shirts is $70 + 90 = 160$. The new cost is $42 + 90 = 132$. Thus, the **change** is $160 - 132 = 28$. So, the percent change is $\frac{28}{160} \cdot 100 = 17.5\%$, choice **A**.

Note: To get the 42 in the second computation we need to discount 70 by 40 percent. Here are two ways to do that.
  (1) Compute 40% of $70 = 0.4 \cdot 70 = 28$, and then subtract $70 - 28 = 42$.
  (2) Compute 60% of $70 = 0.6 \cdot 70 = 42$ (taking a 40% discount of something is the same as taking 60% of that thing).

Warning: Do not accidently use the new value for "change" in the formula. The **change** is the positive difference between the original and new values.

8.

* We can represent the number of liters of green liquid by $19x$ and the number of liters of purple liquid by $6x$ for some number x. Then the total amount of liquid is $25x$ which must be equal to 370. $25x = 370$ implies that $x = 14.8$. Since we want the number of liters of purple liquid, we need to find $6x$. This is $6(14.8) = 88.8$, choice **H**.

Important note: After you find x make sure you look at what the question is asking for. A common error is to give an answer of 14.8 (choice A). But the amount of purple liquid is **not** equal to x. It is equal to $6x$.

Alternate solution: We set up a ratio of the amount of purple liquid to the total liquid.

purple liquid   6 x
total liquid   25   370

$$\frac{6}{25} = \frac{x}{370}$$
$$25x = 2220$$
$$x = \frac{2220}{25} = 88.8$$

This is choice **H**.

9.

Solution by picking numbers: Let's choose two positive integers that are in the ratio of 5 to 4, say 5 and 4. We have $5 + 4 = 9$ and $5 \cdot 4 = 20$. Since 9 is odd, we can eliminate choice A. Since 20 is even, we can eliminate choice D. The answer is therefore B, C, or E.

We need to choose two new numbers that are in the same ratio. A simple way to do this is to multiply our original numbers by an integer, say 2. So, our new numbers are 10 and 8. $10 + 8 = 18$ and $10 \cdot 8 = 80$. Since 18 is even, we can eliminate choice B. So, we are down to either C or E.

Looking at choice C seems to indicate that perhaps we should multiply by 7. So, our new numbers are 35 and 28. $35 \cdot 28 = 980$, which is divisible by 7. We can therefore eliminate choice C, and the answer is choice **E**.

Notes: E is correct because we eliminated the other four choices. The reality of the situation is that we have not actually answered this question. Using the previous method there is no reason to believe that there is no choice of integers that will produce an odd product. In this sense the algebraic method below is more enlightening.

* Algebraic solution: If the ratio of two positive integers is 5 to 4, then the integers can be written as $5x$ and $4x$ for some number x. The sum is $5x + 4x = 9x$, and the product is $(4x)(5x) = 20x^2 = 2(10x^2)$. Since the product has a factor of 2 it is always even and can never be odd. The answer is therefore choice **E**.

For the advanced student: Note that in order for $5x$ and $4x$ to both be integers, x must also be an integer because 5 and 4 have no common factors (contrast this with $2x$ and $4x$ where x can be any multiple of $\frac{1}{2}$). This shows that when we substitute an acceptable value for x in the expression $2(10x^2)$, we will not inadvertently cancel the 2 (we would actually have to cancel $2^2 = 4$ to get an odd number since 2 is also a factor of 10).

10.
* Let's change the form of the resulting fraction to make it easier to get the answer. If we multiply the numerator and denominator of a fraction by the same nonzero number, we get an equivalent fraction. Let's start with 2. So, we see that $\frac{6}{13} = \frac{6 \cdot 2}{13 \cdot 2} = \frac{12}{26}$. Now just observe that $5 + 7 = 12$ and $19 + 7 = 26$. So, $\frac{5+7}{19+7} = \frac{12}{26} = \frac{6}{13}$. So, the answer is 7, choice **G**.

OPTIONAL MATERIAL

The following questions will test your understanding of definitions used in this lesson. These are **not** in the format of ACT questions.

1. Convert each fraction to a decimal and a percent (round each result to two decimal places).

    $\frac{1}{2}$ $\frac{1}{5}$ $\frac{1}{3}$ 1 $\frac{5}{3}$

2. Convert each decimal to a percent and a reduced fraction.

    0.5   0.24   1   1.5   12

3. Convert each percent to a decimal and a reduced fraction.

    5%   0.3%   0.07%   15%   100%

Answers

1. $\frac{1}{2} = 0.5 = 50\%$, $\frac{1}{5} = 0.2 = 20\%$, $\frac{1}{3} = 0.33 = 33.33\%$, $1 = 1 = 100\%$, $\frac{5}{3} = 1.67 = 166.67\%$

2. $0.5 = 50\% = \frac{1}{2}$, $0.24 = 24\% = \frac{6}{25}$, $1 = 100\% = 1$, $1.5 = 150\% = \frac{3}{2}$, $12 = 1200\% = 12$

3. $5\% = 0.05 = \frac{1}{20}$, $.3\% = 0.003 = \frac{3}{1000}$, $0.07\% = 0.0007 = \frac{7}{10,000}$, $15\% = 0.15 = \frac{3}{20}$, $100\% = 1 = 1$

LESSON 22
FUNCTIONS

Reminder: Before beginning this lesson remember to redo the problems from Lessons 2, 6, 10, 14, and 18 that you have marked off. Do not "unmark" a question unless you get it correct.

Functions

A function is simply a rule that for each "input" assigns a specific "output." Functions may be given by equations, tables or graphs.

Note about the notation $f(x)$: The variable x is a placeholder. We evaluate the function f at a specific value by substituting that value in for x.

For example, if $f(x) = 5 - x$, then $f(-3) = 5 - (-3) = 5 + 3 = 8$.

LEVEL 2: FUNCTIONS

1. The functions f and g are defined below. What is the value of $f(8) - g(2)$?

$$f(x) = 2x - 5$$
$$g(x) = x^2 + 3x - 2$$

   A. 0
   B. 1
   C. 2
   D. 3
   E. 4

Solution

Solution $f(8) = 2(8) - 5 = 16 - 5 = 11$.

$g(2) = 2^2 + 3(2) - 2 = 4 + 6 - 2 = 8$.

Therefore, $f(8) - g(2) = 11 - 8 = 3$, choice **D**.

Graphs of Functions

If f is a function, then

$f(a) = b$ is equivalent to "the point (a, b) lies on the graph of f."

Example 1:

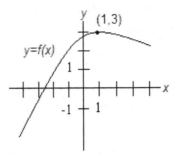

In the figure above we see that the point (1,3) lies on the graph of the function f. Therefore $f(1) = 3$.

Function Facts

Fact 1: The **y-intercept** of the graph of a function $y = f(x)$ is the point on the graph where $x = 0$ (if it exists). There can be at most one y-intercept for the graph of a function. A y-intercept has the form $(0, b)$ for some real number b. Equivalently, $f(0) = b$.

Fact 2: An **x-intercept** of the graph of a function is a point on the graph where $y = 0$. There can be more than one x-intercept for the graph of a function or none at all. An x-intercept has the form $(a, 0)$ for some real number a. Equivalently, $f(a) = 0$.

Example 2:

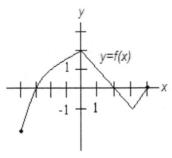

In the figure above we see that the graph of f has y-intercept $(0,2)$ and x-intercepts $(-3,0)$, $(2,0)$ and $(4,0)$.

The numbers −3, 2, and 4 are also called **zeros**, **roots**, or **solutions** of the function.

Note that in example 2, we have $f(-3) = 0$, $f(2) = 0$, and $f(4) = 0$.

Fact 3: If the graph of f is above the x-axis, then $f(x) > 0$. If the graph of f is below the x-axis, then $f(x) < 0$. If the graph of f is higher than the graph of g, then $f(x) > g(x)$.

Example 3: In the figure for example 2 above, observe that $f(x) < 0$ for $-4 \leq x < -3$ and $2 < x < 4$. Also, observe that $f(x) > 0$ for $-3 < x < 2$.

Fact 4: The graph of a function always passes the **vertical line test**: any vertical line can hit the graph *at most* once.

For example, a circle is *never* the graph of a function. It always fails the vertical line test as shown in the figure below.

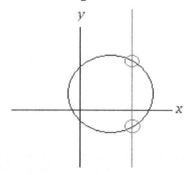

Standard Form for a Quadratic Function

The standard form for a quadratic function is
$$y - k = a(x - h)^2.$$
The graph is a parabola with **vertex** at (h, k). The parabola opens upwards if $a > 0$ and downwards if $a < 0$.

Example 1: Let the function f be defined by $f(x) = 2(x - 1)^2 + 3$. For what value of x will the function f have its minimum value?

The graph of this function is an upward facing parabola with vertex $(1,3)$. Therefore, the answer is $x = 1$.

Remark: Note that in this example $k = 3$ and k is on the right-hand side of the equation instead of on the left.

General Form for a Quadratic Function

The general form for a quadratic function is

$$y = ax^2 + bx + c.$$

The graph of this function is a parabola whose vertex has x-coordinate

$$-\frac{b}{2a}$$

The parabola opens upwards if $a > 0$ and downwards if $a < 0$.

Example 2: Let the function f be defined by $f(x) = -2x^2 - 6x + 5$. For what value of x will the function f have its maximum value?

The graph of this function is a downward facing parabola, and we see that $a = -2$, and $b = -6$. Therefore, the x-coordinate of the vertex is $x = \frac{6}{-4} = -3/2$.

Try to answer the following questions that use function notation. The answers to these questions, followed by full solutions are at the end of this lesson. **Do not** look at the answers until you have attempted these problems yourself. Please remember to mark off any problems you get wrong.

LEVEL 2: FUNCTIONS

2. A function f is defined as $f(x, y, z) = x^2y - y^2z + xz$. What is $f(-2, -1, 3)$?

    F. -13
    G. -7
    H. -5
    J. -1
    K. 1

3. Which of the following graphs could not be the graph of a function?

A. 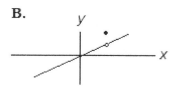 B.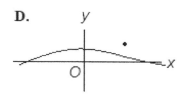

C. D.

E.

4. Suppose that $h(x) = 4x - 5$ and $h(b) = 17$. What is the value of b ?

   F. 4
   G. 5.5
   H. 10
   J. 15
   K. 17.5

LEVEL 3: FUNCTIONS

5. For all real numbers x, let the function h be defined as $h(x) = 5x - 10$. Which of the following is equal to $h(3) + h(5)$?

   A. $h(4)$
   B. $h(6)$
   C. $h(7)$
   D. $h(12)$
   E. $h(20)$

6. The figure below shows the graph of the function g. Which of the following is less than $g(1)$?

F. $g(-3)$
G. $g(-2)$
H. $g(-1)$
J. $g(0)$
K. $g(3)$

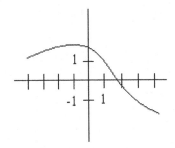

7. Let h be a function such that $h(x) = |3x| + c$ where c is a constant. If $h(2) = -3$, what is the value of $h(-4)$?

A. 1
B. 2
C. 3
D. 4
E. 5

LEVEL 4: FUNCTIONS

8. Let the function g be defined for all real values of x by $g(x) = x(x-1)$. If a is a positive number and $g(a+2) = 56$, what is the value of a?

F. 1
G. 2
H. 3
J. 6
K. 8

9. In the xy-plane, the graph of the function g, with equation $g(x) = px^2 - 25$, passes through the point $(-3, 11)$. What is the value of p?

A. -2
B. 4
C. 5
D. 20
E. 24

$$-3x^2 + bx - 7$$

10. In the *xy*-plane, the graph of the equation above assumes its maximum value at $x = 5$. What is the value of *b*?

    F. -6
    G. -2
    H. 10
    J. 20
    K. 30

Answers

1. D   6. K
2. F   7. C
3. D   8. J
4. G   9. B
5. B   10. K

Full Solutions

2.
*
$$f(-2, -1, 3) = (-2)^2(-1) - (-1)^2(3) + (-2)(3)$$
$$= -4 - 3 - 6 = -13.$$

This is choice **F**.

3.
* Only choice D fails the **vertical line test**. In other words, we can draw a vertical line that hits the graph more than once:

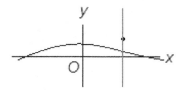

So, the answer is choice **D**.

4.
Solution by starting with choice H: Let's start with choice H and guess that $b = 10$. Then $h(b) = 4b - 5 = 4(10) - 5 = 40 - 5 = 35$. This is too big. So, we can eliminate choices H, J, and K.

233

Let's try choice G next. So, we are guessing that $b = 5.5$. We then have that $h(b) = 4b - 5 = 4(5.5) - 5 = 22 - 5 = 17$. This is correct. So, the answer is choice **G**.

* Algebraic solution: $h(b) = 17$ is equivalent to $4b - 5 = 17$. We add 5 to each side of this equation to get $4b = 22$. We then divide each side of this equation by 4 to get that $b = 5.5$, choice **G**.

5.
Solution by starting with choice C: First note that
$$h(3) = 5(3) - 10 = 5 \text{ and } h(5) = 5(5) - 10 = 15.$$
So, $h(3) + h(5) = 5 + 15 = \mathbf{20}$.

Now, beginning with choice C we see that $h(7) = 5(7) - 10 = 25$. This is a bit too big. So, let's try choice B. We have $h(6) = 5(6) - 10 = 20$. This is correct. Thus, the answer is choice **B**.

Warning: Many students will compute $h(3) + h(5) = 20$ and immediately choose choice E. Do not fall into this trap!

* Algebraic solution: As in the previous solution, direct computation gives $h(3) + h(5) = 20$. Setting $h(x) = 20$ yields $5x - 10 = 20$, so that $5x = 30$, and so $x = \frac{30}{5} = 6$, i.e., $h(6) = 20 = f(3) + f(5)$, choice **B**.

6.
* Let's draw a horizontal line through the point $(1, g(1))$. To do this start on the x-axis at 1 and go straight up until you hit the curve. This height is $g(1)$. Now draw a horizontal line through this point.

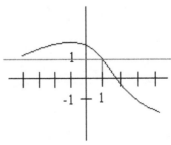

Now, notice that the graph is below this line when $x = 3$. So $g(3)$ is less than $g(1)$. Therefore, the answer is choice **K**.

7.

* $h(2) = |3(2)| + c = 6 + c$. But it is given that $h(2) = -3$. So, $6 + c = -3$, and therefore $c = -9$. So, $h(x) = |3x| - 9$. Finally,
$$h(-4) = |3(-4)| - 9 = |-12| - 9 = 12 - 9 = 3.$$
This is choice **C**.

Recall: $|x|$ is the **absolute value** of x. If x is nonnegative, then $|x| = x$. If x is negative, then $|x| = -x$ (in other words, if x is negative, then taking the absolute value just eliminates the minus sign). For example, $|12| = 12$ and $|-12| = 12$.

8.
* **Solution by starting with choice H:** Let's start with choice H and guess that $a = 3$. Then we have $g(3 + 2) = g(5) = (5)(4) = 20$. This is too small. So, let's guess $a = 6$. Then $g(6 + 2) = g(8) = (8)(7) = 56$ which is correct. Thus, $a = 6$, choice **J**.

Algebraic solution: $g(a + 2) = (a + 2)(a + 1) = a^2 + 3a + 2$. Since $g(a + 2) = 56$, we have $a^2 + 3a + 2 = 56$. Subtracting 56 from each side yields
$$a^2 + 3a - 54 = 0$$
$$(a - 6)(a + 9) = 0$$
So, $a = 6$ or $a = -9$. We reject the negative solution because the question says that a is positive. Thus, $a = 6$, choice **J**.

9.
* Since the graph of g passes through the point $(-3, 11)$, $g(-3) = 11$. But by direct computation
$$g(-3) = p(-3)^2 - 25 = 9p - 25.$$
So $9p - 25 = 11$. Therefore, $9p = 36$, and so $p = 4$, choice **B**.

10.
Solution using the general form for a quadratic function: Using the formula $x = -\frac{b}{2a}$ we have $-\frac{b}{2(-3)} = 5$. So, $b = 30$, choice **K**.

Solution using differential calculus: The derivative of the function $y = -3x^2 + bx - 7$ is $y' = -6x + b$. We set the derivative equal to 0 and plug in $x = 5$ to get $-6(5) + b = 0$, or $b = 30$, choice **K**.

OPTIONAL MATERIAL

Direct Variation

The following are all equivalent ways of saying the same thing:

(1) y varies directly as x
(2) y is directly proportional to x
(3) $y = kx$ for some constant k
(4) $\frac{y}{x}$ is constant
(5) the graph of $y = f(x)$ is a nonvertical line through the origin

For example, in the equation $y = 5x$, y varies directly as x. Here is a partial table of values for this equation.

x	1	2	3	4
y	5	10	15	20

Note that we can tell that this table represents a direct relationship between x and y because $\frac{5}{1} = \frac{10}{2} = \frac{15}{3} = \frac{20}{4}$. Here the **constant of variation** is 5.

Here is a graph of the equation.

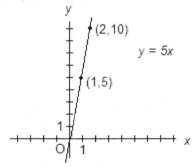

Note that we can tell that this graph represents a direct relationship between x and y because it is a nonvertical line through the origin. The constant of variation is the slope of the line, in this case $m = 5$.

Example: If y varies directly as x and $y = 3$ when $x = 7$, then what is y when $x = 21$?

Solution 1: Since y varies directly as x, $y = kx$ for some constant k. We are given that $y = 3$ when $x = 7$, so that $3 = k(7)$, or $k = \frac{3}{7}$. Thus, $y = \frac{3x}{7}$. When $x = 21$, we have $y = \frac{3(21)}{7} = 9$.

Solution 2: Since y varies directly as x, $\frac{y}{x}$ is a constant. So we get the following ratio: $\frac{3}{7} = \frac{y}{21}$. Cross multiplying gives $63 = 7y$, so that $y = 9$.

Solution 3: The graph of $y = f(x)$ is a line passing through the points $(0,0)$ and $(7,3)$. The slope of this line is $\frac{3-0}{7-0} = \frac{3}{7}$. Writing the equation of the line in slope-intercept form we have $y = \frac{3}{7}x$. As in solution 1, when $x = 21$, we have $y = \frac{3(21)}{7} = 9$.

* Solution 4: To get from $x = 7$ to $x = 21$ we multiply x by 3. So we have to also multiply y by 3. We get $3(3) = 9$.

Inverse Variation

The following are all equivalent ways of saying the same thing:

(1) y varies inversely as x
(2) y is inversely proportional to x
(3) $y = \frac{k}{x}$ for some constant k
(4) xy is constant

The following is a consequence of (1), (2) (3) or (4).

(5) The graph of $y = f(x)$ is a hyperbola.

Note: (5) is not equivalent to (1), (2), (3) or (4).

For example, in the equation $y = \frac{12}{x}$, y varies inversely as x. Here is a partial table of values for this equation.

x	1	2	3	4
y	12	6	4	3

Note that we can tell that this table represents an inverse relationship between x and y because $(1)(12) = (2)(6) = (3)(4) = (4)(3) = 12$. Here the **constant of variation** is 12.

237

Here is a graph of the equation. On the left you can see the full graph. On the right we have a close-up in the first quadrant.

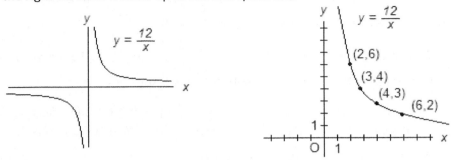

Example: If y varies inversely as x and $y = 8$ when $x = 3$, then what is y when $x = 6$?

Solution 1: Since y varies inversely as x, $y = \frac{k}{x}$ for some constant k. We are given that $y = 8$ when $x = 3$, so that $8 = \frac{k}{3}$, or $k = 24$. Therefore, $y = \frac{24}{x}$. When $x = 6$, we have $y = \frac{24}{6} = 4$.

Solution 2: Since y varies inversely as x, xy is a constant. So we get the following equation: $(3)(8) = 6y$ So $24 = 6y$, and $y = \frac{24}{6} = 4$.

* **Solution 3:** $\frac{(8)(3)}{6} = 4$.

Lesson 23
Geometry

Reminder: Before beginning this lesson remember to redo the problems from Lessons 3, 7, 11, 15, and 19 that you have marked off. Do not "unmark" a question unless you get it correct.

Move the Sides of a Figure Around

A seemingly difficult geometry problem can sometimes be made much easier by moving the sides of the figure around.

Try to answer the following question using this strategy. **Do not** check the solution until you have attempted this question yourself.

LEVEL 2: GEOMETRY

1. What is the perimeter, in meters, of the figure below?

   A. 17
   B. 34
   C. 66
   D. 132
   E. 144

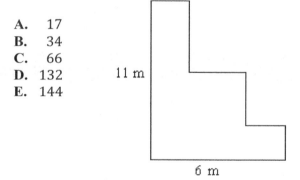

Solution

* Recall that to compute the perimeter of the figure we need to add up the lengths of all 8 line segments in the figure. We "move" the two smaller horizontal segments up and the two smaller vertical segments to the right as shown below.

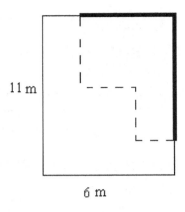

Note that the "bold" length is equal to the "dashed" length. Thus, the perimeter is $(2)(11) + (2)(6) = 22 + 12 = 34$, choice **B**.

Fitting Geometric Objects Inside Another Object

To see how many two-dimensional objects fit inside another two-dimensional object we divide areas. To see how many three-dimensional objects fit inside another three-dimensional object we divide volumes.

Try to answer the following question using this strategy. **Do not** check the solution until you have attempted this question yourself.

LEVEL 3: GEOMETRY

2. How many figures of the size and shape below are needed to completely cover a rectangle measuring 80 inches by 30 inches?

   F. 37
   G. 330
   H. 700
   J. 740
   K. 800

240

Solution

* The area of the given figure is 3 inches^2 and the area of the rectangle is $80 \cdot 30 = 2400$ inches^2. We can see how many of the given figures cover the rectangle by dividing the two areas.

$$\frac{2400}{3} = 800, \text{choice } \mathbf{K}.$$

Note: We can get the area of the given figure by splitting it into 3 squares each with area 1 inch^2 as shown to the right. Then

$1 + 1 + 1 = 3.$

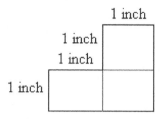

Another way to get the area of the given figure is to think of it as lying inside a square of side length 2 inches as shown below.

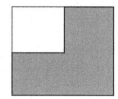

The area of the big square is $2 \cdot 2 = 4$ inches^2, and the area of the little square is $1 \cdot 1 = 1$ inch^2. So, the area of the given figure is $4 - 1 = 3$ inches^2.

The Measure of an Exterior Angle of a Triangle is the Sum of the Measures of the Two Opposite Interior Angles of the Triangle

Try to answer the following question using this strategy. **Do not** check the solution until you have attempted this question yourself.

LEVEL 2: GEOMETRY

3. In $\triangle ABD$ below, if $y = 42$, what is the value of z?

   A. 38
   B. 42
   C. 46
   D. 52
   E. 56

Solutions

* **Quickest solution:** $80 = 42 + z$, and therefore $z = 80 - 42 = 38$, choice **A**.

Alternate method: Angles ACD and ACB form a **linear pair** and are therefore **supplementary**. It follows that angle ACB measures $180 - 80 = 100$ degrees. Since the angle measures of a triangle add up to 180 degrees, it follows that $z = 180 - 42 - 100 = 38$, choice **A**.

The Triangle Rule

The triangle rule states that the length of the third side of a triangle is between the sum and difference of the lengths of the other two sides.

Try to answer the following question using this strategy. **Do not** check the solution until you have attempted this question yourself.

LEVEL 5: GEOMETRY

4. If x is an integer greater than 8, how many different triangles are there with sides of length 3, 9 and x?

   F. One
   G. Two
   H. Three
   J. Four
   K. Five

242

Solution

* The triangle rule tells us that $9 - 3 < x < 9 + 3$. That is, $6 < x < 12$. Since x is an integer greater than 8, x can be 9, 10, or 11. So, there are **three** possibilities, choice **H**.

You're doing great! Let's just practice a bit more. Try to solve each of the following problems. The answers to these problems, followed by full solutions are at the end of this lesson. **Do not** look at the answers until you have attempted these problems yourself. Please remember to mark off any problems you get wrong.

LEVEL 3: GEOMETRY

5. In $\triangle ABC$, the length of $\overline{AB}$ is $\sqrt{82}$ centimeters, and the length of $\overline{BC}$ is $\sqrt{71}$ centimeters. If it can be determined, what is the length, in centimeters, of $\overline{AC}$?

   A. $\sqrt{11}$
   B. $\sqrt{71}$
   C. $\sqrt{82}$
   D. $\sqrt{153}$
   E. Cannot be determined from the given information

6. In the figure below, one side of a triangle is extended. Which of the following is true?

   F. $y = 80$
   G. $z = 80$
   H. $z - y = 80$
   J. $y + z = 80$
   K. $x = y + z$

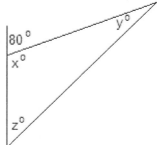

LEVEL 4: GEOMETRY

7. Rectangular bricks measuring $\frac{1}{2}$ meter by $\frac{1}{3}$ meter are sold in boxes containing 8 bricks each. What is the least number of boxes of bricks needed to cover a rectangular area that has dimensions 9 meters by 11 meters?

   A. 3
   B. 17
   C. 74
   D. 75
   E. 132

LEVEL 5: GEOMETRY

8. How many solid wood cubes, each with a total surface area of 150 square centimeters, can be cut from a solid wood cube with a total surface area of 1,350 square centimeters if no wood is lost in the cutting?

   F. 3
   G. 9
   H. 27
   J. 81
   K. 243

9. The lengths of the sides of a triangle are x, 9, and 17, where x is the shortest side. If the triangle is not isosceles, which of the following could be the value of x?

   A. 7.6
   B. 8
   C. 8.7
   D. 9
   E. 9.1

10. In the figure below, what is the average of x, y, z and w in terms of k?

F. $\frac{k}{4}$
G. $\frac{k}{2}$
H. k
J. $2k$
K. $4k$

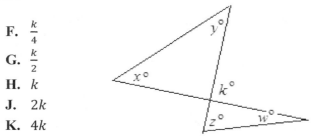

Answers

1. B
2. K
3. A
4. H
5. E
6. J
7. D
8. H
9. C
10. G

Full Solutions

5.
* The triangle rule tells us that $\sqrt{82} - \sqrt{71} < \overline{AC} < \sqrt{82} + \sqrt{71}$. This is all that we can say, however. It follows that the answer is choice **E**.

Notes: (1) If $\triangle ABC$ is a right triangle, with legs AB and BC, then by the Pythagorean Theorem, we have $AC^2 = 82 + 71 = 153$. So $AC = \sqrt{153}$.

(2) If $\triangle ABC$ is a right triangle, and AB is the hypotenuse, then we have $AC^2 = 82 - 71 = 11$. So, $AC = \sqrt{11}$.

(3) Notes 1 and 2 above give two possible results for $\overline{AC}$, verifying that the answer is choice E.

6.
* The measure of an exterior angle of a triangle is the sum of the measures of the two opposite interior angles of the triangle. Therefore, $80 = y + z$, choice **J**.

7.
* The area of a face of one rectangular brick is $(\frac{1}{2})(\frac{1}{3}) = \frac{1}{6}$. The area of the rectangular region we want to cover is $9 \cdot 11 = 99$. We can see how many bricks we need to cover this area by dividing the two areas.

$$99 \div (\tfrac{1}{6}) = 99 \cdot 6 = 594.$$

Now, $\frac{594}{8} = 74.25$. So, the number of boxes needed is 75, choice **D**.

Remark: A common error would be to round 74.25 to 74. This is incorrect because 74 boxes will not contain enough bricks to cover the entire area. Indeed, $8(74) = 592 < 594$.

8.
* We get the surface area of a cube by adding up the areas of the 6 faces. Each face has area x^2, where x is the length of a side of the cube. Therefore, the surface area of a cube is $6x^2$. So, to get the length of a side of each cube we need to solve the equations

$$\begin{array}{ll} 6x^2 = 150 \quad \text{and} & 6x^2 = 1350 \\ x^2 = 25 & x^2 = 225 \\ x = 5 & x = 15 \end{array}$$

Thus, the volume of each cube is $5^3 = 125$ and $15^3 = 3375$, respectively. We can see how many smaller cubes can be cut from the larger cube by dividing the two volumes: $\frac{3375}{125} = 27$, choice **H**.

9.
* **Solution using the triangle rule:** By the triangle rule, we have $17 - 9 < x < 17 + 9$. That is, $8 < x < 26$. Since x is the shortest side, $x < 9$. So, we must choose a number between 8 and 9. Therefore, of the answer choices, the only possible answer is 8.7, choice **C**.

10.
* $k = x + y$, and $k = z + w$, and so $x + y + z + w = 2k$. The average of x, y, z and w is $\frac{x+y+z+w}{4} = \frac{2k}{4} = \frac{k}{2}$, choice **G**.

Remark: Note that the angle labeled k is an exterior angle of both triangles. This is why we initially get two equations involving k.

OPTIONAL MATERIAL

Generalized Pythagorean Theorem

The length d of the long diagonal of a rectangular solid is

$$d^2 = a^2 + b^2 + c^2$$

where a, b and c are the length, width and height of the rectangular solid.

Example: Find the length of the longest line segment with endpoints on a cube with side length 4.

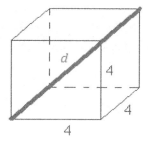

* In this problem, our rectangular solid is a cube. Thus, a, b and c are all equal to 4. So $d^2 = a^2 + b^2 + c^2 = 4^2 + 4^2 + 4^2 = 48 = 16 \cdot 3$. So, $d = \mathbf{4\sqrt{3}}$.

LESSON 24
COUNTING AND PROBABILITY

Reminder: Before beginning this lesson remember to redo the problems from Lessons 4, 8, 12, 16, and 20 that you have marked off. Do not "unmark" a question unless you get it correct.

Review the strategy of **Writing a List** from Lesson 8 and the **Simple Probability Principle** from Lesson 12. Also, recall that the **Counting Principle** says that if one event is followed by a second independent event, the number of possibilities is multiplied. Try to answer each of the following questions using one of these strategies. You may also want to use permutations/combinations in some problems.

LEVEL 1: PROBABILITY

1. There are exactly 24 coins in a bag. There are 8 pennies, 3 nickels, 7 dimes, and the rest are quarters. If one coin is selected at random from the bag, what is the probability that the coin is **not** a quarter?

    A. $\frac{1}{8}$
    B. $\frac{7}{24}$
    C. $\frac{1}{3}$
    D. $\frac{5}{12}$
    E. $\frac{3}{4}$

LEVEL 2: COUNTING AND PROBABILITY

2. A chemist is testing 5 different liquids. For each test, the chemist chooses 2 of the liquids and mixes them together. What is the least number of tests that must be done so that every possible combination of liquids is tested?

    F. 5
    G. 6
    H. 8
    J. 10
    K. 15

3. Of the marbles in a jar, 36 are red. Joseph randomly takes one marble out of the jar. If the probability is $\frac{9}{13}$ that the marble he chooses is red, how many marbles are in the jar?

   A. 39
   B. 52
   C. 78
   D. 104
   E. 117

LEVEL 3: COUNTING AND PROBABILITY

4. A chemist is testing 7 different liquids. For each test, the chemist chooses 4 of the liquids and mixes them together. What is the least number of tests that must be done so that every possible combination of liquids is tested?

   F. 3
   G. 8
   H. 11
   J. 28
   K. 35

$$A, I, T, R, P$$

5. If the letters from the list above are to be randomly ordered, what is the probability that the letters will appear in the order T, A, P, I, R?

   A. $\frac{1}{120}$
   B. $\frac{1}{60}$
   C. $\frac{1}{40}$
   D. $\frac{1}{30}$
   E. $\frac{1}{25}$

6. Set *X* contains only the integers 0 through 180 inclusive. If a number is selected at random from *X*, what is the probability that the number selected will be greater than 114 ?

   F. $\frac{65}{181}$
   G. $\frac{66}{181}$
   H. $\frac{11}{30}$
   J. $\frac{66}{179}$
   K. $\frac{67}{180}$

LEVEL 4: COUNTING

7. Exactly 5 actors try out for the 5 parts in a play. If each actor can perform any one part and no one will perform more than one part, how many different assignments of actors are possible?

   A. 120
   B. 60
   C. 25
   D. 15
   E. 10

8. Any 2 points determine a line. If there are 12 points in a plane, no 3 of which lie on the same line, how many lines are determined by pairs of these 12 points?

   F. 14
   G. 24
   H. 66
   J. 108
   K. 132

LEVEL 5: COUNTING AND PROBABILITY

9. A five-digit number is to be formed using each of the digits 1, 2, 3, 4, and 5 exactly once. How many such numbers are there in which the digits 3 and 4 are not next to each other?

   A. 12
   B. 18
   C. 36
   D. 60
   E. 72

10. The integers 1 through 6 are written on each of six cards. The cards are shuffled and one card is drawn at random. That card is then replaced, the cards are shuffled again and another card is drawn at random. This procedure is repeated one more time (for a total of three times). What is the probability that the sum of the numbers on the three cards drawn was 3, 4 or 5 ?

    F. $\frac{9}{216}$
    G. $\frac{10}{216}$
    H. $\frac{11}{216}$
    J. $\frac{12}{216}$
    K. $\frac{13}{216}$

Answers

1. E
2. J
3. B
4. K
5. A
6. G
7. A
8. H
9. E
10. G

Full solutions to these problems are available for free download here:

www.satprepget800.com/28LesInt

LESSON 25
NUMBER THEORY

Try to solve each of the following problems. The answers to these problems are at the end of this lesson. **Do not** look at the answers until you have attempted these problems yourself. Please remember to mark off any problems you get wrong.

Full solutions to these problems are available for free download here:

www.satprepget800.com/28LesInt

LEVEL 1: NUMBER THEORY

1. What is the least common denominator of $\frac{1}{9}, \frac{5}{6},$ and $\frac{7}{10}$?

   A. 15
   B. 90
   C. 135
   D. 270
   E. 540

2. The price of a house increased from $600,000 to $800,000. The price increased by what percent?

   F. 75%
   G. $66\frac{2}{3}$%
   H. 50%
   J. $33\frac{1}{3}$%
   K. 25%

3. The first term of a sequence is -17. Each term after the first is 4 more than the previous term. What is the first positive number in the sequence?

   A. 1
   B. 2
   C. 3
   D. 4
   E. 5

4. Alex bought a hat that had an original price of $18.00. The store offered a 25% discount on the original price of the hat, and Alex paid 4% sales tax on the discounted price of the hat. How much did Alex pay for the hat, including tax?

   F. $ 4.68
   G. $12.78
   H. $14.04
   J. $14.22
   K. $14.36

5. What is the greatest positive integer that is a divisor of 26, 39, 117, and 169?

   A. 1
   B. 3
   C. 5
   D. 13
   E. 26

LEVEL 2: NUMBER THEORY

6. The ratio of 29 to 5 is equal to the ratio of 203 to what number?

   F. 0.7
   G. 35
   H. 70
   J. 350
   K. 1177.4

7. Danielle's resting heart rate is 65 beats per minute. In scientific notation, how many times would her heart beat in 1 hour, assuming she remains inactive for the full hour?

   A. 6.5×10^1
   B. 65×10^1
   C. 3.9×10^3
   D. 39×10^3
   E. 7.8×10^2

8. The first term in the geometric sequence below is -1. If it can be determined, what is the 5th term of the sequence?

$$-1, 3, -9, \ldots$$

    F. -243
    G. -81
    H. 81
    J. 243
    K. Cannot be determined from the given information

9. A copy machine makes 3200 copies per hour. At this rate, in how many <u>minutes</u> can the copy machine produce 800 copies?

    A. 4
    B. 8
    C. 12
    D. 15
    E. 18

10. A piece of cable k feet in length is cut into exactly 4 pieces, each 3 feet 5 inches in length. What is the value of k ?

    F. $12\frac{2}{3}$
    G. 13
    H. $13\frac{1}{3}$
    J. $13\frac{2}{3}$
    K. 14

11. Which of the following is a simplified form of $\sqrt{28} - \sqrt{175}$?

    A. $-3\sqrt{7}$
    B. $-\sqrt{7}$
    C. $\sqrt{7}$
    D. $3\sqrt{7}$
    E. $5\sqrt{7}$

LEVEL 3: NUMBER THEORY

12. The radius of the Sun is approximately 4.32×10^5 miles and the radius of Jupiter is approximately 4.34×10^4 miles. Which of the following is closest to the difference, in miles, between the diameter of the Sun and the diameter of Jupiter?

    F. 2.0×10^3
    G. 2.0×10^4
    H. 2.0×10^5
    J. 3.9×10^4
    K. 3.9×10^5

13. Daniel is drawing a time line to represent a 1000-year period of time. If he makes the time line 75 inches long and draws it to scale, how many inches will represent 80 years?

    A. 6
    B. 9
    C. 12
    D. 20
    E. 32

14. What percent of 75 is 32 ?

    F. $2\frac{11}{32}\%$
    G. 24%
    H. $37\frac{1}{3}\%$
    J. $42\frac{2}{3}\%$
    K. $234\frac{3}{8}\%$

15. If an integer n is divisible by 21, and 49, what is the next larger integer divisible by these numbers?

    A. $n + 21$
    B. $n + 49$
    C. $n + 70$
    D. $n + 147$
    E. $n + 1029$

16. The number 0.00007 is 1000 times what number?

   F. 7×10^{-9}
   G. 7×10^{-8}
   H. 7×10^{-7}
   J. 7×10^{8}
   K. 7×10^{9}

LEVEL 4: NUMBER THEORY

17. The number 12,121 is the product of the prime numbers 17, 23, and 31. With this knowledge, what is the prime factorization of 145,452?

   A. $2 \cdot 3 \cdot 17 \cdot 23 \cdot 31$
   B. $2^2 \cdot 3 \cdot 17 \cdot 23 \cdot 31$
   C. $12 \cdot 17 \cdot 23 \cdot 31$
   D. $3 \cdot 4 \cdot 17 \cdot 23 \cdot 31$
   E. $2^2 \cdot 3^2 \cdot 17 \cdot 23 \cdot 31$

18. Which of the following complex numbers equals $(\sqrt{2} + 3i)(5 - i)$?

   F. $5\sqrt{2} - 3i$
   G. $5\sqrt{2} + 3i$
   H. $(5\sqrt{2} + 3) + (15 + \sqrt{2})i$
   J. $(5\sqrt{2} + 3) + (15 - \sqrt{2})i$
   K. $(5\sqrt{2} - 3) + (15 + \sqrt{2})i$

19. What is the value of $\log_5 125$?

   A. 3
   B. 4
   C. 6
   D. 10
   E. 16

20. Suppose that k is a positive real number and $\frac{3k^2}{5k^3}$ is a rational number. Which of the following statements about k must be true?

   F. $k = \frac{3}{5}$
   G. $k = 1$
   H. $k = \frac{5}{3}$
   J. k is rational
   K. k is irrational

LEVEL 5: NUMBER THEORY

21. For all pairs of nonzero real numbers a and b, the product of the complex number $a - bi$ and which of the following complex numbers is a real number?

   A. $a + bi$
   B. $a - bi$
   C. $b + ai$
   D. $b - ai$
   E. $ab + i$

22. Consecutive terms of an arithmetic sequence have a positive common difference. The sum of the first 4 terms of the sequence is 200. Which of the following values CANNOT be the first term of the arithmetic sequence?

   F. 46.5
   G. 48
   H. 49.5
   J. 51
   K. None of these can be the first term of the arithmetic sequence.

23. Which of the following expressions equals an irrational number?

   A. $\frac{\sqrt{3}}{\sqrt{27}}$

   B. $\frac{\sqrt{27}}{\sqrt{3}}$

   C. $\sqrt{3} \cdot \sqrt{27}$

   D. $\sqrt{3} + \sqrt{27}$

   E. $\sqrt{3}^2$

24. The integer k is equal to m^2 for some integer m. If k is divisible by 6 and 40, what is the smallest possible positive value of k?

   F. 720
   G. 900
   H. 1200
   J. 1800
   K. 3600

Answers

1. B	5. D	9. D	13. A	17. B	21. A
2. J	6. G	10. J	14. J	18. J	22. J
3. C	7. C	11. A	15. D	19. A	23. D
4. H	8. G	12. K	16. G	20. J	24. K

Full solutions to these problems are available for free download here:

www.satprepget800.com/28LesInt

LESSON 26
ALGEBRA AND FUNCTIONS

Try to solve each of the following problems. The answers to these problems are at the end of this lesson. **Do not** look at the answers until you have attempted these problems yourself. Please remember to mark off any problems you get wrong.

Full solutions to these problems are available for free download here:
www.satprepget800.com/28LesInt

LEVEL 1: ALGEBRA AND FUNCTIONS

1. For what value of x is the equation $7^{5x-2} = 7^{3x}$ true?

   A. 1
   B. 2
   C. 3
   D. 4
   E. 5

2. If $6(x-4) = 7(x-4)$, what is the value of x?

   F. 1
   G. 2
   H. 3
   J. 4
   K. 5

3. If $x + 3 = 10$, then $(x+1)^2 =$

   A. 16
   B. 25
   C. 36
   D. 49
   E. 64

4. Which of the following expressions is equivalent to 11 less than the product of *x* and *y*?

   F. $x + y = 11$
   G. $xy - 11$
   H. $11xy$
   J. $11(x + y)$
   K. $(x + 11)y$

5. If Robert drove *a* miles in *b* hours, which of the following represents his average speed, in miles per hour?

   A. $\frac{a}{b}$
   B. $\frac{b}{a}$
   C. $\frac{1}{ab}$
   D. ab
   E. $a^2 b$

LEVEL 2: ALGEBRA AND FUNCTIONS

6. If $f(x) = 2x^3 + 3x - \sqrt{x}$, what is the value of $f(4)$?

   F. 20
   G. 24
   H. 26
   J. 138
   K. 140

7. Which of the following polynomial equations has solutions -5, 3, and 7 ?

   A. $(x - 7)^2(x - 3)(x + 5)^3$
   B. $(x - 5)(x + 5)^2$
   C. $(x - 5)^3(x + 5)$
   D. $(x - 5)(x + 3)(x + 7)$
   E. $(x + 5)^2(x + 3)(x + 7)$

8. The polynomial $56x^2 + 11x - 15$ is equivalent to the product of $(7x - 3)$ and which of the following binomials?

    F. $49x - 18$
    G. $49x - 12$
    H. $49x + 12$
    J. $8x - 5$
    K. $8x + 5$

LEVEL 3: ALGEBRA AND FUNCTIONS

9. Which of the following expressions is equivalent to $x^{-\frac{2}{3}}$?

    A. $\frac{x^2}{3}$
    B. $\frac{3}{x^2}$
    C. $-\sqrt[3]{x^2}$
    D. $\frac{1}{\sqrt[3]{x^2}}$
    E. $-\frac{1}{\sqrt[3]{x^2}}$

10. What is the determinant of the matrix $\begin{bmatrix} 5 & -6 \\ 3 & -2 \end{bmatrix}$?

    F. -36
    G. -28
    H. 8
    J. 27
    K. 36

11. Which of the following expressions is equivalent to $(5x^3 - 3x^2 + 1) - (3x + 7) - (2x^2 + 1) + (5x^2 + 3x + 8)$?

    A. $5x + 1$
    B. $5x^3 + 1$
    C. $5x^3 + 10x^2 + 1$
    D. $5x^3 - 6x + 1$
    E. $5x^3 + 10x^2 - 6x + 1$

12. If $5x - 6 = |-6|$, how many different values are possible for x?

    F. 0
    G. 1
    H. 2
    J. 3
    K. Infinitely many

13. The graphs of the functions $f(x) = 2x + 2$ and $g(x) = 5 - x$ in the standard (x, y) coordinate plane are lines. If it can be determined, at what point do the graphs intersect?

    A. $(-1, 0)$
    B. $(0, 2)$
    C. $(1, 4)$
    D. $(2, 6)$
    E. Cannot be determined from the given information

14. In the equation $\log_3 45 - \log_3 5 = \log_3 x$, the value of x is?

    F. 6
    G. 7
    H. 8
    J. 9
    K. 10

LEVEL 4: ALGEBRA AND FUNCTIONS

15. The functions f and g are defined as $f(x) = 2x - 5$ and $g(x) = 3x + 1$. Which of the following expressions is equivalent to $f(g(x))$?

    A. $5x - 4$
    B. $6x - 3$
    C. $6x - 14$
    D. $6x^2 - 5$
    E. $6x^2 - 9x - 5$

16. Given j and k such that $(b^3)^j = b^6$ and $(b^k)^3 = b^{12}$ for all positive b, what is b^{-k-j} ?

　　F. $\frac{1}{b^{10}}$
　　G. $\frac{1}{b^6}$
　　H. $\frac{1}{b}$
　　J. b^6
　　K. b^{10}

17. If $x = 5$ is a solution to the equation $x^2 - 3x + a = 0$, then the other solution is

　　A. -3
　　B. -2
　　C. -1
　　D. 0
　　E. 1

18. Let ■ be defined by $x\ ■\ y = \frac{x+y}{x-y}$ for all real numbers x and y, where $x \neq y$. If $1\ ■\ 2 = 2\ ■\ k$, what is the value of k ?

　　F. 0
　　G. 1
　　H. 2
　　J. 3
　　K. 4

19. If $y = 3^x$, which of the following expressions is equivalent to $9^x - 3^{x+2}$ for all positive integer values of x ?

　　A. $3y - 3$
　　B. y^2
　　C. $y^2 - y$
　　D. $y^2 - 3y$
　　E. $y^2 - 9y$

20. What is the matrix product $[a \quad b \quad c] \begin{bmatrix} -1 \\ 0 \\ 1 \end{bmatrix}$?

F. $[-a + c]$
G. $[-a \quad 0 \quad c]$
H. $\begin{bmatrix} -a \\ 0 \\ c \end{bmatrix}$
J. $\begin{bmatrix} -a & -b & -c \\ 0 & 0 & 0 \\ a & b & c \end{bmatrix}$
K. $\begin{bmatrix} -a & 0 & a \\ -b & 0 & b \\ -c & 0 & c \end{bmatrix}$

LEVEL 5: ALGEBRA AND FUNCTIONS

21. Given $f(x) = \frac{x-3}{x^2}$, which of the following expressions is equal to $f(x + 5)$ for all x in its domain?

A. $\frac{x+2}{x^2+10x+25}$
B. $\frac{x+2}{x^2+5}$
C. $\frac{x+2}{2x+10}$
D. $\frac{x-3}{x+5}$
E. $\frac{-x^2+x-3}{x^2}$

22. The magnitude of an earthquake, M, can be modeled by the equation $M = \log \frac{I}{S}$, where I is the intensity of the earthquake and S is a constant. What is the magnitude of an earthquake whose intensity is 10,000 times the value of S?

F. 1
G. 4
H. 10
J. 30
K. 100

23. Consider the function $f(x) = x^2 - 5x + c$. The graph of f in the (x, y) coordinate plane is a parabola whose vertex lies on the x-axis. What is the value of c ?

   A. -6.25
   B. -6
   C. 0
   D. 6
   E. 6.25

24. If $3x = 5 + 2y$ and $4x = 3 - 5y$, what is the value of x ?

   F. $\dfrac{23}{31}$
   G. $\dfrac{37}{41}$
   H. $\dfrac{31}{23}$
   J. $\dfrac{41}{25}$
   K. 31

Answers

1. A	5. A	9. D	13. C	17. B	21. A
2. J	6. J	10. H	14. J	18. K	22. G
3. E	7. A	11. B	15. B	19. E	23. E
4. G	8. K	12. G	16. G	20. F	24. H

Full solutions to these problems are available for free download here:

www.satprepget800.com/28LesInt

Lesson 27
Geometry and Trigonometry

Try to solve each of the following problems. The answers to these problems are at the end of this lesson. **Do not** look at the answers until you have attempted these problems yourself. Please remember to mark off any problems you get wrong.

Full solutions to these problems are available for free download here:

www.satprepget800.com/28LesInt

Level 1: Geometry

1. In the standard (x, y) coordinate plane, what is the midpoint of the line segment that has endpoints $(-2, 5)$ and $(3, -1)$?

    A. $(0, 3)$
    B. $(\frac{1}{2}, 2)$
    C. $(1, 6)$
    D. $(\frac{3}{2}, 1)$
    E. $(5, -5)$

2. If the degree measure of one of the three angles of a triangle is 80° and the other two angles are congruent, what is the measure of one of the congruent angles?

    F. 40°
    G. 50°
    H. 80°
    J. 100°
    K. 120°

3. What is the slope of the line through $(3, -5)$ and $(-2, -1)$ in the standard (x, y) coordinate plane?

   A. -6
   B. $-\frac{5}{4}$
   C. $-\frac{4}{5}$
   D. $\frac{4}{5}$
   E. $\frac{5}{4}$

4. What is the <u>diameter</u> of a circle whose circumference is 4π?

   F. 1
   G. 2
   H. π
   J. 4
   K. 2π

5. In the figure below, A, B, and C lie on the same line. B is the center of the smaller circle, and C is the center of the larger circle. If the diameter of the larger circle is 40, what is the radius of the smaller circle?

   A. 5
   B. 10
   C. 12
   D. 15
   E. 20

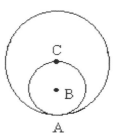

LEVEL 2: GEOMETRY

6. What is the area of a right triangle, in square centimeters, whose sides have lengths 15 cm, 36 cm, and 39 cm?

   F. 270
   G. 292.5
   H. 540
   J. 585
   K. 702

7. The points P, Q, R, and S are collinear, with Q between P and R and with R between Q and S. Given $PR = 11$ in, $QS = 17$ in, and $QR = 4$ in, what is PS, in inches?

   A. 10
   B. 18
   C. 22
   D. 24
   E. 32

8. In the figure below, point Q lies on side PR. If $48 < y < 50$, which of the following is a possible value of x?

   F. 130
   G. 131
   H. 132
   J. 133
   K. 134

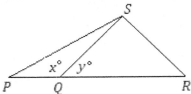

9. In parallelogram $PQRS$ below, $\overline{PR}$ is a diagonal, the measure of $\angle PRS$ is 50°, and the measure of $\angle PQR$ is 110°. What is the measure of $\angle QRP$?

   A. 20°
   B. 40°
   C. 50°
   D. 70°
   E. 110°

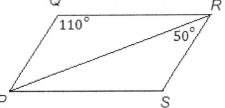

10. In the xy-plane, the point $(5, 0)$ is the center of a circle that has radius 5. Which of the following is NOT a point on the circle?

    F. $(10, 0)$
    G. $(10, -5)$
    H. $(5, 5)$
    J. $(5, -5)$
    K. $(0, 0)$

11. Δ*PST* is equilateral Given that *QR* ∥ *ST*, what is the value of *x* ?

   A. 60°
   B. 95°
   C. 100°
   D. 110°
   E. 120°

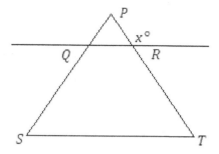

12. In Δ*ABD* below, if $z = 37$, what is the value of *y*?

   F. 38
   G. 75
   H. 90
   J. 100
   K. 105

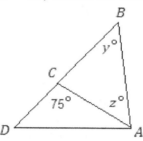

LEVEL 3: GEOMETRY

13. In the standard (x, y) coordinate plane, what is the slope of a line that is perpendicular to the line with equation $2x - 3y = -1$?

   A. -2
   B. $-\frac{3}{2}$
   C. $-\frac{2}{3}$
   D. $\frac{2}{3}$
   E. 3

14. A circle in the standard (x, y) coordinate plane has center $O(-2, -6)$ and passes through the point $P(4, 2)$. What is the length of a <u>diameter</u> of the circle?

    F. $2\sqrt{5}$
    G. $4\sqrt{5}$
    H. 10
    J. 20
    K. 40

15. The volume of a right circular cylinder is 1331π cubic centimeters. If the height and base radius of the cylinder are equal, what is the base diameter of the cylinder, in centimeters?

    A. 22
    B. 20
    C. 11
    D. 10
    E. 7

16. Which of the following is an equation of the line in the xy-plane that passes through the point $(0, -3)$ and is perpendicular to the line $y = -4x + 7$?

    F. $y = -4x - 6$
    G. $y = -4x - 3$
    H. $y = -4x + 3$
    J. $y = \frac{1}{4}x - 3$
    K. $y = \frac{1}{4}x + 6$

17. In the figure below, $k \parallel n$. What is the value of x?

A. 35
B. 70
C. 75
D. 110
E. 145

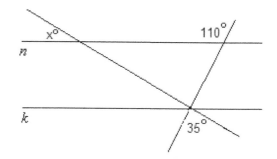

LEVEL 4: GEOMETRY

18. The angle of elevation from the tip of the shadow of a 30 meter tall building to the top of the building has a cosine of $\frac{3}{7}$. What is the length of the shadow to the nearest meter?

    F. 12
    G. 13
    H. 14
    J. 15
    K. 16

19. A cube of sugar with a side length of 2 inches is placed into a glass of water. The glass is shaped like a right circular cylinder with a diameter of 6 inches and a height of 10 inches. Assuming that the glass is filled to the halfway point with water and the sugar cube is completely submerged in the water, which of the following numerical expressions gives the number of cubic inches of water in the glass?

    A. $\pi(5)^3 - 2^3$
    B. $\pi(3)^2(5) - 2^3$
    C. $\pi(3)(5)^2 - 2^3$
    D. $2\pi(3)(5) - 6(2)^2$
    E. $2\pi(3)(5) + \pi(3)^2(12) - 6(2)^2$

20. Point *A* is a vertex of a 9-sided polygon. The polygon has 9 sides of equal length and 9 angles of equal measure. When all possible diagonals are drawn from point *A* in the polygon, how many triangles are formed?

   F. One
   G. Three
   H. Five
   J. Seven
   K. Nine

21. Two circles are shown below. The radius of the smaller circle is 3 meters and the radius of the larger circle is 7 meters. What is the area, in square meters, of the shaded region bounded by the circles?

   A. 9π
   B. 16π
   C. 32π
   D. 40π
   E. 49π

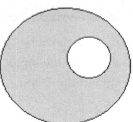

LEVEL 5: GEOMETRY

22. Points *A*, *B*, and *C* lie in a plane. If the distance between *A* and *B* is 16 and the distance between *B* and *C* is 12, which of the following could NOT be the distance between *A* and *C* ?

   I. 3
   II. 27
   III. 28

   F. I only
   G. II only
   H. III only
   J. I and III only
   K. I, II, and III

23. In $\triangle ABC$, the measure of $\angle C$ is 90°, $\tan A = \frac{3}{4}$, and $BC = 21$ centimeters. What is the area of $\triangle ABC$, in square centimeters?

   A. 147
   B. 294
   C. 367.5
   D. 490
   E. 735

24. If $\cos x = k$, then for all x in the interval $0 < x < 90°$, $\tan x =$

   F. $\frac{1}{1+k}$
   G. $\frac{k}{\sqrt{1+k^2}}$
   H. $\frac{1}{\sqrt{1+k^2}}$
   J. $\frac{\sqrt{1-k^2}}{k}$
   K. $\sqrt{1-k^2}$

Answers

1. B	5. B	9. A	13. B	17. C	21. D
2. G	6. F	10. G	14. J	18. H	22. F
3. C	7. D	11. E	15. A	19. B	23. B
4. J	8. G	12. F	16. J	20. J	24. J

Full solutions to these problems are available for free download here:

www.satprepget800.com/28LesInt

Lesson 28
Probability and Statistics

Try to solve each of the following problems. The answers to these problems are at the end of this lesson. **Do not** look at the answers until you have attempted these problems yourself. Please remember to mark off any problems you get wrong.

Full solutions to these problems are available for free download here:

www.satprepget800.com/28LesInt

Level 1: Probability and Statistics

1. The average (arithmetic mean) of five numbers is 510. If the sum of four of the numbers is 1000, what is the fifth number?

    A. 20
    B. 140
    C. 820
    D. 980
    E. 1550

2. In a jar, there are exactly 104 marbles, each of which is yellow, purple, or blue. The probability of randomly selecting a yellow marble from the jar is $\frac{3}{13}$ and the probability of randomly selecting a purple marble from the jar is $\frac{6}{13}$. How many marbles in the jar are blue?

    F. 8
    G. 16
    H. 24
    J. 32
    K. 48

3. Each question on a 3-question quiz offers 4 answers, and exactly 1 answer must be chosen for each question. The quiz has how many possible combinations of answers?

   A. 4
   B. 8
   C. 16
   D. 32
   E. 64

4. A department consisting of 28 faculty members is meeting to choose a chair for the executive committee. The representative, who will be selected at random, CANNOT be any of the 5 faculty members that are already chairs of other committees. What is the probability that Dan, who is NOT the chair of another committee, will be selected?

   F. 0
   G. $\frac{1}{28}$
   H. $\frac{1}{23}$
   J. $\frac{1}{5}$
   K. $\frac{3}{14}$

5. Stickers in the shape of an isosceles triangle, a hexagon, a parallelogram, and a trapezoid are placed into a bucket. If one of these stickers is taken out at random, what is the probability that the shape chosen will have less than 4 vertices?

   A. $\frac{3}{13}$
   B. $\frac{1}{4}$
   C. $\frac{5}{11}$
   D. $\frac{1}{2}$
   E. $\frac{3}{4}$

LEVEL 2: PROBABILITY AND STATISTICS

6. The average (arithmetic mean) of sixteen numbers is 90. If a seventeenth number, 73, is added to the group, what is the average of the seventeen numbers?

    F. 88
    G. 89
    H. 89.5
    J. 90
    K. 90.5

7. Six marbles, each of a different color, are to be lined up in a row. In how many different orders can the marbles be arranged?

    A. 720
    B. 540
    C. 36
    D. 30
    E. 21

8. The average (arithmetic mean) of z, 2, 16, and 21 is z. What is the value of z?

    F. 8
    G. 11
    H. 13
    J. 17
    K. 19

9. A is a set of numbers whose average (arithmetic mean) is 15. B is a set that is generated by multiplying each number in A by 6. What is the average of the numbers in set B?

    A. 15
    B. 21
    C. 45
    D. 81
    E. 90

10. Of the 37 marbles in a jar, the most common color is green. What is the probability that a marble randomly selected from the jar is <u>not</u> green?

    F. $\frac{1}{37}$

    G. $\frac{5}{37}$

    H. $\frac{1}{3}$

    J. $\frac{36}{37}$

    K. It cannot be determined from the information given.

11. What is the average (arithmetic mean) of $9 - k$, 9, and $9 + k$?

    A. 3

    B. 9

    C. 15

    D. $3 + \frac{k}{3}$

    E. $9 + \frac{k}{3}$

LEVEL 3: PROBABILITY AND STATISTICS

12. The mean of a list of 10 numbers is 100. A new list of 10 numbers has the same first 8 numbers as the original list, but the ninth number in the new list is 7 more than the ninth number in the old list, and the tenth number in the new list is 2 less than the tenth number in the original list. What is the average of this new list of numbers?

    F. 98

    G. 100

    H. 100.5

    J. 105

    K. 105.5

13. A jar contains 11 orange jellybeans, 7 yellow jellybeans, and 4 red jellybeans. How many additional yellow jellybeans must be added to the jar so that the probability of randomly selecting a yellow jellybean is $\frac{6}{11}$?

   A. 8
   B. 11
   C. 14
   D. 17
   E. 23

14. The test grades of the 25 students in a math class are shown in the chart below. What is the median test grade for the class?

TEST GRADES OF STUDENTS IN MATH CLASS

Test Grade	60	65	75	95	100
Number of students with that grade	3	12	4	5	1

   F. 65
   G. 70
   H. 75
   J. 85
   K. 95

15. 1000 musicians were polled to determine which of the following instruments they play: piano (P), drums (D), or guitar (G). The Venn diagram below shows the results of the poll. How many musicians said they play at least 2 of the 3 instruments?

   A. 439
   B. 451
   C. 549
   D. 561
   E. 985

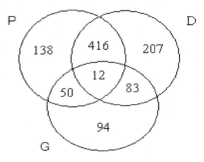

LEVEL 4: PROBABILITY AND STATISTICS

16. Which of the following statements is logically equivalent to the following statement?

    If a pig has wings, then it can fly.

    F. If a pig dos not have wings, then it cannot fly.
    G. If a pig cannot fly, then it does not have wings.
    H. A pig has wings if and only if it can fly.
    J. If a pig does not have wings, then it can fly.
    K. If a pig cannot fly, then it does not have wings.

17. If the average (arithmetic mean) of k and $k + 5$ is b and if the average of k and $k - 9$ is c, what is the average of b and c?

    A. $k - 2$
    B. $k - 1$
    C. k
    D. $k + \frac{1}{2}$
    E. $2k$

18. An urn contains a number of marbles of which 98 are blue, 14 are red, and the remainder are white. If the probability of picking a white marble from this urn at random is $\frac{1}{5}$, how many white marbles are in the urn?

    F. 14
    G. 28
    H. 42
    J. 56
    K. 70

19. The average (arithmetic mean) age of the people in a certain group was 20 years before one of the members left the group and was replaced by someone who is 10 years older than the person who left. If the average age of the group is now 22 years, how many people are in the group?

    A. 1
    B. 2
    C. 3
    D. 4
    E. 5

20. The graph below shows the frequency distribution of a list of randomly generated integers between 0 and 6. Which of the following statements about the mean of the list of integers is true?

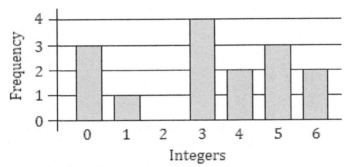

    F. The mean is less than 3.
    G. The mean is 3.
    H. The mean is between 3 and 4.
    J. The mean is 4.
    K. The mean is greater than 4.

LEVEL 5: PROBABILITY AND STATISTICS

21. At Brilliance University, the chess team has 16 members and the math team has 13 members. If a total of 7 students belong to only one of the two teams, how many students belong to both teams?

    A. 7
    B. 11
    C. 15
    D. 22
    E. 24

280

22. The circle graph below shows the distribution of responses to a survey in which a group of men were asked how often they donate to charity. If a man that participated in this survey is selected at random, what is the probability that he donates at least monthly?

    F. 0.33
    G. 0.58
    H. 0.68
    J. 0.73
    K. 0.87

23. The average (arithmetic mean) salary of employees at an advertising firm with P employees in thousands of dollars is 53, and the average salary of employees at an advertising firm with Q employees in thousands of dollars is 95. When the salaries of both firms are combined, the average salary in thousands of dollars is 83. What is the value of $\frac{P}{Q}$?

    A. $\frac{1}{10}$
    B. $\frac{1}{5}$
    C. $\frac{53}{148}$
    D. $\frac{2}{5}$
    E. $\frac{53}{95}$

24. Joe and Dave are playing a game where two 6-sided dice are rolled. Joe will be awarded 3 points for each of the two dice that shows a six as the top face. Let the random variable x represent the total number of points that Joe receives on any toss of the dice. What is the expected value of x?

    F. 0
    G. 1
    H. 2.5
    J. 5
    K. 10

Answers

1. E	5. B	9. E	13. B	17. B	21. B
2. J	6. G	10. K	14. F	18. G	22. F
3. E	7. A	11. B	15. D	19. E	23. D
4. H	8. H	12. H	16. K	20. H	24. G

Full solutions to these problems are available for free download here:

www.satprepget800.com/28LesInt

AFTERWORD
YOUR ROAD TO SUCCESS

Congratulations! By completing the lessons in this book you have given yourself a significant advantage in ACT math. Go ahead and take a practice ACT. The math score you get should be much higher than the score you received before completing these lessons.

I hope that you have been marking off all the questions that you've been getting wrong. You should continue to go back and redo each of those problems every few days until you can get each one right on your own.

If you feel confident that you can get most of the questions in this book correct, then it is time to move on to the advanced book in this series. The advanced book can take you right up to a 36 in ACT math.

If you decide to use different materials for practice problems, please remember to try to solve each problem that you attempt in more than one way. After all, the actual answer is not very important. What is important is to learn as many techniques as possible. This is the best way to simultaneously increase your current score, and increase your level of mathematical maturity.

I really want to thank you for putting your trust in me and my materials, and I want to assure you that you have made excellent use of your time by studying with this book. I wish you the best of luck on the ACT, on getting into your choice college, and in life.

Steve Warner, Ph.D.
steve@SATPrepGet800.com

ACTIONS TO COMPLETE AFTER YOU HAVE READ THIS BOOK

1. **Take another practice ACT**

   You should see a substantial improvement in your score.

2. **Continue to practice ACT math problems for 10 to 20 minutes each day**

   You may want to purchase *28 SAT Math Lessons to Improve Your Score in One Month – Advanced Course*.

3. **Like my Facebook page**

   This page is updated regularly with ACT prep advice, tips, tricks, strategies, and practice problems. Visit the following webpage and click the 'like' button.

   # www.facebook.com/ACTPrepGet800

4. **Review this book**

   If this book helped you, please post your positive feedback on the site you purchased it from; e.g. Amazon, Barnes and Noble, etc.

5. **Claim your FREE bonuses**

   If you have not done so yet, visit the following webpage and enter your email address to receive solutions to all the supplemental problems in this book and other materials.

   # www.satprepget800.com/28LesInt

About the Author

Dr. Steve Warner, a New York native, earned his Ph.D. at Rutgers University in Pure Mathematics in May, 2001. While a graduate student, Dr. Warner won the TA Teaching Excellence Award.

After Rutgers, Dr. Warner joined the Penn State Mathematics Department as an Assistant Professor. In September, 2002, Dr. Warner returned to New York to accept an Assistant Professor position at Hofstra University. By September 2007, Dr. Warner had received tenure and was promoted to Associate Professor. He has taught undergraduate and graduate courses in Precalculus, Calculus, Linear Algebra, Differential Equations, Mathematical Logic, Set Theory and Abstract Algebra.

Over that time, Dr. Warner participated in a five year NSF grant, "The MSTP Project," to study and improve mathematics and science curriculum in poorly performing junior high schools. He also published several articles in scholarly journals, specifically on Mathematical Logic.

Dr. Warner has more than 15 years of experience in general math tutoring and tutoring for standardized tests such as the SAT, ACT and AP Calculus exams. He has tutored students both individually and in group settings.

In February, 2010 Dr. Warner released his first SAT prep book "The 32 Most Effective SAT Math Strategies," and in 2012 founded Get 800 Test Prep. Since then Dr. Warner has written books for the SAT, ACT, SAT Math Subject Tests and AP Calculus exams.

Dr. Steve Warner can be reached at

steve@SATPrepGet800.com

BOOKS BY DR. STEVE WARNER

 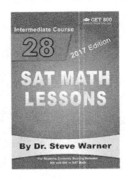 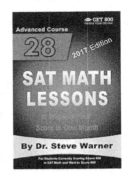

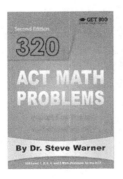 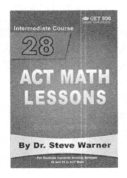 

www.Get800TestPrep.com

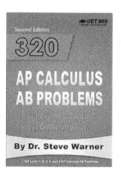
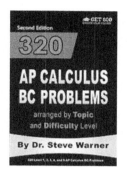

Made in the USA
Coppell, TX
29 March 2021